Praise for *Hands-On AWS CDK*

AWS CDK has an empowering role. With many young people globally as agents of change utilizing tech-driven solutions that cross borders, this book is a welcome toolkit. As cloud native technologies such as AWS CDK continue to evolve, they open up new opportunities for young developers around the world to participate in building scalable, automated infrastructure. By leveraging the power of programming languages, youth can contribute to the global movement of technology-driven international development, creating more accessible, efficient, and sustainable solutions for the future.

—*Eunice Ajambo, economist, United Nations*

This is an exceptional resource that not only demystifies cloud infrastructure but equips you to build real, impactful solutions with confidence. The practical, project-driven approach makes it a must-read for anyone serious about mastering cloud native development in AWS.

—*Jeffrey Rosenbaugh, senior director of professional services, Lucid Software*

Finally, a hands-on, project-based CDK book that takes readers on a very enjoyable journey to learning the AWS CDK. The writing style, content breadth, and depth applied to a fun and useful project make the book hard to put down, except to get your hands on the keyboard to get coding.

—*Andy Taylor, senior network solutions architect at AWS and self-confessed network automation nerd*

Hands-On AWS CDK offers a brilliantly structured and project-driven approach, making it the ultimate guide for developers to master cloud native application development using AWS CDK while building real-world, portfolio-ready projects. With its emphasis on hands-on learning, practical examples, and thoughtful explanations, this book not only teaches the technical aspects of AWS CDK but also fosters a deeper understanding of modern cloud practices, including automation, security, and generative AI integration.

—*Gwanhoo Lee, PhD, chair of the department of Information Technology and Analytics, American University*

Hands-On AWS CDK works for everyone, whether you're just starting out or you're a seasoned pro. Beginners can follow the step-by-step projects to build their skills, while experienced developers can jump around to find exactly what they need. It's a practical guide that grows with you as you learn.

—*Andrew Humphreys, director of product management, HyperTunnel*

Hands-On AWS CDK

*Building Cloud Native Applications with
Infrastructure as Code*

Sam Ward Biddle and Kyle T. Jones

Hands-On AWS CDK

by Sam Ward Biddle and Kyle T. Jones

Published by O'Reilly Media, Inc., 1005 Gravenstein Highway North, Sebastopol, CA 95472.

O'Reilly books may be purchased for educational, business, or sales promotional use. Online editions are also available for most titles (*http://oreilly.com*). For more information, contact our corporate/institutional sales department: 800-998-9938 or *corporate@oreilly.com*.

Acquisitions Editor: Megan Laddusaw	**Indexer:** nSight, Inc.
Development Editor: Michele Cronin	**Interior Designer:** David Futato
Production Editor: Aleeya Rahman	**Cover Designer:** Karen Montgomery
Copyeditor: Krsta Technology Solutions	**Illustrator:** Kate Dullea
Proofreader: Audrey Doyle	

April   2025:   First Edition

Revision History for the First Edition

2025-04-14:   First Release

See *https://www.oreilly.com/catalog/errata.csp?isbn=0636920963257* for release details.

978-1-098-15877-4

[LSI]

Table of Contents

Preface

The AWS Cloud Development Kit (CDK) is an open source software development framework that enables developers to define cloud infrastructure using familiar programming languages such as Python, TypeScript, Java, C#, and others instead of traditional JSON or YAML templates. The development of AWS CDK has evolved over time, driven by the need for a more efficient and familiar way to define and manage cloud resources.

The idea for the CDK originated from customer feedback and the recognition that traditional Infrastructure as Code (IaC) tools using static configuration files had limitations in terms of expressiveness, reusability, and productivity. AWS CDK was introduced in 2018 as a new approach to IaC, allowing developers to define cloud infrastructure using their preferred programming languages, leveraging the full power of their language's features and ecosystem.

Since its initial release, AWS CDK has undergone continuous development and improvement. AWS has actively engaged with the community to gather feedback and make updates to the framework based on user needs. AWS CDK has seen regular updates with new features, bug fixes, and improvements to its performance, stability, and usability.

The development of AWS CDK has also been influenced by the growing adoption of cloud native application development practices, such as DevOps and GitOps, which emphasize automation, repeatability, and versioning of infrastructure configurations as code. AWS CDK has integrated with popular development tools and practices, including integrated development environments (IDEs), source code repositories, continuous integration and continuous deployment (CI/CD) pipelines, and AWS CloudFormation, to provide a seamless and efficient experience for developers.

AWS CDK has been extended to support multiple programming languages, allowing developers to choose the language that best fits their team's skills and preferences. This has expanded the adoption of AWS CDK across a wide range of development communities, making it a popular choice for defining cloud infrastructure in a more familiar and productive way.

How This Book Is Structured

This book follows a "project-first" approach. Feel free to skip to Chapter 1 if you want to get straight to building, and return to the Preface when you have questions. If you like guidance before you start building, read on. This book is an all-in-one project-based practical introduction to AWS CDK written for builders by builders. Through the course of this book, you will build two complete and well-architected cloud native applications.

The first project is a digital Home Energy Coach complete with a data pipeline, serverless web application with authentication, and recommendation engine that we will build together bit by bit over the course of the book. Want to see what you will build? You can take a look at some artifacts from the sample project at *https://github.com/hands-on-aws-cdk-book/hands-on-aws-cdk-book-projects*.

This is also where you will find the code for the projects in this book. We recommend bookmarking this repository, and if you think it's useful, you can even give it a star.

We will start from scratch and progressively add additional elements to the project with each chapter. The second project is your own version of the first project. It will be unique to you and is intended to solve a problem specific to your interests, business, or engineering responsibilities. As you will see, the magic of CDK is in how common constructs can be used to build a variety of solutions.

Throughout the book, we will encourage you to document, write tests, and push your projects to a GitHub repository that will become your CDK portfolio. Share your portfolio with current or prospective employers, friends, or the open source community. We invite you to join the Hands-on AWS CDK community and share links to your projects, screenshots, and video tours. We love demos.

Why CDK?

The AWS CDK is a unique IaC solution that offers several benefits compared to other IaC providers, such as traditional JSON or YAML templates, as well as other popular frameworks like Terraform or CloudFormation:

Familiar programming languages
    CDK allows developers to define cloud infrastructure using familiar programming languages like Python, TypeScript, Java, C#, and others. This makes it easier for developers to leverage their existing programming skills and knowledge, resulting in increased productivity and a reduced learning curve.

Higher-level abstractions

CDK provides higher-level abstractions, known as *constructs*, that encapsulate common cloud patterns and best practices. This enables developers to define infrastructure using reusable and composable components, making it easier to create and manage complex infrastructure configurations with less code.

Improved productivity

CDK's programming language–based approach and higher-level abstractions make it more productive for developers to define, manage, and update IaC. CDK's rich ecosystem of libraries and community-contributed constructs also provides a wide range of pre-built components that can be easily reused, further accelerating development and reducing duplication of efforts.

Seamless integration

CDK seamlessly integrates with popular development tools and practices, such as IDEs, source code repositories, CI/CD pipelines, and AWS CloudFormation. This allows for a smooth and efficient workflow, enabling developers to easily integrate infrastructure changes into their existing development processes and workflows.

Full AWS service coverage

CDK provides comprehensive coverage of AWS services, allowing developers to define and manage a wide range of cloud resources using the same programming language and constructs. This makes it a unified and consistent way to define infrastructure across different AWS services, reducing the need to switch between different tools or configurations.

Flexibility and portability

CDK allows developers to define infrastructure using programming languages, which provides flexibility and portability. CDK code can be easily reused across different AWS accounts, regions, or projects and can also be deployed to multiple cloud environments, making it a versatile choice for multicloud or hybrid cloud scenarios.

Like you, we came to CDK a little unsure of what we were getting into. We were familiar with other tools such as Ansible, CloudFormation, Terraform, and even the occasional shell script for orchestration. But CDK quickly won us over because it made building cloud infrastructure much more similar to writing object-oriented application code. At AWS, there is less of a divide between "platform" and "application" teams, which we find tends to result in tighter integration between the software and the infrastructure. This has a lot of benefits including more reliable, secure, and cost-effective applications.

We are passionate about teaching others the benefits of CDK and how to use it. On a personal level, we love CDK for some additional reasons:

Building with CDK is fun

Honestly—writing code still feels like magic, and orchestrating cloud services from a code editor feels like being a magician. We still can't get over how fun it is to go from idea or business challenge to cloud native solution in an afternoon or a week or a month by writing CDK. Just wait till you get your first taste in Chapters 1 and 2.

CDK is open source and you can contribute to it

We love that CDK is open source and that you can contribute documentation, improvements, or even brand-new constructs. We have contributed several constructs to the public CDK libraries and to additional private libraries, and we have built several open source solutions for customers using CDK.

CDK allows you to benefit from the flexibility and reusability of an object-oriented programming language

We covered this earlier, but it's worth reiterating on a personal level. It. Is. So. Awesome. To define, instantiate, and extend classes rather than copying and pasting declarative syntax. Writing CDK in object-oriented programming languages makes development quicker, and less prone to error, and is quite honestly more elegant, fun, concise, and effective. Just wait till you try it out. We think you won't want to go back.

CDK makes collaboration easier

We have seen a lot of customers struggle with a siloed infrastructure development process, constantly reinventing the wheel, and experiencing difficulty maintaining consistent infrastructure operations. It's very difficult to reuse declarative syntax in CloudFormation of Terraform templates, which often leads to a centralized and slow process of cloud adoption. CDK makes this a lot easier because teams can maintain central construct libraries that can be used as packages and maintained centrally while developers use them for their own projects. We have seen this accelerate development velocity while also improving security, financial operations, and cloud operations.

CDK lets software developers also own/understand infrastructure

Because CDK combines application logic with infrastructure, CDK helps reduce the need to silo infrastructure into ticketing systems that divide IT and Application teams. We have seen, and experienced, the power of CDK to let developers own and/or understand infrastructure, which often improves overall reliability, helps optimize cost, and contributes to greater agility in the development cycle.

If you weren't convinced that CDK is worth your time before reading this section, we hope you are now. We are confident that by the time you finish Chapters 1 and 2 and you've built your first two projects, you will be proudly flying the CDK flag. Are there CDK flags? *Maybe there should be.* Now that we have expressed our love and appreciation for CDK, we will further explain why we wrote this book and why we think you should keep on reading it.

Why We Wrote This Book

This is the book we wish had existed when we started learning CDK. We came together around the idea for this book because we wanted to build real projects in a context that was engaging and informative, and we wanted to feel well prepared to build real production cloud applications using CDK. Since such a book didn't exist, we decided to write it for you. We know that time efficiency is important when you're building a new technology. This book is meant to be a one-stop guide to learn the what, why, and how of CDK and build real projects that you can show or share as a digital portfolio.

Who This Book Is For

This book is for developers, students, hobbyists, and the cloud-curious. This book is for people who have tried AWS CloudFormation, Terraform, Ansible, and many other tools but wanted something more like object-oriented programming and less declarative. This book is for teams looking to adopt CDK. If you made it this far, this book is for you.

How to Use This Book

The book is a tool for you to use in the ways that best suit your needs. Here are some options for how you might use the book, but you get to decide how you use it:

- Read this book sequentially from cover to cover.
- Read this book as a reference text, consulting specific chapters as you need them.
- Read this book as a free-for-all, picking random chapters and following along with projects as you go.

We want this book to serve as a useful reference even after you have completed the projects. Our goal is for you to learn how CDK works, not to memorize specific recipes that produce standard outcomes. You can look those up as needed. If we were picking up the text for the first time, we would get comfortable with a computer to work on, a favorite beverage, and a quiet place. We would probably complete a chapter and corresponding project each in a single sitting, until we had built our own portfolio project. After reading once, we would return to the text as a reference when building personal and work projects. We might recommend specific chapters to a curious friend and lend the book to them, always sure to get it back to lend to the next person.

Why Projects First?

You might find that this book is structured a little differently from your traditional technical guide or text. We put the projects at the very beginning of each chapter so that you can get "hands-on" first (as the title suggests). This means that some project sections may have you asking yourself, "Why am I doing this?"; "What does this even mean?"; and "Can you give me the theory and concepts, please?"

We wrote the book this way for three reasons:

- We talked with a lot of our target audience and they told us that they often just skip ahead to projects anyway.
- In our teaching practice, we both have seen the "flipped classroom," "expedition-ary learning," and "constructivist" models work really well for learners who want to accelerate their skill development while developing long-term knowledge and understanding.
- We wanted to keep your attention and make the book feel a bit like a guided adventure.

Each chapter begins with a brief description of the project and learning goals. Then, we get straight into "now do this." Don't panic. We will explain what happened after the project. We included comments in the project code, and each project includes a completed and annotated "exemplar" that you can reference as you go. You may find that the things we ask you to do feel unfamiliar, challenging, or ambiguous. Trust us. If you complete the exercises and read the text for each chapter, then we think you will walk away with a deeper understanding of how to build something new with CDK, what it all means, why it works, and how to extend your knowledge within your own projects and contexts.

Documentation

If you have ever inherited undocumented code and struggled to make sense of it, you probably wished the person before you had taken some extra time to document each function, variable, and class with inline comments. If you have ever struggled through deploying a repository for the first time, you also probably wish the creator had thoroughly documented every step with copy/paste commands and visual dia-grams. No fun.

There are competing theories on the role of documentation in code. Some people say that code should be *self-documenting*, meaning that the code itself is written so intuitively and clearly that very little additional documentation is needed. Within an organization, or even a shared project, this is sometimes possible. But we have found that the best way to write ergonomic, easy-to-understand, and easy-to-extend IaC is to document thoroughly within the code and within a README file.

Documenting your code is a great way to deepen your own understanding of what your code is doing. When you write docstrings in TypeScript, you are forced to explain, in simple terms, what each class, function, and variable means; what services they deploy; and how to use them. Throughout this book, you will use JSDocs to document your code.

This is the standard requirement for all open source contributions to the standard AWS CDK Library, and it has the added benefit of providing tab-completion typing within code editors. This means that the JSDoc strings that you write will pop up with little explanations of your code, making it easier for others to extend, use, and reuse the code that you write. Whatever your stance is on documenting code, try our approach to documentation. You might like it. And in either case, you will learn something from the exercise.

Testing

There are several schools of thought on testing code, especially IaC. Some engineers believe that every unit of code should have tests, and that every application should have several tests including end-to-end, functional, and integration tests. Some developers practice *test-driven development*, in which they write a test *before* they write the deployable components of their code. We are test-driven development people.

Each project will start small with a simple architecture. As we add more modules, the application will gradually become more complex. We use the AWS Well-Architected Framework (*https://oreil.ly/KmYcO*) as a guide for creating applications that do their job in the best way possible.

The AWS Well-Architected Framework is a structured set of design principles to align applications to best practices. The framework has six pillars: Operational Excellence, Security, Reliability, Performance Efficiency, Cost Optimization, and Sustainability.

What You Will Build

Imagine you are the lead cloud architect, developer, and technical project manager for a cloud native software solution. You are tasked with building an open source software platform to help individuals track, analyze, and understand their home energy usage. This application needs to be relevant to homeowners, renters, and local utilities.

The application will allow users to upload home energy use data in CSV format and as image files of a utility bill. Your boss asks you to deploy the platform using IaC on AWS (even though your boss is not 100% sure what that means). Your coworkers, Sam and Kyle, recommend that you use AWS CDK in TypeScript and that you write with application logic in JavaScript.

By the end of the book, you will have two portfolio-ready projects that you can maintain on your public GitHub page to demonstrate your cloud development skills. The projects will prepare you with the skills and concepts necessary to build your own cloud native CDK application in the culminating capstone project chapter at the end of this book. In the next section, you will learn about the technical details and AWS services that will be used in the project.

End of Chapter Organization

Each chapter ends with several key elements, which we outline here.

Getting Unstuck

In each chapter, we provide a Getting Unstuck section that provides trouble-shooting tips and resources for common issues that may arise during the project.

Chapter Synth

Each chapter will end with a `chapter synth` section. It's a CDK pun. You will get it soon. If you already think that is a funny joke, this book is going really well. If you have a better joke, please submit your issue to the project's GitHub repository.

Review

The chapter synth begins with a review of the topics covered at the end of each chapter to help solidify your knowledge and skills. It is our way of reminding you of what you learned in the chapter and to set the stage for the review questions and extension activities.

Discussion

Each chapter includes optional discussion questions. It is an open book quiz (Hint: use this book), but if a question is challenging for you, we recommend reviewing the corresponding parts of the chapter.

Extension Activities

We include optional extension activities at the end of each chapter. These activities often involve applying your knowledge in a new context. Try them out right away. Or don't. You can always bookmark these and return to them later.

Conclusion

We wrote this book to help you build amazing things using AWS CDK. You can read it in order, out of order, or as a choose-your-own-adventure text. Each chapter begins with a project by design. We think it is more fun this way.

Conventions Used in This Book

The following typographical conventions are used in this book:

Italic
> Indicates new terms, URLs, email addresses, filenames, and file extensions.

`Constant width`
> Used for program listings, as well as within paragraphs, to refer to program elements such as variable or function names, databases, data types, environment variables, statements, and keywords.

`<>`
> Shows text that should be replaced with user-supplied values or by values determined by context.

 This element signifies a tip or suggestion.

 This element signifies a general note.

 This element indicates a warning or caution.

Using Code Examples

All code in this book is available on GitHub with additional comments and notes; these materials can be download at *https://github.com/hands-on-aws-cdk-book/hands-on-aws-cdk-book-projects*.

If you have a technical question or a problem using the code examples, please send email to *support@oreilly.com*.

This book is here to help you get your job done. In general, if example code is offered with this book, you may use it in your programs and documentation. You do not need to contact us for permission unless you're reproducing a significant portion of the code. For example, writing a program that uses several chunks of code from this book does not require permission. Selling or distributing examples from O'Reilly books does require permission. Answering a question by citing this book and quoting example code does not require permission. Incorporating a significant amount of example code from this book into your product's documentation does require permission.

We appreciate, but generally do not require, attribution. An attribution usually includes the title, author, publisher, and ISBN. For example: "*Hands-On AWS CDK* by Sam Ward Biddle and Kyle T. Jones (O'Reilly). Copyright 2025 Sam Ward Biddle and Kyle T. Jones, 978-1-098-15877-4."

If you feel your use of code examples falls outside fair use or the permission given above, feel free to contact us at *permissions@oreilly.com*.

O'Reilly Online Learning

 For more than 40 years, *O'Reilly Media* has provided technology and business training, knowledge, and insight to help companies succeed.

Our unique network of experts and innovators share their knowledge and expertise through books, articles, and our online learning platform. O'Reilly's online learning platform gives you on-demand access to live training courses, in-depth learning paths, interactive coding environments, and a vast collection of text and video from O'Reilly and 200+ other publishers. For more information, visit *https://oreilly.com*.

How to Contact Us

Please address comments and questions concerning this book to the publisher:

O'Reilly Media, Inc.
1005 Gravenstein Highway North
Sebastopol, CA 95472
800-889-8969 (in the United States or Canada)
707-827-7019 (international or local)
707-829-0104 (fax)
support@oreilly.com
https://oreilly.com/about/contact.html

We have a web page for this book, where we list errata, examples, and any additional information. You can access this page at *https://oreil.ly/handsonawscdk*.

For news and information about our books and courses, visit *https://oreilly.com*.

Find us on LinkedIn: *https://linkedin.com/company/oreilly-media*.

Watch us on YouTube: *https://youtube.com/oreillymedia*.

Acknowledgments

The authors acknowledge the many people who helped make this book a reality.

We, and this book, benefited immensely from feedback from Andy Taylor, Julian Setiawan, Prasad Gandham, Jon Terry, and Jason Hardy. Needless to say, any errors are ours alone.

At O'Reilly, Michele Cronin shepherded us through the publication process with good cheer and the right amount of prodding. Aleeya Rahman took our book through the early release and production phases. We also thank Megan Laddusaw for seeing the potential for a book on CDK and initiating our project at O'Reilly.

Finally, we are thankful for the patience and support of our families—Chanel and Carmelo and Amanda, Annamarie, Christopher, and Sarah. Special thanks to our writing companions Sunny and Leila.

## CHAPTER 1

Getting Started with CDK

This book is project driven. We want you to get hands-on and learn by building. We start by introducing the project that you will be building throughout the book. After introducing the project, we will get you all set up with your development environment and prerequisites so that we can begin building in Chapter 2. In this chapter, we will cover just a bit more background so that we can hit the keyboard right away with all the subsequent chapters.

We want to give a friendly warning that if you are brand new to cloud development, IT administration, or AWS, this chapter may feel challenging. If you have some experience, this may be a bit more accessible, but some concepts may still be new. In designing the book, we made conscious decisions to avoid the "easy route" if it was going to instill bad habits for security and cost optimization. This means the learning curve may feel a bit steep in this first chapter, but in the long run, you will be a stronger cloud developer for it. That said, please do provide feedback where we can make the directions simpler or clearer; we are always looking for ways to make these topics more accessible while still providing expert-level knowledge and skills.

Let's take a deep breath and go step by step. In this chapter, you will learn:

- How to set up your AWS account
- How to set up the AWS Command Line Interface (CLI)
- How to set up your development environment
- How to set up your first project

To get started you will need:

- A computer running macOS, Linux, or Windows
- An internet connection

What You Will Build

There are two major projects in this book, each consisting of several smaller projects, or microservices. The first project will be one we do together. We will call this Project 1, or the Shared Project. This project will be your own version of an application unofficially named Home Energy Coach, but you can call it something different as you make it your own.

Each chapter will focus on a step-by-step tutorial where we teach you CDK *concepts* while building new features into our application. By the start of the penultimate chapter, you will have a full application that will be mostly the same as any other person who finishes this book. In the final chapter, you will have an opportunity to select your own use case and design, build, and deploy an application that is unique to you. This is Project 2—the Portfolio Project. Think of the first project, or the Shared Project, as preparation for your own creative endeavor—building a solution to a problem you are familiar with or would like to explore.

In this section, we will introduce you to the Shared Project, which will occupy every chapter of this book except for the last. Just keep in mind that everything you are learning is meant to prepare you for the exciting task of building your own project with AWS CDK. Don't worry, we will guide you through the whole process and even share some starter case studies if you need some ideas to get started. Read on for all the details of our shared project. We will revisit Project 2 (aka your Portfolio Project) in the final chapters.

We will make occasional references to Project 2, the Portfolio Project, throughout the book. As you are learning and building and following directions, we want you to be constantly asking yourself, "How can I use this in a different way for my own project?"

Project 1: The Shared Project

Throughout this book, you will be asked to take on the role of lead cloud architect, developer, and technical project manager for a cloud native software solution. You are tasked with building an open source software platform to help individuals track, analyze, and understand their home energy usage. This application needs to be relevant to homeowners, renters, or anyone else who uses electricity in the place they call home. This platform will be deployed as IaC on AWS and built using AWS CDK in TypeScript, with application logic written in JavaScript. The application you build will allow users to upload home energy use data in CSV format and as utility bill image files.

The application will record energy use over time; display it in simple graphics on a web page; and utilize a chatbot interface, search, natural language processing, and generative AI to make energy optimization recommendations based on the user's defined energy goals. This solution will combine elements of serverless API development, web application development, AI/ML, DevOps, and data analytics. You will also get to interact with free external APIs for foundational large language models and real-time carbon emissions measurement. The project will be deployed via a GitHub Actions pipeline and will utilize unit, infrastructure, integration, and end-to-end functional testing. The project will allow you to make personalized customizations by following the extension activities with each chapter.

If you're wondering, "But is this really how someone would deploy a real application on AWS?" the answer is emphatically YES! We wrote this book to be the guide we never had when developing real AWS solutions used in industries and enterprises. This is an accelerated introduction that prepares you to build real applications for real businesses. Have fun with it. We had a lot of fun building it.

By the end of the book, you will have a portfolio-ready project that you can maintain on your public GitHub page to demonstrate your cloud development skills. The project will also prepare you with all of the necessary skills and concepts to build your own cloud native CDK application in the culminating capstone project chapter at the end of this book. In the next section, you will learn about the technical details and AWS services that will be used in the project.

Figure 1-1 shows the Home Energy Coach application that we will build incrementally. Don't worry if this doesn't make sense right now. We will go step by step in the coming chapters.

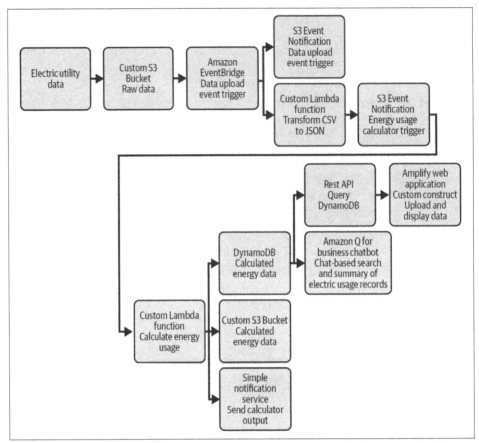

Figure 1-1. Architecture for the final project we are building. Each chapter will add features to our application.

Electric Utility Usage Data
> CSV files in standard format with electric utility usage data. The project repository includes examples and a template for you to input your own utility usage data.

Custom S3 Raw Data Bucket
> Raw data landing zone for electric utility usage .csv files. This bucket uses S3 event notifications to trigger our data pipeline.

S3 Event Notifications: Upload Event Trigger
> Trigger for data transformation and notifications.

Simple Notification Service: Data upload status notification
Email and optional SMS (text message) notifications about data upload status. These notifications are sent to the email and contact list you set up in the AWS console.

Custom Lambda Function: Transform raw data
Transforms raw data into a standard format that can be used for calculations.

S3 Event Notification: Energy usage calculator trigger
When transformed data is uploaded to the S3 bucket this event triggers the next.

Custom Lambda Function: Calculate energy usage
Completes a calculation totaling energy usage.

Custom DynamoDB Table
Stores calculated energy usage for transactional access.

Custom S3 Bucket: Store calculated energy usage data
Stores calculated energy usage for analytical access. This is a simplified data lake that can be used for forecasting, data visualization, and analytics. This serves a different purpose from the analytical database and is stored and a lower cost with the expectation of less frequent access.

Simple Notification Service: Notify calculated energy output
Email and optional SMS (text message) notifications about calculated energy usage.

API Gateway: REST API
Provides authenticated access to calculated energy usage data in standard format.

Level 3 Generative AI Chatbot Construct
Combines search, chatbot, and generative AI to provide summaries and recommendations about energy usage data. Uses a combination of keyword search and context, and one-shot prompting to provide recommendations and insights about energy usage.

AWS Amplify Web Application: Energy coach application front end
Frontend web and mobile page to interact with, query, and analyze electric usage data.

Project 2: The Portfolio Project

The second project in this book is your own. We will provide some case studies and ideas to get you started, but ultimately you will be responsible for designing, building, and deploying your own cloud native application using AWS CDK. This project will be an opportunity to demonstrate your creativity, interests, and expertise. We invite you to take what you learn in Project 1 and extend, remix, and rethink it in a new context. In the final chapter, we will guide you through the process of coming up with an idea, understanding your users and what they need, and building it. We encourage you to begin thinking about your project now, and to keep it in mind as you work through the rest of the book.

Prepare Your Learning Environment

Throughout the book, we will refer to a project code repository hosted on Git-Hub called `hands-on-aws-cdk-book-projects`. We recommend opening this project repository and starring and bookmarking it on GitHub. By the end of this book, you may even feel inspired to contribute to the project repository. More on that later. For now, you will want to open the repository so that you can refer to it throughout the book. This repository includes synthetic datasets that you will need to use in the project and includes completed versions of each project with extensive inline code comments.

The project repository can be found at: *https://oreil.ly/hands-on-aws-cdk-book*. The directory structure is shown in Example 1-1.

Example 1-1. Project repository directory structure

```
hands-on-aws-cdk-book-projects
├── app
│   └── infrastructure <-- this is where the projects will be
│       └── resources <-- this includes setup resources from chapter 1
├── synthetic-data <-- this contains the synthetic data you will use
├── CONTRIBUTING.md <-- guide for contributors (could be you!)
├── README.md <-- readme for the repository with links to all chapter projects
└── .gitignore <-- tells git which files to ignore
```

Each chapter directs you to review specific components of the final project. In many cases, this code will have some additional resources that you have not yet built but are present in the final project. We strongly recommend that you use the main branch of the project repository as your "source of truth" for correct and complete code. The code samples in the book are meant to be illustrative, but may not always have the most up-to-date changes. Each section of code in the sample repository has a README, with FAQs, and detailed comments and examples. Please refer to the sample project code any time you get stuck in the project.

You can use this in a few different ways:

- Keep the project repository open at all times and refer back to it regularly with each new step of the project. Use the project as an exemplar or a way to get unstuck if you're not sure. Use this approach if you like to have a strong example to guide your work every step of the way.

- Keep the project repository bookmarked and open it at the end of each chapter to check your work against an example. Use this approach if you like to work with some ambiguity and prefer to use your own resources and check your work only at the end.

You will need the project repository for datasets, and you should bookmark it as a vital reference for your final project. We will also update sample projects should there be any changes to technologies or dependencies within the project code. We also invite you to review the project README and try deploying the final application as you complete the project on your own. This is a great way to look ahead and anticipate what you will be building.

Set Up Your Cloud Development Environment

To get started you will learn to set up your cloud development environment with VS Code, Git, and AWS CLI so that you can begin building cloud infrastructure. After you get set up, you can build your first project! This is the Cloud Development Kit (CDK) equivalent to "Hello, World!"

You will use the environment you set up here to build, manage, and deploy CDK projects in the rest of this book.

Set Up Your AWS Account

Setting up an AWS (Amazon Web Services) account and generating access keys is a crucial step for developers who plan to use AWS services for cloud development. AWS provides a wide range of cloud computing services, including computing power, storage, databases, networking, and more, that can be used to build and deploy applications.

Here's a brief overview of how to set up an AWS account and generate access keys for development:

1. Sign up for an AWS account. To do this, visit the AWS website (*https://aws.amazon.com*) and click the Create an AWS Account button. Follow the instructions to provide the required information, such as email address, password, and payment details.

2. Provide payment information. AWS requires a valid payment method, such as a credit card, to verify your identity during the account setup process. You will not be charged unless you use paid services beyond the Free Tier. *Don't worry. We will show you how to set up a budget to avoid surprise bills.*

3. Complete the identity verification process. As part of the account setup, AWS may require additional identity verification, which can be done in the form of phone verification or by uploading identification documents.

Great! Now you have set up your AWS account with what is known as your root user. Next, we will set up an AWS budget to avoid surprise bills. Soon you will log out of this user and *NEVER, EVER, EVER* log back in to do development work. We will show you how to set up an admin user for development work in an upcoming section. But first, budgets.

Set Up Your AWS Budgets

When starting out with AWS, it's easy to unintentionally go outside the boundaries of the Free Tier and get charged more than expected. To avoid surprise bills, set up budgets to keep your usage in check. Here's how to set budgets in AWS:

1. Log in to your AWS account.

2. Use the top search bar to search for *Budgets* and select the Billing and Cost Management service (Figure 1-2).

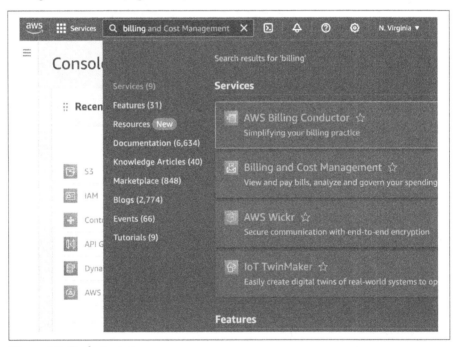

Figure 1-2. Budget setup

3. On the left sidebar, click Budgets under Budgets and Planning. You will likely need to activate Cost Explorer to activate Budgets, so click the link to do so.

4. Select "Create budget" and "Monthly cost budget."

5. Select "Use a template (simplified)" and "Monthly cost budget."

6. Give your budget a name; something like "cdk-learning-budget."

7. Set the Budgeted amount, such as $10. For this project, your costs will depend mostly on how much you use your app. If you set a budget of $50/month, this should be a good starting point. Most of the services we use will be within the Free Tier, so you can also set your budget as $0. This will alert you before going over the Free Tier (see Figure 1-3).

8. Enter your email so that you receive email alerts.

9. Review the budget settings, then select "Create budget."

Seriously, do not skip the budget-creation step. There are two types of cloud developers (well, many more than two, but bear with us): 1) the kind who use budgets, and 2) the kind who have accidentally spent some enormous sum of money on misconfigured resources when they were first learning, costing themselves or their employers a ton of money.

Be the first kind, not the second. Some lessons stick better when you learn them the hard way. Some are only embarrassing. Just trust us. We both learned the hard way so that you don't have to.

Now your AWS account has spending guardrails! The dashboard will track your usage across services and alert you as the budget limit nears. You can explore AWS freely without worrying about surprise overages. Next up, you will create your admin user using AWS Identity and Access Management (IAM) (*https://aws.amazon.com/iam*). This is the user you will log in with to carry out administrative tasks. You will never log in with your root user again.

Figure 1-3. Budget creation

Create an Admin IAM User

When you first create an AWS account, you sign in with root user credentials. But it's risky to use the powerful root account for everyday work! Please visit the official AWS IAM documentation (*https://oreil.ly/oxOvR*), which describes the most secure practices for setting up an Administrator account.

Sign In and Generate Keys for Your CDK Developer User

You are going to enable console access and access keys. This is the user you will assume for all development for the rest of this book:

1. Select "Enable console access" and follow all instructions to set up and enable multifactor authentication for console access.

2. Select "Create access key."

3. Under "Use case," select Command Line Interface (CLI) and select the checkbox indicating that you understand the other recommended methods and choose this one. Click Next.

4. Under "Description tag," add a brief description, such as `<your-initials>Cdk DeveloperCliKeys<date><year>`.

5. Select "Create keys." Save the CSV or copy/paste the access keys because you will need them for the next step.

 DO save the keys somewhere temporary so that you can use them in a few minutes. *DO NOT* save the keys permanently on your machine. You should permanently delete them as soon as you confirm that they are working locally.

Now your user is ready for CDK deployment! Its keys authenticate your cdk terminal sessions.

Wow! That was a long and tedious process, right? We know. It's like that for a reason. Security and identity and access management require friction. The meticulously detailed process of setting up IAM role, policy, user, and access keys is what allows us to maintain principle of least privilege (PoLP) effectively. We thought hard about making this "easier" for our readers so that you could "focus on development." Through experience, we have seen the dangers of outsourcing IAM setup and management. Any strong cloud developer needs to be familiar with IAM and be comfortable troubleshooting when permissions aren't quite right. If you don't know IAM, you will have a big gap in your cloud development and security skill set, so this is a great time to get familiar through practice. To read more about setting up IAM, review the official AWS IAM user guide (*https://oreil.ly/MTg7J*).

With your limited-privilege IAM user set up, you can develop safely knowing exactly what CDK access is permitted. As a final step, you will set up the AWS CLI so that you can begin building on your local machine.

Set Up the AWS CLI

In this book, we will set up the AWS CLI to store our credentials locally in a profile and access AWS from the command line. This step assumes some knowledge of your operating system's command line.

Brief Intro to Command-Line Environments

A command-line environment, also known as a command-line interface (CLI) or text-based interface, is a way of interacting with a computer operating system or software application using text commands. In a command-line environment, users input commands through a text-based interface, typically in a terminal or command prompt window, and the system responds with output or performs the requested task.

Command-line environments have been used for decades and are still widely used today, especially in operating systems like Unix, Linux, and macOS, as well as in networking devices, servers, and programming environments. They provide a powerful and efficient means of interacting with a computer system, allowing users to execute commands, run scripts, manage files and directories, configure system settings, and perform a wide range of additional tasks.

Command-line environments are useful for flexibility and automation. Users can chain together multiple commands, create scripts, and automate repetitive tasks, which can save time and effort. Command-line environments are also highly efficient, as they often require fewer system resources compared to graphical user interfaces (GUIs), making them suitable for systems with limited resources or remote access.

Command-line environments can also be complex and require users to have knowledge of specific commands and syntax. They may not be as user-friendly as GUIs, especially for novice users. Nevertheless, mastering command-line environments can be highly beneficial for system administrators, developers, and power users who require fine-grained control over their systems and want to automate tasks efficiently.

Here's a brief overview of how to set up the AWS CLI and begin deploying AWS resources:

1. Install the AWS CLI. The AWS CLI can be installed on various operating systems, including Windows, macOS, and Linux. Follow the AWS documentation (*https:// oreil.ly/kZjaw*) for instructions on how to install the AWS CLI on your preferred operating system. The current edition of this book uses AWS CLIv2, so even if you have the AWS CLI installed, it is important to ensure that you have the latest version. You can check by running `aws --version` in your terminal. This should return `aws-cli/2.13.13` or greater.

2. Configure the AWS CLI. After installing the AWS CLI, you need to configure it with your AWS account credentials. This includes providing your AWS Access Key ID, Secret Access Key, default region, and default output format. You can configure the AWS CLI by using the `aws configure` command and following the prompts, or by manually editing the AWS CLI configuration files.

Try it out now using the Key and Secret from the previous step. Follow the prompts to save your developer keys to your AWS configuration file locally:

```
aws configure
```

You should see prompts that look like this:

```
AWS Access Key ID [None]: <insert your key ID when prompted>
AWS Secret Access Key [None]: <insert your secret key when prompted>
Default region name [None]: <insert us-east-2 or another region>
Default output format [None]: <leave this as blank to select default>
```

If you are not sure which region to use, try us-east-2 (located in Ohio). AWS divides the world into regions, which are nodes on the AWS network. There are four regions located in the United States, and there are also other regions across the globe. You generally want to choose a region that is close to where you are working to reduce latency, but there are also times when you might want to work in another region based on the project you are developing.

Verify that everything is set up by checking your assumed identity:

```
aws sts get-caller-identity
# this should print your AWS account ID to the console
```

Once the AWS CLI is configured, you can verify the setup by running a simple AWS CLI command, such as `aws s3 ls`, to list the objects in an S3 bucket. If the command executes successfully and returns the expected results, it indicates that your AWS CLI setup is correct.

With the AWS CLI set up, you can start deploying AWS resources using the AWS CLI commands. AWS CLI provides a wide range of commands to manage various AWS services, such as EC2 instances, S3 buckets, CloudFormation stacks, and more. You can use these commands to create, configure, update, and delete AWS resources as needed for your development and deployment workflows.

One of the key benefits of using the AWS CLI is the ability to automate AWS operations using scripts or other automation tools. You can write scripts or use tools like AWS CloudFormation, AWS software development kits (SDKs), or other IaC frameworks to automate the deployment and management of AWS resources, making it efficient and repeatable. In our case, we will do all of these things, but mostly wrapped in CDK.

Leapp Secrets Manager

For extra security with your IAM keys, consider installing the Leapp secrets manager (*https://oreil.ly/7jp1s*). It's kind of like a personal password manager, but for your AWS credentials. Once you start developing on AWS, you will likely have a lot of AWS accounts to work in. Leapp makes it easy to manage all of your keys and rotate them as needed.

Set Up Your Local Development Environment

Developers need a place to develop. One widely used integrated development environment (IDE) for CDK development is Visual Studio Code (VS Code), which provides a rich set of features for code editing, debugging, and version control.

There are lots of IDEs to choose from. We use VS Code throughout the book, but you can use whichever IDE you prefer. Some other common IDEs are GitHub Codespaces and Atom.

Set Up Visual Studio Code

To set up VS Code for CDK development follow these steps:

1. Install VS Code. From the official VS Code website (*https://code.visualstu dio.com*), download and install the version of VS Code for your operating system.

2. Install CDK Extensions. VS Code has several extensions specifically designed for CDK development, such as AWS Toolkit and CDK Explorer. Install these extensions from the VS Code Extensions Marketplace to enhance your CDK development experience.

3. Install Node.js. CDK is built on Node.js, so make sure you have Node.js installed on your development machine. You can download and install Node.js from the official website (*https://nodejs.org*). We also cover this in the next section.

4. Install the CDK Toolkit. The CDK Toolkit is a CLI that is used to interact with CDK applications. Install it globally on your machine using npm (Node Package Manager) by running the command `npm install -g aws-cdk`.

With these steps, you can set up VS Code as an IDE for CDK development and start building cloud applications using the power of IAC with CDK.

Set Up Git and GitHub

Setting up Git and GitHub is an essential step for version control and collaborative software development. Git is a distributed version control system that allows developers to track changes, collaborate, and manage source code efficiently, while GitHub is a popular web-based hosting service for Git repositories, providing a platform for collaboration and sharing of code among team members.

We use GitHub in this book, but you can use any Git repo that you like. Other popular Git repos include GitLab (*https://www.gitlab.com*), Bitbucket (*https://bitbucket.org*), and AWS Code-Commit (*https://aws.amazon.com/codecommit*).

Git can be installed on various operating systems, including Windows, macOS, and Linux. Follow the Git documentation for instructions on how to install Git on your preferred operating system. There is also an instructive guide for setting up Git locally (*https://oreil.ly/jjp2v*).

After installing Git, you need to configure it with your name and email address, which will be associated with your Git commits. You can configure Git using the `git config` command and providing your name and email address as arguments.

If you don't have a GitHub account, sign up for a free account on the GitHub website. You will need a GitHub account to host and share your Git repositories on GitHub. We will encourage you to use this throughout your project. Git-based version control is an important part of any cloud developer's workflows.

Setting up Git and GitHub simplifies version control and collaboration. Even if you are a one-person development team, using Git allows you to track changes and share code easily. It streamlines the development workflow, and we will use it throughout this book.

> There are lots of tutorials about Git if you want to dive deeper. We like the tutorial from Software Carpentry (*https://oreil.ly/thwIC*).

Install Prerequisite Packages and Software

We are almost ready to start building. The next section guides you through installation of prerequisite software and packages. The great news is that you only have to do this once on a given machine, and then you can build lots of things whenever you want.

Install Node and npm

Make sure you have Node.js and npm (*https://oreil.ly/spHjg*) running on your machine. We installed them in previous steps, but it's always good to double-check:

```
node --version
npm --version
```

Both commands should produce an output stating the version of the package.

We will be building all of our applications using TypeScript, which will be installed by default as a dependency for the CDK. TypeScript is a typed superset of JavaScript that compiles to plain JavaScript. It adds optional static typing, classes, interfaces, and other features to standard JavaScript syntax for larger-scale development. TypeScript also adds type safety and scalability to JavaScript, making it well suited for IaC development.

Its optional typing provides guardrails when coding—it catches errors during compilation that would otherwise cause runtime crashes. This helps catch infrastructure bugs before provisioning. The class-based object orientation also helps organize all the infrastructure constructs needed for IaC solutions like CDK. TypeScript provides guardrails and organization on top of JavaScript for more robust IaC development.

Install CDK

Now that you have all the CDK prerequisites, the final step is to install the CDK CLI, and the `aws-cdk-lib` core library of constructs.

Start by installing the `aws-cdk` CLI globally on your machine. This way, you can use it when creating new projects. It will help scaffold many processes of building with CDK:

```
npm install -g aws-cdk
cdk --version
```

Next, install the `aws-cdk-lib` core library. This consists of the core level 1, level 2, and level 3 (L1, L2, and L3) constructs contributed by AWS and the open source community, maintained by the AWS CDK team and core contributors:

```
npm install aws-cdk-lib
```

Now that you have installed all of the prerequisite software, you are ready to start building. Before we build, it is essential that you understand the L1, L2, and L3 CDK construct categories. In the next section, we will explore L1, L2, and L3 constructs with a simple example. Don't worry if the difference isn't immediately clear to you. You are about to get a lot of practice with these topics.

Infrastructure as Code and Automation

In the context of IaC, automation can greatly simplify and accelerate the process of creating, deploying, and managing infrastructure resources in the cloud. CDK provides a declarative language for defining IaC, which can then be applied to automatically provision and manage cloud resources in a consistent and repeatable way.

By automating the process of infrastructure provisioning, CDK can reduce the risk of human error and inconsistency that can occur when tasks are performed manually. This is particularly important in complex environments where multiple resources must be provisioned and configured correctly in order to work together.

Automation also allows teams to focus on higher-value activities such as innovation and development, rather than manual provisioning and management of infrastructure. With CDK, teams can make infrastructure changes quickly and easily, enabling them to respond to changing business needs in real time.

Additionally, automation can help reduce costs by optimizing resource utilization, eliminating manual processes, and reducing labor costs. CDK can help companies save money and resources by automating the process of infrastructure management and provisioning, enabling them to scale more efficiently and effectively.

How Infrastructure as Code Works

With IaC, builders define infrastructure resources such as servers, databases, and networking components using code, rather than manually provisioning them through a web console or CLI.

IaC works by defining the desired state of infrastructure in a declarative configuration language, which is then applied to create or modify resources in the cloud. The CDK code defines the relationships and dependencies between resources, enabling CDK to automatically manage the order in which resources are provisioned and configured.

The benefits of IaC include increased efficiency, consistency, and scalability. By using code to define infrastructure resources, teams can automate the provisioning and management of infrastructure, reducing the risk of human error and enabling them to scale more efficiently. Additionally, IaC provides version control and audit trail capabilities, making it easier to track and manage infrastructure changes over time.

IaC also enables teams to work collaboratively and efficiently, with code serving as a shared language for communicating infrastructure changes and requirements. With CDK, teams can work together to define infrastructure resources using a common syntax, enabling them to streamline the process of infrastructure management and provisioning.

How CDK Works on AWS

CDK works on AWS by leveraging the AWS API to automate the provisioning and management of infrastructure resources in the cloud. CDK provides a declarative configuration language that allows users to define their desired infrastructure state as code, and then applies that code to create, modify, and delete resources on AWS.

To use CDK on AWS, users first define their AWS credentials and configuration settings in a CDK configuration file. This file specifies the resources to be created and their properties, as well as any dependencies and relationships between resources. The CDK configuration file is then used to generate a plan, which outlines the changes that CDK will make to the existing infrastructure in order to bring it into the desired state.

Once the plan has been reviewed and approved, CDK applies the changes to the infrastructure in a safe and predictable manner. CDK uses the AWS API to provision and configure resources in the correct order, ensuring that dependencies are met and that resources are provisioned correctly. CDK also provides support for AWS-specific features, such as auto-scaling groups, elastic load balancers, and VPC, allowing users to manage complex AWS infrastructure with ease. Additionally, CDK can be integrated with other AWS services, such as CloudWatch and S3, to enable monitoring and storage of CDK state files.

Overall, CDK provides a powerful and flexible way to manage infrastructure on AWS, allowing users to automate the provisioning and management of resources at scale while maintaining consistency and predictability.

AWS CloudFormation, AWS CDK, and Terraform

AWS CloudFormation, AWS CDK, and Terraform are all IaC tools that enable users to define, provision, and manage cloud resources in a declarative and automated way.

The AWS CDK provides a high-level object-oriented abstraction over AWS Cloud-Formation. Using the CDK, developers can define IaC using a programming language such as TypeScript or Python, and then use the AWS CDK Toolkit to generate CloudFormation templates and deploy them to AWS. Terraform is a popular open source tool that can be used to provision and manage infrastructure on a variety of cloud providers, including AWS. Terraform uses a declarative configuration language to define infrastructure resources, and it can be used to automate the provisioning of resources in a safe and predictable manner.

AWS CloudFormation is a native AWS IaC tool that provides a JSON- or YAML-based declarative language to describe and provision infrastructure resources. Cloud-Formation templates can be used to automate the creation of complex architectures and can be version controlled and reused across multiple environments.

While each tool has its own strengths and weaknesses, they all provide powerful ways to automate the management of infrastructure on AWS. Terraform offers a wide range of providers and a powerful configuration language, while the AWS CDK offers a programming language–based approach to IaC, and CloudFormation provides a native, AWS-focused solution. Ultimately, the choice between these tools will depend on the specific needs and preferences of each individual organization.

Getting Unstuck

What if I can't log in as my IAM user?
> Double check that you're using the correct login URL for IAM users. It should look something like this: `https://<account-id>.signin.aws.amazon.com/console`. You can find this in the IAM dashboard under Users > your user > Security credentials. If you're still being redirected to the root login, try using an incognito window to ensure cached credentials aren't interfering. Also make sure the user has the correct permissions, ideally the `Administrator Access` policy for this setup.

What do I do if I get an error when installing CDK?
> Make sure you've installed Node.js and npm first. Run `node --version` and `npm --version` to confirm. If those are working, try installing CDK globally using `npm`

install -g aws-cdk. If that fails, you might have a permissions issue—try running the install command with sudo (on Mac/Linux) or with elevated privileges on Windows.

What if I can't see the Budgets section in the AWS Console?
In many cases, it's because you haven't enabled the Cost Explorer yet. Go to the Billing dashboard, click Cost Explorer, and activate it. Once enabled, the Budgets feature will become available. After that, you can set up your monthly limit and email alerts.

What if I'm overwhelmed by all the setup steps?
That's completely normal. It's a lot to take in. Take a breath, and remember that most of this setup is a one-time task. If you get stuck, open the GitHub repo that comes with this book. You can compare your work with the reference branches and use the example configuration files as a guide. And don't forget: this chapter isn't about building something perfect—it's about getting ready to build. You're doing great.

Chapter Synth

In this chapter, you learned:

- How to set up an AWS account
- How to set up an IAM user for CDK development
- How to access your AWS IAM user for CDK development from the command line
- How to install all of your software prerequisites
- How to set up your development environment

Now you are ready to build your first very simple CDK application. Let's go!

Discussion

1. What kinds of projects could you build with CDK? How would using CDK for IaC make it easier or faster to deploy code?

2. Review the official CDK developer docs (*https://cdk.dev*). Try to find one example of an L1 construct, one of an L2 construct, and one of an L3 construct.

3. How are CDK, CloudFormation, and the Cloud Control API related? How are they different?

Extension Activities

This chapter introduced AWS CDK. You will get a lot of hands-on experience throughout this book. Before we dive deeper, consider these extension activities:

1. Visit the official CDK documentation (*https://oreil.ly/1pMCE*) and consider following some of the Getting Started tutorials.

2. Try writing your own brief CDK Getting Started guide. Try to fit all the steps into a single page or onto a single sheet of paper. What special tips would you highlight?

3. Find someone (preferably someone who is interested) and explain to them the benefits of AWS CDK and how it can help businesses innovate.

## CHAPTER 2

Hello, CDK!

In this chapter, you will begin building the CDK equivalent of "Hello, World!"—a rite of passage in programming. This will be your first complete CDK application, so there will be a lot of new terms and commands to learn. To start, you will build a simple object store that accepts a text file, triggers an on-demand cloud function called a Lambda function, and prints a greeting to the logs for your function. You will then extend this simple program to serve as the foundation of your Home Energy Coach program. In this chapter, you will deploy the Lambda function that says "Hello." To get started, you will need to initialize your first CDK project.

Through this project, you will learn:

- How to initialize and bootstrap a new CDK application
- How to create a CDK stack and integrate it with your CDK application
- How to use the `aws-cdk-lib` standard library
- How to synthesize, deploy, and destroy a CDK application
- The definitions of *app*, *stack*, *construct*, and *context* in CDK

To get started, you will need:

- The GitHub Repo (*https://oreil.ly/hands-on-aws-cdk-ch2*)

Project Architecture: Build a "Hello, CDK" Lambda Function

In this first project segment, you will build a simple microservice that accepts a *.txt* file as an input to an S3 bucket, uses Amazon EventBridge to trigger an AWS Lambda function, and prints a greeting to the CloudWatch log screen each time. Figure 2-1 represents this.

Figure 2-1. High-level architecture for our simple "Hello, CDK" Lambda function. We will build on this design in the coming chapters.

This is the simplest application we will build, so it just shows one box with a Lambda function. In the next chapter, we will extend this into an event-driven architecture. You will learn a lot about CDK through deploying this one application, though, so enjoy yourself.

Generate a New CDK Application

Time to build. Initialize your CDK application using the cdk init command with a few flags to create your project as a TypeScript project with basic boilerplate code. Yes, you can do all of this manually, but it will go much more quickly if you use the boilerplate template and modify as you need. Later in the book we will show you how to create your own boilerplate templates.

Begin by navigating to the directory that you want to work from. We recommend creating a directory called *hands-on-aws-cdk-book* and opening this within your VS Code file explorer.

Make a directory called *hello-cdk*. Later we will rename our application home-energy-coach and you will learn how to rename your application. For now, just start with hello-cdk:

```
mkdir hello-cdk
cd hello-cdk
```

Now initialize your CDK application using the TypeScript boilerplate:

```
cdk init app --language typescript
```

You did it! You now have a CDK application to begin working with. This process uses the CDK Toolkit to generate a boilerplate project for TypeScript. It builds a full starter folder structure for a CDK application. For now, we will make minimal modifications to this structure to build our "Hello, CDK" project. In future chapters, you will customize this more to meet the requirements of a complex architecture composed of several microservices.

When you first bootstrap the application, it will have the structure shown in Example 2-1 by default. You don't have to do anything—this is all made for you automatically.

Example 2-1. CDK application directory structure

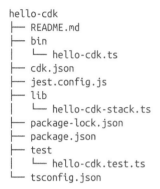

```
hello-cdk
├── README.md
├── bin
│   └── hello-cdk.ts
├── cdk.json
├── jest.config.js
├── lib
│   └── hello-cdk-stack.ts
├── package-lock.json
├── package.json
├── test
│   └── hello-cdk.test.ts
└── tsconfig.json
```

The Structure of a CDK Application

CDK apps are organized into components, including the application, stacks, constructs, and the structure of the repository:

Application

The CDK application is the entry point of your app and represents the overall infrastructure you want to deploy. It can contain one or more stacks, which are the building blocks of your infrastructure. The application is typically defined in a single file, often named *app.ts* or *main.ts*, and is responsible for orchestrating the deployment of all the stacks in your app.

Stacks

Stacks are the basic units of deployment in CDK and represent a set of AWS resources that are deployed together. Each stack is defined as a class in TypeScript or Python, and it can contain one or more constructs. Stacks can have dependencies on other stacks and can be deployed independently or as part of a larger app.

Constructs

Constructs are reusable components that represent AWS resources or higher-level abstractions, such as custom patterns or application components. Constructs can be used to define the resources and configuration of your infrastructure, and they can be composed together to create more complex and reusable infrastructure patterns. Constructs can be written as classes in Type-

Script or Python, and they encapsulate the details of creating and configuring AWS resources.

Repository structure

The structure of a CDK app repository typically includes the CDK app code, configuration files, and any additional files required for deployment. The app code, including the application, stacks, and constructs, is typically organized into separate directories or modules, depending on the complexity of the app. Configuration files, such as *cdk.json* or *cdk.context.json*, can be used to define deployment settings or input parameters. Additionally, the repository may include other files such as README, LICENSE, and *.gitignore* files, as well as any other files required for the app's functionality or deployment process.

CDK apps are designed to be modular, allowing for reusability, scalability, and maintainability. CDK provides a clear separation of concerns between the app, stacks, and constructs, making it easier to manage and deploy IaC using the CDK framework.

Let's take a closer look at the entry point for your CDK application. Open the file located at */bin/hello-cdk.ts*. You will see the code shown in Example 2-2. You don't have to copy this. It was created automatically when you typed `cdk init app --language typescript`.

Example 2-2. CDK application boilerplate

```
#!/usr/bin/env node ❶
import 'source-map-support/register'; ❷
import * as cdk from 'aws-cdk-lib'; ❸
import { HelloCdkStack } from '../lib/hello-cdk-stack'; ❹

const app = new cdk.App(); ❺
new HelloCdk(app, 'HelloCdk', { ❻
  // env: { account: process.env.CDK_DEFAULT_ACCOUNT,
  //        region: process.env.CDK_DEFAULT_REGION },
  env: { account: '123456789012', region: 'us-east-1' }, ❼
}); ❽
```

❶ This line specifies that the file should be executed as a Node.js script.

❷ Here, we import source map support to get JavaScript (JS) stack traces for TypeScript (TS) errors.

❸ This line imports the AWS CDK Construct Library.

❹ This line imports the `HelloCdkStack` class from the *hello-cdk-stack.ts* file.

❺ Here, we create a new CDK app instance.

❻ This creates a new instance of the `HelloCdkStack`, passing in the CDK app and stack name.

❼ This line defines the `env` prop, which accepts an object to define which AWS account and region your application is deployed to. See more details on this in the following note.

❽ We finally close the `HelloCdkStack` class definition. In all subsequent examples, this will be implied and not explained.

This initializes and defines the CDK app and stack that will be synthesized into an AWS CloudFormation template.

Notice that the boilerplate defines the CDK environment in commented-out code. This is because there are two ways to define your environment:

```
env: { account: process.env.CDK_DEFAULT_ACCOUNT,
       region: process.env.CDK_DEFAULT_REGION }
```

And also:

```
env: { account: '123456789012', region: 'us-east-1' }
```

Example 2-2 defines the environment by passing local environment variables to your CDK app. So, this will pass the environment variables assumed by your AWS CLI profile locally on your machine. This can also be helpful if you want to dynamically pass an account and region to your CDK application in a pipeline. We will do this later! This is the method we will use to deploy our application.

Example 2-3 defines the environment through a hardcoded account number and region. This would be useful if you wanted to deploy a CDK application through a pipeline defined in one account, but wanted to standardize the account that it is deployed into. Generally we find that defining your environment using local variables gives you more flexibility, so we will use this method in the book.

You will need to uncomment the environment input code so that your local environment variables are passed to the application. Uncomment the following line by removing the double slash from the beginning of the line:

```
// env: { account: process.env.CDK_DEFAULT_ACCOUNT,
          region: process.env.CDK_DEFAULT_REGION }
```

You can also delete all of the other comments. Your *./bin/hello-cdk.ts* file should now look like Example 2-3.

Example 2-3. Updated CDK application entry point boilerplate

```
#!/usr/bin/env node
import 'source-map-support/register';
import * as cdk from 'aws-cdk-lib';
import { HelloCdkStack } from '../lib/hello-cdk-stack';

const app = new cdk.App();
new HelloCdkStack(app, 'HelloCdkStack', {

  env: { account: process.env.CDK_DEFAULT_ACCOUNT,
         region: process.env.CDK_DEFAULT_REGION },

});
```

Understanding Application Stacks

A *stack* in AWS CDK is a collection of AWS resources defined and managed together. It represents a single unit of deployment in CloudFormation. Each CDK stack is synthesized into a CloudFormation template, which AWS CloudFormation uses to provision and manage the resources. Stacks are essential because they allow you to logically group related resources together.

Resources within a stack can be isolated from other stacks, enabling more granular control and separation of concerns. For example, you might have a separate stack for networking resources (virtual private clouds, subnets) and another for application resources (EC2 instances, S3 buckets).

AWS CDK allows stacks to reference resources in other stacks. This is useful when sharing a resource, such as a VPC, between multiple applications.

Each stack can be deployed to different AWS environments (regions or accounts), making it easier to maintain infrastructure across multiple environments (development, staging, production).

Now let's take a look at the application stack that was created as part of the boilerplate. Navigate to */lib/hello-cdk-stack.ts*. Example 2-4 shows what you will see. Again, this was made automatically and you don't need to copy this code.

Example 2-4. CDK stack boilerplate

```
import * as cdk from 'aws-cdk-lib';
import { Construct } from 'constructs';
// import * as sqs from 'aws-cdk-lib/aws-sqs';

export class HelloCdkStack extends cdk.Stack { ❶
  constructor(scope: Construct, id: string, props?: cdk.StackProps) { ❷
    super(scope, id, props); ❸
```

```
    // The code that defines your stack goes here

    // example resource
    // const queue = new sqs.Queue(this, 'HelloCdkQueue', {
    //   visibilityTimeout: cdk.Duration.seconds(300)
    // });
  }
}
```

Let's examine what is going on here. We start by importing the AWS CDK Construct Library. Then, we import the `Construct` class from the Constructs library.

In this snippet, we have commented out the import of the CDK SQS module. This is an example of an L2 construct, and we will explore using these in more detail in this chapter:

❶ This line defines the `HelloCdkStack` class extending `cdk.Stack`. This basically extends many common features of a stack, and you will see how we can use this when creating our own stacks and constructs.

❷ This is the constructor method with `scope`, `id`, and optional `props`. In TypeScript and the AWS CDK, the constructor is like a recipe that tells the computer how to make a new thing. It needs a main container (called `scope`) and a special name (called `id`), and you can add extra details (called `props`) if you want the thing to behave in a special way.

❸ We call the parent `cdk.Stack` constructor here. This is a way of telling your new thing to use the main instructions from its higher-up (parent). This ensures that the necessary container (`scope`), a unique name (`id`), and any additional specifications (`props`) are used correctly to create the new thing. It's like building on the essential directions given by the higher-up.

Installing Dependencies

Now you are going to prepare your application for deployment by installing, building, and synthesizing. When you create a new CDK application from boilerplate, the npm modules are already installed, but we're going to run the command anyway to get you in the habit of doing it:

```
npm install # installs dependencies
npm run build # builds your typescript
```

If you prefer Yarn or other tools, you can use those instead. The `npm install` command installs all the dependencies listed in the *package.json* file.

You can move this all into one line if you like with: npm install && npm run build.

Building a CDK Application

In a CDK TypeScript project, when you run the command npm run build, you're telling the npm to execute a predefined build script. This script typically triggers the TypeScript compiler to translate your TypeScript code into JavaScript code that can be understood and executed by the computer.

Specifically, the npm run build command compiles your CDK TypeScript project, checking for any errors and generating the necessary JavaScript files. This is important because TypeScript is a "typed" language that helps catch mistakes before code runs, and the build step transforms TypeScript code into the more universally compatible JavaScript format. Once the build process is done, you'll have the necessary files ready to deploy and run your AWS CDK application.

When you run npm run build, you will notice that there are suddenly a whole bunch of extra files in your project. These will have the same names as your existing files, but now two extra files for every *.ts* file with *.d.ts* and *.js* extensions.

The TypeScript compiler transforms your *.ts* files into *.js* files. These are the actual JavaScript code that your computer can run. The *.js* files are what your project uses when it's actually running or being deployed. The *.d.ts* files are *declaration* files. They don't contain executable code, but they provide information about your TypeScript code to other parts of your project or external tools. They act like a guide, helping tools and other code understand the types, classes, and functions you've defined in your TypeScript code.

Running npm run build is often skipped, which can lead to issues later on. We recommend standardizing this step in your workflow to ensure that your TypeScript code is compiled correctly before deploying your application. In Chapter 11, we cover testing CDK applications and adding precommit hooks, which basically run some scripts automatically for you each time you commit to Git. This is a great way to ensure that you always run your build step before deploying your application.

When you are updating files, you should only make changes to the files that end in *.ts*. The other files will be regenerated each time you build your project. You can also choose to ignore these files by modifying the *.gitignore* file. One thing to note: if you ignore *.js* files, this could affect Lambda functions that use JavaScript. There are ways to help manage this, but let's just say that if you stay up until 3 a.m. wondering why your Lambda code is missing from your remote environment, it might be because of *.gitignore*.

Bootstrap Your CDK Application

Before you can deploy your CDK application, you need to bootstrap it. *Bootstrapping* is the process of preparing your CDK app for deployment by creating a CloudFormation stack that contains the necessary resources for deploying CDK apps. This includes an S3 bucket for storing CDK assets, such as CloudFormation templates and Lambda function code, and an IAM role for the CDK Toolkit to use when deploying resources to AWS.

To bootstrap your CDK application, run the following command:

```
cdk bootstrap
```

This will create a CloudFormation stack in your AWS account that contains the required resources for deploying CDK apps. The CDK Toolkit will use this stack to store assets and manage deployments. You only need to bootstrap your CDK app once, and you can reuse the same stack for deploying multiple CDK apps.

Let's take a quick look at what this creates in the AWS Console. Each time we look to see what we've deployed, we will follow a similar process:

1. Go to the AWS Management Console and open the CloudFormation service by searching for *CloudFormation*.
2. Click Stacks and look for a stack called CDKToolkit (see Figure 2-2).
3. Open the CDKToolkit stack details and select the Resources tab.

If you are the curious type, you might want to look more closely at what is created with this toolkit. This is some of the "magic" that happens behind the scenes with CDK. While it's interesting to look closely at what's in here, we strongly recommend not making any changes to this stack. This is a special stack that CDK uses to manage your deployments, and making changes to it could cause issues with your CDK deployments.

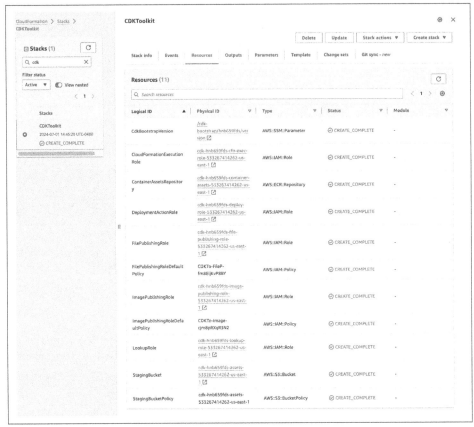

Figure 2-2. CDK Toolkit

Synthesize Your CDK Application

You have installed dependencies and used the TypeScript compiler to generate your JavaScript files. Now you will synthesize your CDK application:

```
cdk synth
```

Let's take a look at what happens when you synthesize your application by running cdk synth (Figure 2-3).

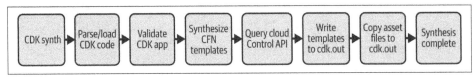

Figure 2-3. CDK synth process

When cdk synth is run, the CDK Toolkit starts by parsing and loading the CDK code. It discovers all stacks, resources, and so on, that were defined. The toolkit then validates the app, checking for issues like circular dependencies or invalid property values. Next, it begins synthesizing each stack defined in the app into a CloudFormation template in JSON or YAML format. To generate the templates, it queries the Cloud Control API to get required information, such as available instance types for the target account and region.

The resulting CloudFormation templates are written to the *cdk.out* directory. This directory will contain a template file for each stack defined in the app. In addition to the templates, *cdk.out* will include copies of all asset files that were referenced in the CDK app, such as the Lambda source code. After synthesis completes successfully, the CloudFormation templates in *cdk.out* can be deployed using cdk deploy to provision the resources defined in the CDK app.

Now we get to start building. You can either follow along by modifying the boilerplate you were given, or just delete the contents of the file and write from scratch. We like writing from scratch because it forces you to really understand each section and each step.

Project Tutorial: Deploy a "Hello, CDK" Lambda Function

Next up, we are going to create a Lambda function that will print, "Hello, CDK" to the console each time it is fired. We will begin by modifying our existing *stack-hello-cdk.ts* file to add a Lambda function resource, or construct, within that stack.

AWS Lambda is a serverless compute service that runs code in response to events like HTTP requests or updates to S3 buckets. The code runs in ephemeral containers that are provisioned when invoked and shut down afterward. Resources are allocated automatically based on usage. Lambda functions can be authored in languages like Node.js, Python, Go, and Java. The code is uploaded as a deployment package to AWS. We will use a lot of Lambda functions in this book because they are one of the most powerful tools available for building performant, cost-optimized, and agile cloud solutions. We will also be able to keep your AWS bill very low because Lambda functions can easily stay within the AWS Free Tier since they only fire when they are needed, and they don't require you to keep a server running at all times.

Lambda functions are like tiny virtual workers who sleep until you give them a job to do. When you need some work done, you ring a bell, which wakes up a worker; they do the task, and then they go back to sleep. You only pay for the seconds they are awake working. The more bells you ring, the more workers are awakened to handle the jobs simultaneously.

The AWS CDK Toolkit makes it easy to define Lambda functions in code. You configure the runtime, memory, timeout, handler method, and code location. CDK will deploy the code as a Lambda function and wire up any triggers you define like S3 events. When the CDK app is synthesized, the Lambda function gets created in the resulting CloudFormation template.

One of the advantages of working with AWS CDK is that you can easily define your Lambda functions within the same codebase as your infrastructure. This allows your developers to more easily manage application logic and infrastructure instead of defaulting to traditional methods of managing logic and infrastructure separately. We see this as one of the most powerful uses of CDK, so we are giving you a lot of experience with it.

You will need to edit and rename the stack generated for you in boilerplate. Rename the file at */lib/hello-cdk-stack.ts* to */lib/lib/stack-hello-cdk.ts*. We recommend prepending each filename with either *app*, *stack*, or *construct*. Because there are so many components in a CDK application, we find that it helps to always see what level of abstraction you are working on first, and standard naming conventions help reduce choices, which can be a nice thing for you as a developer and anyone who reads your code and wants to contribute to it. You will also notice that the CDK Toolkit will automatically ask you if you want to update your references to match the changed file name. Select Yes.

Define Your Lambda Function Infrastructure

Now you will build and deploy a Lambda function that, when triggered, prints "Hello, CDK". We start by creating the Lambda function infrastructure, and in the following section we will write the Lambda handler code. Open *./lib/stack-hello-cdk.ts* and begin writing your code, as shown in Example 2-5.

Example 2-5. "Hello, CDK" Lambda function infrastructure

```
import * as cdk from "aws-cdk-lib";
import { aws_lambda as lambda } from "aws-cdk-lib";
import * as path from "path";

export class HelloCdkStack extends cdk.Stack {
  constructor(scope: cdk.App, id: string, props?: cdk.StackProps) {
    super(scope, id, props);

    const helloCdkLambda = new lambda.Function(
      this, "HelloCdkLambda", {
      runtime: lambda.Runtime.NODEJS_20_X,
      handler: "index.main",
      code: lambda.Code.fromAsset(
        path.join(__dirname, "./lambda/lambda-hello-cdk")
      ),
    });
  }
}
```

Let's take a closer look at what we just defined. First, we import the AWS CDK Lambda construct library. This allows us to define Lambda functions in CDK. Then, we import the Node.js `path` module. This is used to generate local filepaths:

Next, we define a `Stack` class extending the base CDK `Stack` class. This creates a CDK stack that will contain resources. Then, we define the `Stack` constructor method. This will be called to initialize the stack.

Define Your Lambda Function Application Logic

Now we are ready to create a new Lambda function construct assigned to constant `helloCdkLambda`. The constructor params name and identify the resource. Once we create the function, we configure the Lambda runtime to Node.js 20.*x*. This runtime executes the Lambda code. We need to specify the Lambda handler method name. This is the code executed when the function is invoked. Finally, we set the Lambda code by pointing to a local directory containing the code.

But that's not all! Now that we have defined our Lambda function infrastructure, we also need to write the code that will be packaged up and deployed as a Lambda function:

1. In the *stack-hello-cdk* directory, create a new directory called */lambda*.

2. In the */lambda* directory, create a file called *index.js*.

3. Navigate to this directory and intitialize a new npm environment with `npm init`. Note that this is now required with the latest node runtimes available in Lambda as of 2025.

4. Here you will need to install the AWS SDK for JavaScript client for S3 with `npm install @aws-sdk/client-s3`.

In this function, you will write your Lambda code as defined in Example 2-6. This will be brand-new code, so you can still start writing your code.

Example 2-6. "Hello, CDK" Lambda function handler

```
async function main(event) { ❶
  const msg = "Hello, CDK!" ❷
  console.log(msg) ❸
  return { ❹
    body: JSON.stringify({message: msg}),
    statusCode: 200,
    };
  };

module.exports = {main};
```

Let's break down what we just did here:

❶ We define an asynchronous function called `main` that accepts an `event` object as an input parameter.

❷ We define a constant variable `msg` that has the message string in it.

❸ We log this message to the console—in this case, the AWS CloudWatch Logs.

❹ We return an object that contains a `body` that consists of a JSON-formatted string with a key of `message` and a value of `Hello, CDK!`. The object also has a `statusCode` of `200`, which is an HTML status code indicating that the request is OK.

 See the Mozilla documentation for more on HTML status codes (*https://oreil.ly/T_HV5*). This will become useful with our Lambda functions when we start using them to carry out API requests.

In summary, we are passing an `event` object to the function called `main`, and that function is going to simply print "Hello, CDK!" to the console, which will be located in the AWS CloudWatch Logs in the AWS Console. We will show you how to check this message very soon!

Deploy Your Function

Time to test it out! The steps here will be the same each time, but we're going to keep writing them just to make sure you commit them to memory. Build, synthesize, and then deploy your application to see what you get:

```
npm run build
cdk synth
cdk deploy --all
```

While only three lines of code, this block has a lot going on. Let's see what we deployed:

1. Log in to the AWS Management Console and open the CloudFormation service by searching for *CloudFormation*.

2. Click Stacks and look for a stack called HelloCdk (see Figure 2-4).

Figure 2-4. "Hello, CDK" stack creation

3. Open the HelloCdk Stack details.

4. In the Resources tab, look for an S3 bucket called HelloCdkS3Bucket and a Lambda function called HelloCdkLambda (see Figure 2-5).

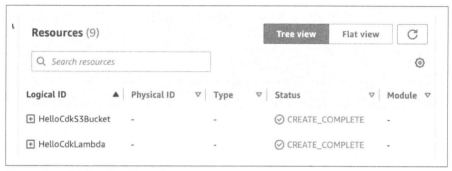

Figure 2-5. "Hello, CDK" stack resources

5. Click the physical ID of the S3 bucket to view it in the S3 console.

6. Click the physical ID of the Lambda function to view it in the Lambda console.

7. In the Events tab, review the event history and note any errors.

8. Click the Template tab to see the synthesized CloudFormation template. It can be helpful to review this CloudFormation template, as you can see in one place all of the resources you created with CDK.

Test Your Function

Let's test out our Lambda function by navigating to the Lambda Service in the AWS Management Console:

1. Click on Functions in the lefthand navigation pane and locate HelloCdkLambda. It will be listed as a function and have a name like `HelloCdk-HelloCdkLambda-<random string>` (see Figure 2-6).

| | HelloCdkStack-
HelloCdkLambdaCCB7
D852-MRAmeZVTZoP4 | - | Zip | Node.js 18.x | 13 minutes ago |

Figure 2-6. "Hello, CDK" stack Lambda

2. Click the function name to open the details.

3. On the Code tab, quickly verify that the source code matches what you created with a "Hello, CDK!" message.

4. Open the Test tab and click the Test button to execute the function.

5. In the test event JSON editor, leave the default empty event. Give the test event a name like "HelloCdkTestEvent" and click Save.

6. Click the Test button again to invoke the function. You should see the output of your function under "Execution result."

7. Verify that the Response section contains the print output "Hello, CDK!". You should see something like Figure 2-7:

```
{
  "body": "{\"message\":\"Hello, CDK\"}",
  "statusCode": 200
}
```

```
Test Event Name
HelloCdkTestEvent

Response
{
  "body": "{\"message\":\"Hello, CDK!\"}",
  "statusCode": 200
}

Function Logs
START RequestId: 30944aac-8adb-426e-b9ce-b4a9f760f05f Version: $LATEST
2024-07-01T19:05:42.139Z    30944aac-8adb-426e-b9ce-b4a9f760f05f    INFO    Hello, CDK!
END RequestId: 30944aac-8adb-426e-b9ce-b4a9f760f05f
REPORT RequestId: 30944aac-8adb-426e-b9ce-b4a9f760f05f  Duration: 13.37 ms  Billed Duration: 14 ms
```

Figure 2-7. "Hello, CDK" Lambda test execution result

 To really prime your AWS skills you can also review the logs from your Lambda function by selecting Monitor in the middle menu bar. This will take you to the CloudWatch Logs for your Lambda function. You can see the logs from your function execution here. This is a great way to debug your function and see what is happening when it runs. This will come in handy later.

Congratulations! You have now deployed an AWS CDK application with one resource. It may seem like a small victory, but this is a big moment. Building infrastructure with code is kind of like being a magician. While this is a simple application, we think you're really going to like how quickly we can add complexity with relative ease.

 Enabling active tracing in Lambda provides debug logs and request tracing when testing a function in the Lambda console. It's useful to enable when testing to get maximum visibility into how the function executes and identify any problems. The added logging and tracing data is kept for one hour before being deleted. We will cover logging and observability in greater detail later in the book, but it's helpful to start getting used to reading logs now:

CDK Documentation

When working with the AWS CDK, it's important to refer to the official CDK documentation (*https://oreil.ly/219uQ*) to get relevant information and choose the right constructs for your project.

There are many resources available. Here are our tips on how to effectively use the CDK docs. Begin by searching for specific constructs. The CDK documentation provides a search functionality that allows you to search for specific constructs based on their names, keywords, or use cases. This can help you quickly find the right constructs that align with your project requirements.

Read the construct documentation (yep, we said "read the docs"). Once you have identified relevant constructs, make sure to thoroughly read their documentation to understand their purpose, properties, methods, and examples. The documentation typically includes code snippets, usage examples, and best practices that can help you effectively use the constructs in your CDK app.

CDK constructs are organized in a hierarchy of levels (L1, L2, L3) and modules. Understanding the hierarchy can help you choose the right level of abstraction for your project. For example, L1 constructs provide a direct mapping to CloudFormation resources, L2 constructs provide higher-level abstractions with common AWS patterns, and L3 constructs are custom constructs built by the developer. Choose the construct level that best fits your requirements.

There is a rich ecosystem of CDK libraries and modules maintained by the community that provide additional constructs for various AWS services and use cases. These libraries can provide valuable pre-built constructs that can save development time and effort. Make sure to check the CDK library and module documentation for relevant constructs that may be useful in your project.

The CDK documentation also includes best practices, guidelines, and recommendations on how to effectively use CDK constructs in your projects. Following these best practices can help you avoid common pitfalls and ensure that your CDK app is well architected and maintainable.

CDK documentation is a valuable resource for getting relevant information on CDK constructs and choosing the right constructs for your project. Make sure you thoroughly read and understand the documentation to effectively use CDK constructs and build scalable and maintainable AWS infrastructure with the CDK.

Basic CDK Commands

The AWS CDK provides a set of command-line tools that you can use to interact with your CDK app and deploy infrastructure resources to AWS. Here are some basic CDK commands and their descriptions:

cdk init
> Initializes a new CDK app in the current directory, creating the necessary files and folder structure

cdk synth
> Synthesizes your CDK app into CloudFormation templates, which represent the AWS resources that will be deployed

cdk diff
> Compares the current state of your CDK app with the deployed stack in AWS and shows the differences between them, highlighting any changes that will be made during the next deployment

cdk deploy
> Deploys the CDK app to AWS, creating or updating the stack based on the synthesized CloudFormation templates

cdk destroy
> Deletes the deployed stack and all its associated resources from AWS, effectively tearing down the infrastructure created by the CDK app

cdk list
> Lists all the stacks deployed by the CDK app in your AWS account

cdk bootstrap
> Creates or updates an Simple Storage Service (S3) bucket in your AWS account that is used for storing CDK Toolkit assets, such as CloudFormation templates and Lambda functions

```
cdk context
```
Sets context values for your CDK app, which can be used to configure app-specific settings

```
cdk doctor
```
Checks your CDK app for common issues and provides recommendations on how to fix them

These basic CDK commands help you build, deploy, and manage your CDK app and its associated resources in AWS. It is worth learning these so that you can recall them as needed. We will use many of these throughout the course of the book. When in doubt, you can always use `cdk --help` for general info, or for a specific command, you can use the `help` flag with the command name, as in `cdk deploy --help`.

CDK to CloudFormation

CDK is an abstraction layer over CloudFormation (CFn). When you deploy a CDK app, AWS is synthesizing the CDK into CloudFormation under the hood.

The synthesized CloudFormation templates generated by the `cdk synth` command capture the infrastructure defined in your CDK app as a set of declarative configuration files. These templates adhere to the CloudFormation syntax and can be used to create, update, or delete the corresponding AWS resources. The CDK app's constructs are translated into CloudFormation resources, properties, and parameters in the synthesized templates. During the `cdk deploy` command, CloudFormation uses these templates to create or update the specified stack in AWS, effectively provisioning the infrastructure resources defined in your CDK app.

CDK allows you to define your app's infrastructure using higher-level constructs, such as L2 or L3 constructs, which provide a more abstract and concise way to define resources compared to CloudFormation templates. The CDK automatically translates these constructs into CloudFormation templates during the `cdk synth` command, making it easier to manage and deploy complex infrastructure using code.

Getting Unstuck

What do I do if I get an error when deploying my CDK application?
The first step is to review the log outputs in your console. This is typically a good place to start because it gives you CDK-specific insights about any errors you're encountering. For simple issues, this will usually do the job. For more complex issues, we also recommend going to the CloudFormation section of the AWS Console. Often the CloudFormation logs will be more detailed than the CDK outputs. We encourage you to first try figuring out the issue by reading the documentation before you start googling or generative AI-ing. This will help

your learning, and as of February 2025, many large language models still give pretty inaccurate guidance for debugging CDK. Be careful, you could go down quite a rabbit hole. If you can't find the answer in the documentation, the AWS forums are a great place to ask questions.

What if my Lambda function doesn't print "Hello, CDK!" to the console?
This could be happening for a few reasons. First, check the Lambda function code to ensure that the message is being printed correctly. Make sure that the handler method is correctly defined and that the code is being executed when the function is invoked. Next, check the CloudWatch Logs for the Lambda function to see if there are any errors or issues with the function execution. If you're still having trouble, review the CDK app code and the Lambda function configuration to ensure that everything is set up correctly. If you're still stuck, try reaching out to the AWS forums or support for additional help.

What if I get an error about needing to conduct a CDK bootstrap?
This means that your CDK app is not properly configured to deploy to AWS. The CDK bootstrap process creates the necessary resources in your AWS account, such as an S3 bucket and an IAM role, that are required for deploying CDK apps. To resolve this error, run the `cdk bootstrap` command in your CDK app directory to create the required resources in your AWS account. Once the bootstrap process is complete, you should be able to deploy your CDK app without any issues.

Chapter Synth

In this chapter, you learned:

- How to initialize and bootstrap a new CDK application
- How to create a CDK stack and integrate it with your CDK application
- How to use the `aws-cdk-lib` standard library
- How to synthesize, deploy, and destroy a CDK application
- The definitions of *app*, *stack*, *construct*, and *context* in CDK

Discussion

1. How does CDK speed up the process of building and deploying a Lambda function?
2. What are the steps to synthesize, deploy, and destroy a CDK application?
3. What is the difference between a CDK app, stack, and construct?
4. When might you use a CDK context in an application?

Extension Activities

In this chapter, you built a simple Lambda function. Now try making some changes to the function:

1. Change the message printed to the console.

2. Try using a different runtime for the Lambda function, such as Python or Java.

3. Try writing your output as a log instead of a printed message. You can use `console.error()` to write to the log or `console.info()` to write to the info log.

4. Read the Lambda construct documentation and identify three other configurations you can change.

5. Write a loop to deploy two Lambda functions based on a list of greetings. You can use an array of greetings and loop through them to deploy multiple Lambda functions within your CDK code.

## CHAPTER 3

Introducing CDK and AWS Constructs

In this chapter, you will continue building your "Hello, World!" application by adding object storage and an event notification to trigger your "Hello, CDK" function. This will constitute a basic event-driven architecture, allowing you to upload a document and trigger an event. You will build the components of this project in three different ways so that you can learn about Level 1, 2, and 3 (L1, L2, and L3) CDK constructs. At the end of this project, you will have established the first event-driven process for your Home Energy Coach application.

Through this project, you will learn:

- How to deploy AWS resources using L1, L2, and L3 constructs
- How to connect multiple CDK constructs into an event-driven architecture

To get started, you will need:

- The GitHub Repo (*https://oreil.ly/hands-on-aws-cdk-ch3*)

Project Architecture: Greeting S3 Bucket

This is how it all gets started. In this project segment, we are going to set up the most basic building block of CDK that will take data from S3 and print a message. While Figure 3-1 is simple, we will build from here over the coming chapters.

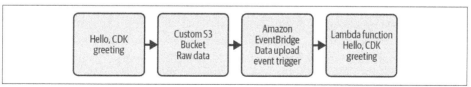

Figure 3-1. The starting place for the "Hello, CDK" application

These are the three steps we'll follow:

1. S3 bucket to upload raw data
2. Event notification to trigger Lambda function
3. Lambda function to print "Hello, CDK"

Note that you will construct this architecture and revise it multiple times to see the L1, L2, and L3 approaches to deploying an S3 bucket.

Defining L1, L2, and L3 Constructs

For CDK, we use the term *constructs* for reusable building blocks that are used to define and configure AWS resources as infrastructure code. Constructs are organized into different levels, commonly referred to as L1, L2, and L3 constructs, each with its own characteristics and use cases:

Level 1 (L1) constructs

L1 constructs, also known as CloudFormation resources, provide a direct mapping to the AWS CloudFormation resource types. They are generated from AWS CloudFormation templates and represent the raw, low-level AWS resources, such as EC2 instances, S3 buckets, or RDS databases. L1 constructs are defined in the `@aws-cdk/aws-cloudformation` module and are used for specifying resources and their properties using CloudFormation-like syntax.

Level 2 (L2) constructs

L2 constructs, also known as the AWS Construct Library, provide a higher-level, more abstracted way of defining AWS resources. They are pre-built, reusable constructs that encapsulate common AWS patterns or best practices, and they are designed to be more developer friendly and expressive compared to L1 constructs. L2 constructs are defined in the `@aws-cdk/aws-_<service>_` modules, such as `@aws-cdk/aws-s3` or `@aws-cdk/aws-dynamodb`, and can be easily imported and used in CDK apps.

Level 3 (L3) constructs

L3 constructs, also known as application constructs or custom constructs, are constructs that are built on top of L1 and L2 constructs to provide higher-level abstractions specific to an application or domain. L3 constructs are created by developers and can be shared and reused across different CDK apps or projects. They encapsulate custom logic, configurations, or patterns that are not available in the existing L1 or L2 constructs, allowing for greater flexibility and customization in defining AWS infrastructure. L3 constructs are also called patterns, so if you see that, don't worry. They mean the same thing.

L1 constructs provide a direct mapping to CloudFormation resources; L2 constructs are pre-built, reusable constructs that encapsulate common AWS patterns; and L3 constructs are custom constructs built on top of L1 and L2 constructs to provide higher-level abstractions specific to an application or domain. The use of different construct levels allows for flexibility, reusability, and expressiveness when defining IaC using the CDK.

Project Tutorial: Deploy an S3 Bucket

Now we will go into greater detail using our S3 bucket as a starting example. We are going to build the S3 bucket for our dynamic greeting, which will later become the S3 bucket to kick off our data pipeline. We are going to build this bucket in three different ways so that you can see the differences between building with L1, L2, and L3 constructs.

Project Preparation

Open *./lib/stack-hello-cdk.ts* in your editor and update the code starting with ``.

Level 1 Construct

To start, we will build our S3 bucket using the L1 construct. This is the most basic way to build an S3 bucket. It is a direct mapping to the CloudFormation `AWS::S3::Bucket` resource type. It can be used to define an S3 bucket with its properties, such as bucket name, access control, and bucket policies, in a CDK app:

```
import * as cdk from "aws-cdk-lib";
import { CfnBucket } from 'aws-cdk-lib/aws-s3';
import * as path from "path";

export class HelloCdkStack extends cdk.Stack {
  constructor(scope: cdk.App, id: string, props?: cdk.StackProps) {
    super(scope, id, props);

    // Level 1 (L1) construct for S3 Bucket
    // Note: Hard-coded names can collide.
    // Consider omitting `bucketName` for auto-generated names.
    const rawDataBucket = new CfnBucket(this, 'rawDataBucket', {
      bucketName: 'raw-data-landing-zone-greeting',
      accessControl: 'Private',
      // other bucket properties
    });

    // Additional code (e.g., Lambda) can go here if needed
  }
}
```

It is a best practice to always set the _accessControl_ to _Private_. Later we will talk about how you can grant access to objects in a bucket as needed.

This L1 construct isn't so bad to build, but an L2 version would be a bit easier. Before we do that, let's review the L1 construct in the console. Go to the S3 console and search for the bucket you just created. You can also search for the bucket in the AWS Console search bar. Alternatively, you can take a look at the CloudFormation stack that was created.

Level 2 Construct

The bucket from @aws-cdk/aws-s3 is an L2 construct that provides a higher-level abstraction for an S3 bucket compared to the L1 construct. It encapsulates common AWS patterns and best practices, such as default encryption, versioning, and CORS configuration, making it more developer friendly and expressive. The following is example usage in a CDK app:

```
import { Bucket } from 'aws-cdk-lib/aws-s3';

const s3Bucket = new Bucket(stack, 'MyS3Bucket', {
  bucketName: 'my-s3-bucket',
  encryption: BucketEncryption.KMS,
  versioned: true,
});
```

Now let's go try it out with the L2 construct. Go ahead and remove the L1 construct and replace it with the L2 construct as done here:

```
import * as cdk from "aws-cdk-lib";
import { aws_lambda as lambda } from "aws-cdk-lib";
import { Bucket, BucketEncryption } from "aws-cdk-lib/aws-s3";
import * as path from "path";

export class HelloCdkStack extends cdk.Stack {
  constructor(scope: cdk.App, id: string, props?: cdk.StackProps) {
    super(scope, id, props);

    // Level 2 (L2) construct for S3 Bucket
    const rawDataBucket = new Bucket(this, 'MyS3Bucket', {
      bucketName: 'my-s3-bucket',
      encryption: BucketEncryption.KMS,
      versioned: true,
    });

    // Existing Lambda function code remains here
  }
}
```

Now that you have built this using an L2 construct, let's have a look at an example of an L3 construct. Remember, L3 constructs are custom constructs that are built on top of L1 and L2 constructs to provide higher-level abstractions specific to an application or domain. In this particular case, we are going to build a custom construct that will create an S3 bucket with specific configurations and some other resources as well. We will see this again when we encounter custom constructs in the following chapters.

Level 3 Construct

The MyCustomS3Bucket is an L3 construct that is custom-built by the developer to encapsulate custom logic, configurations, or patterns specific to the application or domain. It can be used to define a higher-level abstraction for a complex component, such as a serverless application, a microservice, or an architecture pattern, in the CDK app.

Here is an example of an L3 construct that is a custom construct for an S3 bucket. In this particular case, our construct includes an access logs bucket, versioning, and lifecycle rules. While we could write out this configuration every time we need an S3 bucket, it is much easier to create a custom construct that we can reuse. More importantly, when working within a shared development environment, this construct reduces the risk of misconfiguration and security issues. If each developer uses this construct to create an S3 bucket, then all S3 buckets will be created with the same settings. Similarly, if we need to change the settings for all S3 buckets, we can do so in one place across the entire project or even across the entire organization. Take a look at the construct itself, and then look at how it is used:

```
import * as cdk from 'aws-cdk-lib';
import { Construct } from 'constructs';
import * as s3 from 'aws-cdk-lib/aws-s3';

/**
 * Properties for the MyCustomS3Bucket construct
 */
export interface MyCustomS3BucketProps {
  /**
   * The physical name of the S3 bucket.
   */
  bucketName: string;

  /**
   * Number of days after which objects expire.
   *
   * @default 90
   */
  expirationDays?: number;
}

/**
```

```
 * A custom L3 construct that creates an S3 bucket with specific configurations.
 */
export class MyCustomS3Bucket extends Construct {
  /**
   * The main S3 bucket created by this construct.
   */
  public readonly bucket: s3.Bucket;

  /**
   * The associated access logs bucket.
   */
  public readonly accessLogsBucket: s3.Bucket;

  constructor(scope: Construct, id: string, props: MyCustomS3BucketProps) {
    super(scope, id);

    // Create the access logs bucket
    this.accessLogsBucket = new s3.Bucket(this, 'AccessLogsBucket', {
      encryption: s3.BucketEncryption.S3_MANAGED,
      versioned: true,
    });

    // Create the main S3 bucket with
    // lifecycle rules and access logs configured
    this.bucket = new s3.Bucket(this, 'CustomBucket', {
      bucketName: props.bucketName,
      encryption: s3.BucketEncryption.S3_MANAGED,
      accessLogs: {
        bucket: this.accessLogsBucket,
      },
      versioned: true,
      lifecycleRules: [
        {
          expiration: cdk.Duration.days(props.expirationDays ?? 90),
          transitions: [
            {
              storageClass: s3.StorageClass.INTELLIGENT_TIERING,
              transitionAfter: cdk.Duration.days(30),
            },
          ],
        },
      ],
    });
  }
}
```

This represents a more complex set of configurations, but as an L3 construct, it can be used in a very simple way. Review this example usage in a CDK app:

```
import * as cdk from 'aws-cdk-lib';
import { Construct } from 'constructs';
import { MyCustomS3Bucket } from './my-custom-s3-bucket';
```

```
export class MyStack extends cdk.Stack {
  constructor(scope: Construct, id: string, props?: cdk.StackProps) {
    super(scope, id, props);

    // Using the custom L3 construct
    const myCustomS3 = new MyCustomS3Bucket(this, 'MyCustomS3', {
      bucketName: 'my-custom-bucket',
      expirationDays: 120,
    });
  }
}
```

The L3 construct MyCustomS3Bucket showcases the value of higher-level abstractions in CDK development, particularly in joining multiple components. Here's why it's particularly useful:

Encapsulation of best practices

The L3 construct encapsulates several S3 bucket best practices, such as enabling encryption, versioning, and lifecycle rules. This ensures that every S3 bucket created with this construct follows these standards without the developer having to remember to apply them each time.

Joining multiple components

This L3 construct demonstrates how to combine multiple AWS resources into a single, cohesive unit:

- It creates a main S3 bucket for data storage.

- It automatically creates an associated access logs bucket.

- It applies a bucket policy to enforce HTTPS-only access.

By joining these components, the construct provides a complete solution for secure S3 storage with logging.

Simplification of complex configurations

The construct combines multiple L2 constructs and configurations into a single, easy-to-use component. Instead of separately specifying encryption, versioning, lifecycle rules, access logging, and security policies, developers can create a fully configured set of buckets with a single line of code.

Consistency across projects

By using this L3 construct, teams can ensure that all S3 buckets in their organization are created with consistent settings and associated resources, reducing the risk of misconfiguration and security issues.

Improved readability

The usage example demonstrates how an L3 construct can significantly simplify the code in the main stack. Instead of dozens of lines configuring multiple S3 buckets and their relationships, there's just one line creating the custom bucket setup.

Reusability

Once created, this L3 construct can be easily reused across multiple stacks or even different projects, saving time and reducing code duplication. The joined components (main bucket, logs bucket, and policy) are always created together, ensuring consistency.

Abstraction of complexity

The L3 construct hides the complexity of the underlying configurations and relationships between components. Developers using this construct don't need to understand all the details of S3 bucket configuration or how to properly set up access logging; they can simply use the preconfigured construct.

Easier maintenance

If there's a need to update the standard configuration for S3 buckets (e.g., changing the lifecycle rules or modifying the relationship between the main bucket and logs bucket), it can be done in one place—the L3 construct—rather than updating multiple stacks individually.

Enforcing architectural decisions

By encapsulating multiple components and their relationships, L3 constructs can enforce architectural decisions. In this case, the construct ensures that every main bucket always has an associated logs bucket and HTTPS-only policy, implementing a specific security architecture.

By leveraging L3 constructs like `MyCustomS3Bucket` to join multiple components, developers can create more maintainable, consistent, and efficient CDK applications. These constructs promote best practices across their organization and ensure that related resources are always created and configured together, reducing the chance of incomplete or inconsistent deployments.

Why Use L1, L2, and L3 Constructs?

L1, L2, and L3 constructs provide different levels of abstraction and flexibility when defining AWS resources as infrastructure code using the CDK. Each construct level has its own characteristics and use cases, and they can be used together to build complex and scalable applications in a more efficient and developer-friendly way.

L1 constructs provide a direct mapping to CloudFormation resources and are useful for defining raw, low-level AWS resources with CloudFormation-like syntax. They are generated from AWS CloudFormation templates and are used for specifying resources and their properties using CloudFormation resource types. Sometimes, if an AWS service or product is new, you might need to use an L1 construct to access it. But there are benefits to this level of specificity. L1 constructs can be handy if you are building out a custom construct library for your team and want to set your own "sane" defaults or want to configure a resource in a way that is not supported by the L2 construct. L1 constructs are also helpful if you want to have highly granular control over the resource properties and configurations or if you are transitioning from existing CloudFormation templates to CDK.

L2 constructs provide a higher-level, more abstracted way of defining AWS resources and are designed to be more developer friendly and expressive compared to L1 constructs. They are pre-built, reusable constructs that encapsulate common AWS patterns or best practices, such as default encryption, versioning, and CORS configuration, making it easier to define and configure AWS resources in a CDK app. L2 constructs are defined in the @aws-cdk/aws-<service> modules, such as @aws-cdk/aws-s3 or @aws-cdk/aws-dynamodb, and can be easily imported and used in CDK apps. L2 constructs are useful if you want to quickly define and deploy AWS resources without having to write low-level CloudFormation code or if you want to follow best practices and conventions when defining IaC.

L3 constructs provide custom constructs that are built on top of L1 and L2 constructs to provide higher-level abstractions specific to an application or domain. They are created by developers and can be shared and reused across different CDK apps or projects. L3 constructs encapsulate custom logic, configurations, or patterns that are not available in the existing L1 or L2 constructs, allowing for greater flexibility and customization in defining AWS infrastructure. L3 constructs are useful if you want to define complex components, such as a serverless application, a microservice, or an architecture pattern, in a CDK app or if you want to create reusable constructs that can be shared and extended by other developers within your team or beyond.

A strong understanding of L1, L2, and L3 constructs is essential for building scalable, maintainable, and efficient CDK applications. By using the right construct level for the right use case, you can create robust and flexible IaC that meets your application requirements and development needs. It's also important to understand what is happening under the hood so that you can troubleshoot and optimize your CDK applications effectively.

Documenting Your Code

It is a best practice to document your CDK code using JSDoc comments to provide context, explanations, and examples for other developers who may work on or review your code. JSDoc comments are a standard way to document JavaScript code and are supported by most IDEs and code editors, such as VS Code, IntelliJ IDEA, and WebStorm. The benefits of documenting your CDK code include:

Improved code readability

JSDoc comments help make your code more readable and understandable by providing additional context, explanations, and examples for each construct, method, or property.

Better code maintainability

JSDoc comments help other developers understand the purpose, usage, and behavior of your CDK code, making it easier to maintain, extend, and troubleshoot in the future.

Enhanced code collaboration

JSDoc comments serve as a form of documentation that can be shared and reviewed by other developers, enabling better collaboration and knowledge sharing within your team or organization.

Documentation also gives you a chance as the developer to think through what you have built or written. It is a good practice to document your code as you write it, rather than waiting until the end of a project or task. This way, you can capture your thoughts, decisions, and considerations in real time, making it easier to remember and explain your code later on. If you can't explain your own code through clear documentation, then you may need to refactor or simplify it. Or maybe you just don't fully understand it. Either way, documentation is a good way to check your own understanding.

A well-known quotation from physicist Richard Feynman is often paraphrased as, "If you can't explain it simply, you don't understand it well enough." He recommended to his students and readers a technique called the *Feynman technique*, in which you explain a concept in simple terms as if you were teaching it to someone else. This is a great way to check your understanding of a concept or topic, and it can be applied to writing documentation for your code as well.

Here is an example of how you can document your CDK code using JSDoc comments:

```
import * as cdk from 'aws-cdk-lib';
import { Construct } from 'constructs';
import * as s3 from 'aws-cdk-lib/aws-s3';

/**
 * Properties for the MyBucket construct
 */
export interface MyBucketProps {
  /**
   * The name of the S3 bucket.
   */
  readonly bucketName: string;

  /**
```

```
  * Whether to enable versioning for the bucket.
  *
  * @default false
  */
 readonly versioned?: boolean;

 /**
  * The removal policy for the bucket.
  *
  * @default cdk.RemovalPolicy.RETAIN
  */
 readonly removalPolicy?: cdk.RemovalPolicy;
}

/**
 * A custom construct that creates an
 S3 bucket with specific configurations.
 */
export class MyBucket extends Construct {
  /**
   * The S3 bucket created by this construct.
   */
  public readonly bucket: s3.Bucket;

  /**
   * Constructs a new instance of the MyBucket construct.
   *
   * @param {Construct} scope - The scope in which to define this construct.
   * @param {string} id - The scoped construct ID.
   * @param {MyBucketProps} props - Properties for the S3 bucket.
   */
  constructor(scope: Construct, id: string, props: MyBucketProps) {
    super(scope, id);

    this.bucket = new s3.Bucket(this, 'MyBucket', {
      bucketName: props.bucketName,
      versioned: props.versioned ?? false,
      removalPolicy: props.removalPolicy ?? cdk.RemovalPolicy.RETAIN,
    });
  }
}
```

JSDoc annotations are used to document the MyBucketProps interface and the
MyBucket class. For the interface, each property is described, including optional
properties annotated with @default values. The MyBucket class includes a description
of the class itself and detailed annotations for the constructor parameters using
the @param tag. These JSDoc comments provide clear and comprehensive documentation,
making it easier for developers to understand the purpose and usage of the
construct and its properties, enhancing maintainability and collaboration.

You can use similar JSDoc comments to document other parts of your CDK project, such as additional classes, methods, or any custom configurations. Documentation helps improve the understandability and maintainability of your CDK project, making it easier for other developers to work with and extend in the future.

Getting Unstuck

I deployed my S3 bucket, but I got an error stating that the bucket already exists. What should I do?

All S3 bucket names globally have to be unique. You will get an error when deploying the stack if you name your bucket with one that already exists in your CDK app. S3 has the concept of *physical names* and *logical names*. The S3 bucket name is the physical name and each one must be globally unique. The logical name is the name you give the bucket in your CDK code. You can have two buckets with the same logical name in the same stack. The CDK will automatically append a unique identifier to the logical name to make sure that the physical names are unique. This is why we always recommend using logical names and omitting the name string for buckets. By leaving out the name field, the CDK will automatically generate a unique name for you. The collision of named resources is a common source of issues with cloud development, so it's really useful to rely on the CDK to do the naming for you unless there is some really compelling reason not to.

There is no existing construct for the service I want to use. What should I do?

You can create a custom L3 construct to define the resource in your CDK app. This involves creating a new class that extends the Construct class and defining the resource properties, configurations, and logic within the class. You can then use the custom construct in your CDK app to create the resource with the desired settings. Custom constructs provide a way to define custom resources or configurations that are not available in the existing CDK constructs, allowing for greater flexibility and customization in defining AWS infrastructure. More on this in the next chapter.

I'm trying to add an event notification to my S3 bucket to trigger my Lambda function, but it's not working. What could be the issue?

Several things can cause this issue. First, check if you've granted the necessary permissions for S3 to invoke your Lambda function. You need to add a resource-based policy to your Lambda function, allowing S3 to invoke it. Check that the event type you've specified (e.g., s3:ObjectCreated:*) matches the action you're performing on the bucket. At this point, you should check that the bucket and Lambda function are in the same region. Double-check the bucket name and Lambda function Amazon Resource Name (ARN) in your notification configuration. If you've checked all these and it's still not working, you might want to enable CloudTrail and check the logs for any errors or permission issues.

I'm getting a circular dependency error when trying to connect my S3 bucket to my Lambda function. How can I resolve this?

Circular dependencies occur when two or more resources depend on each other. Start by trying to break the circular dependency by introducing a new construct that both resources can depend on. You can use the `Fn.importValue()` function to import values from one stack to another, which can help break circular references. If you have a lot going on with the code, then consider splitting your resources into separate stacks. If the circular dependency is between the S3 bucket and the Lambda function, you might need to create the Lambda function first, then the S3 bucket, and finally add the event notification to the bucket in a separate step. Remember, CDK needs to be able to determine a clear order of resource creation, so avoiding circular dependencies is crucial.

My CDK deployment is failing with a resource handler returned message that reads: "The specified bucket does not exist." What's going wrong?

This error usually occurs when you're trying to perform an operation on a bucket that doesn't exist yet or has been deleted. To start, check that you're not referencing the bucket before it's created in your CDK code. If you're using a bucket name, make sure it's unique and hasn't been used before (even if deleted, S3 bucket names are globally unique and can't be reused immediately). If you're updating an existing stack, make sure the bucket wasn't manually deleted outside of CDK. You can check if you're in the correct AWS account and region where the bucket is supposed to exist. If none of these solve the issue, try destroying the stack completely (`cdk destroy`) and redeploying it from scratch.

Chapter Synth

In this chapter, you learned:

- How to deploy AWS resources using L1, L2, and L3 constructs
- The differences between construct levels and when to use each
- How to connect multiple CDK constructs into an event-driven architecture
- Best practices for documenting CDK code

Now you are ready to continue building more complex architectures with CDK!

Discussion

1. Compare and contrast L1, L2, and L3 constructs. When would you choose to use each type? What are the trade-offs?

2. Why might you want to create a custom L3 construct instead of using existing L1 or L2 constructs? What scenarios would benefit most from custom constructs?

3. How does documentation using JSDoc comments improve CDK code maintainability and team collaboration? What key elements should be included in CDK documentation?

4. Review an existing CDK construct library and identify one L3 construct. What is the construct? What is the purpose of the construct? What other AWS resources are involved?

Extension Activities

Here are some additional activities to consider now that you have completed this chapter:

1. Take the S3 bucket L2 construct we built and extend it with additional features like lifecycle rules, encryption settings, or cross-region replication. Document your additions with JSDoc comments.

2. Create your own custom L3 construct that combines an S3 bucket with other AWS services (like Lambda or Simple Notification Service [SNS]). What patterns or combinations would be useful for common use cases?

3. Compare implementing the same infrastructure using pure CloudFormation versus CDK constructs. What advantages and challenges do you notice with each approach?

4. Research popular open source CDK construct libraries (like CDK Patterns or AWS Solutions constructs). How do they implement L3 constructs? What can you learn from their approaches?

5. Try to find an existing L1 construct and convert it to an L2 construct. What is the difference in the code? What is the benefit of the L2 construct?

## CHAPTER 4

Integrating CDK Constructs

In this chapter, you will integrate multiple CDK constructs to create a dynamic greeting by uploading data to your S3 bucket. This will be the final modification to your "Hello, World" CDK application. You'll chain together an S3 bucket, an EventBridge notification, and a Lambda function to return a dynamic greeting. Later we'll modify this event-driven architecture to accept utility data and calculate usage patterns.

An S3 event notification is a way to trigger an AWS Lambda function when an object is uploaded to an S3 bucket. This is a common pattern for building event-driven architectures.

You can think of an S3 event notification as a universal remote control with buttons that trigger actions in different applications. When you press a button, a signal goes to the remote control hub. The hub then sends commands to take appropriate actions in the linked apps and services for that button.

An event notification makes it easier to build serverless architectures. Services can generate events when something happens, and rules can route them to serverless compute like Lambda to take action on those events. This decouples and scales applications by avoiding direct dependencies. Event notifications handle all the event ingestion, buffering, routing, and delivery reliability. It eliminates complexity so that you can focus on writing code to react to events.

In our application, we will use S3 event notifications to fire events when data is uploaded to our S3 bucket. We will start this with just a simple text file. This will be a major upgrade to our application since it will allow us to greet anyone by name! Later in our project we will modify this a bit to kick off a data pipeline that will perform calculations.

Project Architecture: Dynamic Lambda Greeting

In previous segments, we hardcoded the name for the greeting. In this segment, we will set up the structure so that the name can be dynamic. Admittedly, this is still a simple use case, but this illustrates how we can use event-driven architecture and Amazon Lambda to customize the application.

Figure 4-1 shows the logical architecture for this part of the project. A user will put raw data into an S3 bucket, which will send a notification to EventBridge. That will, in turn, trigger the "Hello, CDK" function, which will trigger a Lambda function to print "Hello, {your name}".

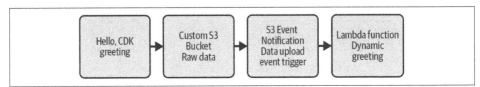

Figure 4-1. Architecture for this part of the project

This architecture is the scaffolding for our bigger project. Once we know how to do this, we can start adding more triggers, more functions, and more nifty features.

Add an S3 Event Notification

The code in Example 4-1 creates the S3 Event notification. Our goal is to use CDK to design and build applications that follow sustainable architecture principles, focusing on scalability, reliability, and performance efficiency. In future chapters, we will add additional CDK constructs to implement cloud native architectural patterns and microservices. This approach is more sustainable in terms of resource utilization, energy consumption, and environmental impact compared to a monolithic application.

Example 4-1. "Hello, CDK" S3 bucket

```
import * as cdk from "aws-cdk-lib";
import * as s3 from "aws-cdk-lib/aws-s3";
import * as lambda from "aws-cdk-lib/aws-lambda";
import * as s3n from "aws-cdk-lib/aws-s3-notifications"; ❶
import * as path from "path";

export class HelloCdkStack extends cdk.Stack { ❷
  /**
   * Constructor for the stack
   * @param {cdk.App} scope - The CDK application scope
   * @param {string} id - Stack ID
   * @param {cdk.StackProps} props - Optional stack properties
   */
```

```
    constructor(scope: cdk.App, id: string, props?: cdk.StackProps) { ❸
      super(scope, id, props);

      const helloCdkS3Bucket = new s3.Bucket(this, "HelloCdkS3Bucket", { ❹

        removalPolicy: cdk.RemovalPolicy.DESTROY,
        autoDeleteObjects: true,
        lifecycleRules: [
          {
            expiration: cdk.Duration.days(1),
          },
        ],

      });

      const helloCdkLambdaFunction = new lambda.Function(this, "HelloCdkLambda", { ❺
        description:
          ```Lambda function generates
          a dynamic greeting by retrieving the text from an
          S3 object and when triggered by S3 event```,
        runtime: lambda.Runtime.NODEJS_18_X,
        handler: "index.main",
        code: lambda.Code.fromAsset(
          path.join(__dirname, "./lambda/lambda-hello-cdk")
        ),
      });

      helloCdkS3Bucket.grantRead(helloCdkLambdaFunction); ❻

      helloCdkS3Bucket.addEventNotification(
        s3.EventType.OBJECT_CREATED,
        new s3n.LambdaDestination(helloCdkLambdaFunction),
        { suffix: ".txt" }
      );

      new cdk.CfnOutput(this, "bucketName", {
        value: helloCdkS3Bucket.bucketName,
      }); ❼

  }
}
```

Let's break down what this code does to augment our previous version of the
HelloCdk stack. First, we import the required AWS CDK modules: the core CDK
Library, along with the S3, Lambda, and S3 Notifications modules (imported as s3,
lambda, and s3n, respectively). We also import the Node.js path module, which we'll
use to specify the Lambda function's code location:

❶ The S3 Notifications module (as s3n) is imported from aws-cdk-lib, which
provides constructs for configuring S3 bucket event notifications.
```

② The `HelloCdkStack` class extends the base CDK `Stack`. It represents cloud resources as a single deployable unit.

③ The constructor accepts the CDK app's scope, a stack ID, and optional stack properties.

④ We create an S3 bucket named `HelloCdkS3Bucket` to upload greetings. As part of the bucket configuration, we set it to be destroyed when the stack is deleted, and we enable auto-deletion of objects upon stack removal. We also set a lifecycle policy to expire objects after one day.

⑤ We create a Lambda function named `HelloCdkLambda` and set configurations like a runtime environment (Node.js 18.*x*), a handler method, and its code location. We also include a description, which is helpful for others to understand the purpose of the Lambda function. We need to make sure Lambda has read access to the `HelloCdkS3Bucket`, which we accomplish with the `grantRead` method.

⑥ Here, we define the Lambda invocation on the S3 event when a new `.txt` object is created in the S3 bucket.

⑦ With this line, we output the S3 bucket name, which can be helpful for referencing it after the stack is deployed.

In simple terms, we add an event that triggers each time a *.txt* file is uploaded to our S3 bucket. We grant our Lambda function access to the bucket and its contents, allowing it to read the uploaded file and print a dynamic greeting based on its contents.

Removal Policies and Destroy on Delete

Most L2 and L3 CDK constructs that handle data default to retaining that data even if you destroy or delete your CDK stacks. This is designed to prevent accidental data loss when changes are made. However, during the early stages of CDK development, as you deploy, destroy, and revise stacks, you might end up with an accumulation of numerous S3 buckets, database tables, and other resources.

Since we're still in the early stages, and our application is currently an event-driven architecture that doesn't require data persistence yet, we won't persist any data for now. Later in the book we'll guide you through various options for managing data retention, such as destroying, retaining, or taking snapshots upon deletion. By the end, you'll implement a CDK aspect that deletes data stores during development but retains them in production. Think of a CDK aspect as a filter applied during stack synthesis. More details on this will come later.

We've built our infrastructure as code. Now, we need our Lambda function. You will get this code from the project sample code on GitHub.

1. Navigate to the GitHub repository (*https://oreil.ly/B-6pZ*). Notice that, in our project repository, the final directory structure looks a little different than your project will look now. That's okay. You're going to build a lot of new things, but for now, focus on the hello-cdk stack.

2. Review the README for this stack and navigate to the Lambda function code. Here, you will see some simple code that takes the S3 bucket event notification as input, extracts the bucket, gets the object that was uploaded, reads the contents of the file as if it were a *.txt* file, and prints a simple greeting statement.

3. Review the code to make sure you understand it and transfer it to your project directory structure. You will need to create a Lambda directory and an index file. You will also need to install your AWS SDK dependencies. Follow the instruction in the README for more support if required.

Time to test our application! Try synthesizing and deploying your application from memory. One of the great features of the CDK Toolkit is that it provides immediate feedback if you encounter an issue. If you get stuck, don't worry—simply refer back to the earlier steps in the chapter.

Open the CloudFormation service in the AWS Console. You should notice a familiar pattern: our stack is still present, but now an additional resource is included. This time, let's test our Lambda function by uploading a few files and observing the results:

1. Open a text editor and create a file called *test.txt*.

2. Add your name to the file and save it locally. The file should look like this:

```
<Firstname Lastname>
```

In the S3 console, locate the bucket called `HelloCdkBucket`. Then, click Upload and select the *test.txt* file (Figure 4-2).

Figure 4-2. "Hello, CDK" bucket upload part 1

Soon you will upload the file and see the greeting in the Lambda function logs. But don't upload your file yet! First, we want to look at each part of the architecture so that we can trace the event from the S3 bucket to the Lambda function output (Figure 4-3).

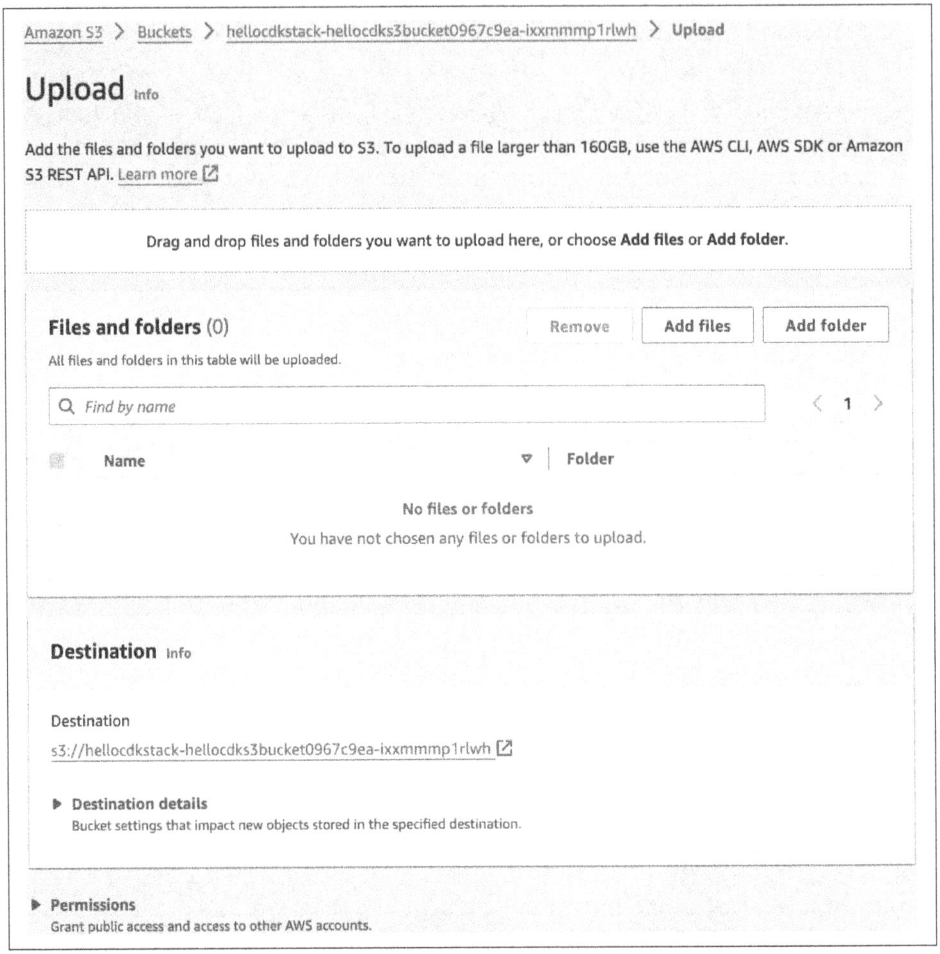

Figure 4-3. "Hello, CDK" bucket upload part 2

Now, open the Lambda console and locate the `HelloCdkLambda` function (Figure 4-4). It will be called something like `HelloCdkStack-HelloCdkLambdaAABB123-abc123`, except the letters and numbers at the end will be different. See the following tip for more details.

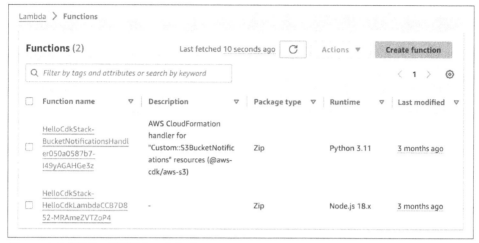

Figure 4-4. "Hello, CDK" Lambda function

At this point, switch to the Monitor tab and expand the metrics. You will want to take note of the current metrics values. Since you haven't triggered your function yet, you should see that the Invocations metric is at 0 (Figure 4-5).

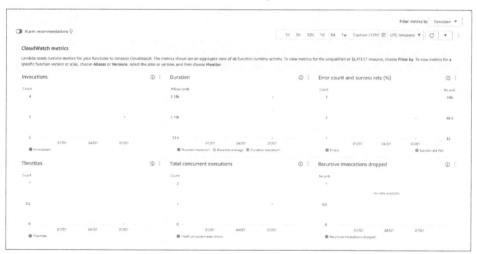

Figure 4-5. "Hello, CDK" Lambda function metrics

Now return to the Lambda function in the console. Here you will see a visual depiction of the S3 event notification that is connected to your Lambda function (Figure 4-6).

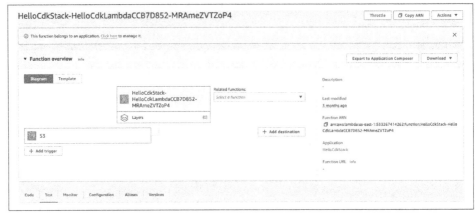

Figure 4-6. "Hello, CDK" Lambda S3 event

If you click on the S3 event notification, you will see the details of the event (Figure 4-7). This is a great way to troubleshoot your application if it isn't working as expected. By looking at the event details, you can verify the configuration of the event notification and see if the event is working as expected. This is, in general, a good practice when troubleshooting event-driven applications. In most cases, you can find your way into the AWS Console or at least CloudWatch to see the event details. If, for some reason, your event isn't firing the way you expect, you can go and trace each step of the event to see where the issue is.

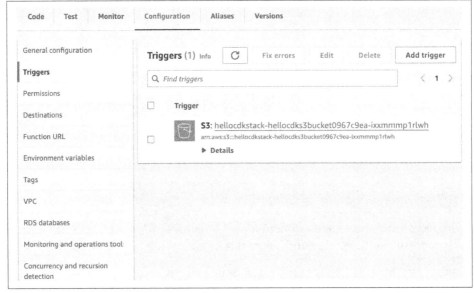

Figure 4-7. "Hello, CDK" Lambda S3 event details

Great! Now you are ready to upload your file. Go back to the S3 console and upload the *test.txt* file. Once you have uploaded the file, go back to the Lambda console and check the metrics. You should see that the Invocations metric has increased. This means that the function has been triggered. Go to CloudWatch Logs and view the log group for the function (Figure 4-8). Look for a recent log stream and inspect the contents. At this point, you need to check if execution of the function resulted in the "Hello, CDK!" message being printed. This confirms that the S3 event properly invoked the Lambda function via Event Notifications.

Figure 4-8. "Hello, CDK" Lambda function logs

Try the same steps, but this time try creating a new file called *test.md*, a markdown file. Put your name in the markdown file and upload it using similar steps. What do you expect to happen? Why does this happen? Is there a way you can modify the function to handle situations like this?

Have you noticed the naming conventions used with CDK resources yet? There are multiple types of identifiers and names. The two we will focus on are *physical IDs* and *logical IDs*. Physical IDs are used to reference resources across applications where the resource name needs to be predictable in all situations. For instance, if application A needs to reference an S3 bucket in application B, you might need to name it VeryImportantS3Bucket, and no matter how many times you deploy, you need the name to stay the same.

This would matter a lot if application B always had to reference VeryImportant S3Bucket. The *problem* with this type of identifier is also its strength—it is always the same. This means that if you make changes to your application or create new buckets, the names can collide, resulting in accidental references, failed deployments, and various other issues.

Logical IDs, on the other hand, are dynamically constructed each time a new resource is deployed. If there are significant changes to that resource, it may receive a new logical ID, which will also be passed to all the resources that depend on it during an update. In this example, your S3 bucket will follow the naming pattern _<stack>-<resource><unique-identifier>_. So, your S3 bucket might be called

`VeryImportantStack-VeryImportantS3BucketAABB123-abc123`. This approach dramatically reduces the chance of resource conflicts, collisions, or duplications and is considered the most stable naming convention, which is why CDK does this by default.

 Here are some tips on how to let CDK name resources for you:

- Avoid changing the logical ID of an AWS CloudFormation resource after creation, as it may result in resource deletion, service interruptions, or data loss.

- When using AWS CDK, avoid explicitly setting resource names; if you do, changing an immutable configuration could gridlock your stack. Instead, either rename the resource or delete and redeploy the stack to move forward.

- Allow CDK to auto-generate resource names to avoid issues during updates, but explicitly set resource names when referring to resources from another application.

Using Parameters and Overrides

Parameters in CloudFormation allow you to customize the behavior of your stacks at deployment time. CDK provides a convenient way to define these parameters, making it easier to manage configurations without changing your code.

You can define parameters directly in your CDK stack. When you deploy your stack, you can provide parameter values using the CLI. Using parameters in this way adds flexibility to your IaC.

Overrides are another feature that allows you to modify specific properties of resources at deployment time. This can be especially useful if you change a property based on the deployment environment (e.g., development versus production). To use overrides, you can set properties on your resources after they have been defined. Overrides can be helpful when integrating existing resources or making small adjustments without redefining your entire stack.

When defining parameters, you can provide default values to streamline the deployment process. This is particularly useful in development environments where standard configurations are used. By providing defaults, users can deploy without specifying every parameter, reducing the chance of errors.

AWS CloudFormation allows you to specify constraints on parameters, such as minimum or maximum values for numerical inputs or allowed values for string inputs. By implementing validation directly in your CDK parameters, you can catch configuration errors early in the deployment process.

In more complex applications, you might have parameters that depend on each other. For example, the type of instance you want to deploy may depend on the selected environment. You can implement logic in your CDK code to handle these dependencies and validate that the input parameters make sense together.

Getting Unstuck

I've deployed my stack, but I don't see any EventBridge rules in the AWS Console. What could be the issue?

There are a few things to check to resolve this. First, make sure you've actually added the EventBridge notification to your S3 bucket in your CDK code. Look for something like `helloCdkS3Bucket.addEventNotification()` in your stack. You can check that you've deployed the latest version of your stack by running `cdk diff` to see if there are any pending changes. Go ahead and check your IAM role to make sure it has the necessary permissions to create EventBridge rules. As always, you can check if there are any error messages in the CloudFormation console or in the CDK deployment output. Finally, if none of these solve the issue, try destroying and redeploying your stack.

My Lambda function isn't being triggered when I upload a file to the S3 bucket. How can I troubleshoot this?

Check if the file you're uploading matches the suffix specified in the event notification (*.txt* in this case). Verify that the Lambda function has the necessary permissions to be invoked by S3. Look for the resource-based policy on your Lambda function. In the S3 console, look at the properties of your bucket and check if the event notifications are set up correctly. You can try uploading a file manually through the AWS Console to rule out any issues with your upload process. Check the CloudWatch Logs for your Lambda function to see if there are any error messages.

I'm getting a "circular dependency detected" error when I try to deploy my stack. What's causing this and how can I fix it?

Circular dependencies occur when two or more resources depend on each other. For starters, review your code to identify where the circular dependency might be. It's often between the S3 bucket and the Lambda function. Next, try creating the Lambda function first, then the S3 bucket, and finally add the event notification to the bucket. If the circular dependency persists, you might need to split your stack into multiple stacks to break the dependency cycle. You can use `Fn.importValue()` to import values from one stack to another, which can help break circular references. Finally, consider using a custom resource to create the event notification after both the S3 bucket and Lambda function have been created.

My Lambda function is being triggered, but it's not reading the content of the uploaded file. What could be wrong?

There are several potential issues to check. First, make sure you've granted the necessary permissions for the Lambda function to read from the S3 bucket. Look for `helloCdkS3Bucket.grantRead(helloCdkLambdaFunction)` in your stack. Then, check if your Lambda function code is correctly retrieving the S3 object. It should use the AWS SDK to get the object content. Next, verify that the Lambda function's execution role has the necessary IAM permissions to read from S3. As always, review the CloudWatch Logs—they are super useful for debugging. Finally, try increasing the Lambda function's timeout if the file is large and might be taking too long to read.

In the next chapter, we will add more complexity to our application by adding a new trigger and a new function. This will allow us to start building a data pipeline that will calculate utility usage patterns. This is a common use case for event-driven architectures and will give you a good foundation for building more complex applications.

Chapter Synth

In this chapter, you learned:

- How to deploy an EventBridge notification
- How to pass parameters between CDK constructs
- How to integrate multiple CDK constructs
- How to use CDK to create an event-driven architecture
- The difference between physical and logical IDs in CDK

Discussion

1. In this chapter, you strung together the inputs and outputs of several CDK constructs. How would you add more user interactivity using these constructs?

2. What is the difference between an event-driven application and a polling application? What are the benefits?

3. Describe the method for passing data between CDK constructs. At what point does this happen in the synthesis process?

4. How would you modify the application to accept multiple files and print a greeting for each uploaded file?

5. How would you modify the application to accept a file with multiple names and print a greeting for each name in the file?

6. Articulate the difference between a physical ID and a logical ID in CDK. How does CDK use these IDs to manage resources?

Extension Activities

Now that you have completed this chapter, try to modify the application to:

1. Print the name in the greeting from a list.

2. Print a greeting based on the time of day.

3. Accept files in different formats and/or reject files if they do not meet the format specification.

4. Use a hardcoded greeting in the Lambda function and see if you can get it to print a greeting without using the S3 bucket.

5. Integrate with an external API to tell the user the current weather based on location.

6. Select an additional API to integrate with and add a new greeting based on the data from that API.

7. Add an SNS notification so that any errors in the Lambda function are sent to an email address.

Building Multistack CDK Applications

In this chapter, you will modify your "Hello, CDK" application to form the foundation of the Home Energy Coach application. You will create CDK stacks for shared resources and the data pipeline. You will build upon your existing application by repurposing your S3 bucket and Lambda function as a data pipeline. This pipeline will allow you to upload home energy usage data and receive a summary of total energy consumed. You can either use a provided sample dataset or fill in the data template with information from your own utility bill. This chapter will prepare you for the next one, where you will learn multiple ways to package Lambda functions.

The projects are going to get progressively more involved, starting here. There is a jump from the earlier intro chapters to what you will make in this chapter. We know it is tough, but take your time, and we are confident you will be able to continue building cool stuff.

Project Architecture: Data Pipeline Microservice

In this project segment, you will build a data pipeline microservice that allows a user to upload a .csv file containing home energy usage data to an S3 bucket. The system uses Amazon EventBridge to trigger an AWS Lambda function, which then summarizes the total energy used in kilowatt hours (kWh). Figure 5-1 illustrates the application flow up to this point. We use EventBridge to take specific actions based on the incoming data.

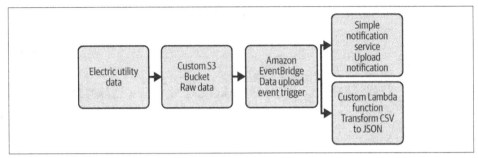

Figure 5-1. Serverless data pipeline architecture

The diagram illustrates the main components of our serverless data pipeline. We store the electric utility data in the S3 bucket. As data is added to the bucket, it automatically triggers a workflow to send the user a notification and kick off the workflow to convert the CSV into JSON.

Create a Shared Resources Stack

We recommend organizing your multistack CDK applications into clearly defined stacks, each with its own purpose. You can think of each stack as a microservice. While a stack may depend on data passed from another stack to function, it is best to minimize or limit cross-stack dependencies whenever possible. However, in some cases, there are resources that are used by multiple stacks.

You can organize these resources into a "shared resources" stack. This shared resources stack will deploy consistently, even when you're working with subcomponents of your application. CDK nicely manages all of this for you. You can include shared storage, notification topics, and authentication resources in this stack. For the Home Energy Coach project, we will include an S3 bucket designated as a "landing bucket" for raw data and an SNS topic that will be used for several notifications across the application.

You can define stack dependencies to enforce synchronous synthesis. Stack dependencies allow you to specify the order in which stacks are synthesized during deployment, ensuring that dependent stacks are created or updated before the dependent stacks that rely on them.

There is no "right way" to handle shared resources, but our general rule is:

- If only one stack will use the resource, put it in that stack.
- If more than one stack will use the resource, put it in shared resources.

Rename Your CDK Application

Let's begin by renaming our existing application. This will also help you understand the inner workings of the CDK application structure:

1. Rename the application directory from *hello-cdk* to *home-energy-coach*.

2. Change the application name in *cdk.json* and *package.json*. This is how CDK identifies your application and builds and deploys everything.

3. Rebuild your *package.lock.json* to keep it consistent with the *package.json* by running `npm install`. They'll probably sync up eventually anyway, but we prefer to be proactive—both in this book and in life.

Redefine the Application Entry Point

The entry point is the main file that gets executed when the library is imported or required in a CDK application. It typically defines the public API of the library and exposes the functions, classes, or objects that users can access. So far, we've been working with default entry points, but now we want to take more control and define a custom entry point for each stack.

Rename the bin/main app entry point located at *./bin/hello-cdk.ts* from *hello-cdk.ts* to *main.ts*. This is a matter of choice and style. We prefer using "main" because it clearly identifies this as the primary app file. And just a note: you can deploy multiple applications within a single CDK repository. We won't be doing that in this project, but it's good to know for future reference.

Restructure Your Application for Multiple Stacks

Multistack deployments in CDK involve deploying several CDK stacks within a single CDK application. Each stack in a CDK application can represent a distinct unit of deployment—like a group of resources or a specific environment.

This simplifies things. For instance, stacks can be written in different programming languages like TypeScript, Python, Java, or C#, leveraging CDK's language-specific libraries. You can also pass outputs from one stack to another, allowing for the creation of more complex and scalable cloud infrastructure deployments. CDK makes it easy to manage dependencies, outputs, and configurations across multiple stacks, all within a single application.

Before we build our data pipeline microservice, we need to set up a clean project structure that supports multistack development. It's common to break projects into multiple CDK stacks as projects grow and become more complicated. Each stack should focus on a specific task like data processing, APIs, authentication, or machine learning. This makes your project easier to manage and scale. In this section, we'll restructure the initial "Hello CDK" stack into a more modular format and prepare our codebase for multiple stacks by creating dedicated folders for each one. Let's walk through the steps to get that set up:

1. Rename the stack located at *./lib/hello-cdk.ts* to *stack-data-pipeline.ts*.

2. Next, create a directory called *stacks* in the *./lib* directory. This is where we'll organize all of our stacks. Soon, you'll have more than one stack, so it's best to keep things tidy from the start.

3. Create another directory, called *stack-data-pipeline*, in the *./lib/stacks* directory. This is where your data pipeline stack and all its related files will be stored.

4. Move the *stack-data-pipeline.ts* file into the *./lib/stacks* directory. Nice and organized, right? We like to use the same name for the stack file and the directory where it lives. While this isn't required, it helps maintain consistent naming conventions, making it easier for anyone new to the project to quickly understand the structure and what each file represents at a glance.

Reusable CDK Libraries and Stack Organization

AWS CDK helps structure cloud infrastructure so that the code is maintainable, scalable, and team-friendly. One of CDK's strengths is its support for reusable libraries and constructs that capture common patterns or business logic. Here are three best practices to keep in mind as you build stacks and reusable components to help you save time and reduce duplication across your CDK applications:

Use cross-stack references judiciously.
   While it's possible to reference resources from one stack in another, be cautious not to create too many dependencies between stacks. This can lead to tight coupling and make it harder to update or deploy stacks independently.

Organize stacks logically.
   Group resources in a way that makes sense for your application. Common patterns include separating networking, computing, storage, and database resources into different stacks.

Deploy stacks independently.
   In large projects, you may want to deploy stacks independently rather than all at once. CDK makes it easy to deploy individual stacks using the `cdk deploy` command.

Create a Shared Resources Stack

CDK offers a wide range of built-in and community-contributed libraries that can be used as shared resources across different CDK applications. You can create reusable constructs or libraries that encapsulate common patterns or best practices specific to your organization and share them among your development teams. This not only promotes consistency but also accelerates development by allowing teams to reuse well-tested and validated code across various CDK applications.

1. Create a directory in the *./lib/stacks* directory and call it *stack-shared-resources*.

2. Create your shared resources stack file in the *./lib/stacks/stack-shared-resources* directory and call it *stack-shared-resources.ts*.

Now we have a multistack directory structure ready to go (Figure 5-2). Let's add some new stacks, starting with our shared resources stack.

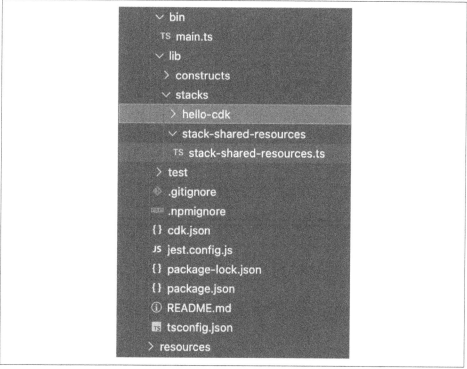

Figure 5-2. Directory structure for shared resources stack

Since this is a shared resources stack, we'll need to pass its output to other stacks. We'll achieve this by passing the output as props to other stacks. At this point, we will begin reshaping our `hello-cdk` stack into something more specific for our application. You can either remove it and rewrite from scratch, or work to modify it for the data pipeline. We'll dive deeper into context later in this chapter.

All of the code in Example 5-1 is new, but in some cases, we'll be building constructs similar to those we created in our "Hello, CDK" stack. For more practice, we recommend writing everything from scratch so that you can reinforce your learning. Please consult the shared resources stack within the project sample code on GitHub for the full implementation with detailed documentation and explanation.

Example 5-1. Shared resources stack

```
import * as cdk from "aws-cdk-lib"; ❶
import { aws_s3 as s3 } from "aws-cdk-lib";
import { aws_sns as sns } from "aws-cdk-lib";
import { aws_sns_subscriptions as subscriptions } from "aws-cdk-lib";

export interface SharedResourcesStackProps extends cdk.StackProps { ❷
  readonly adminEmailAddress: string;
}

/**
 * The stack class extends the base CDK Stack
 */
export class SharedResourcesStack extends cdk.Stack { ❸
  /**
   * Constructor for the stack
   * @param {cdk.App} scope - The CDK application scope
   * @param {string} id - Stack ID
   * @param {SharedResourcesStackProps} props - Stack properties
   * including adminEmailAddress
   */

  // These are the properties that will be made available to other stacks ❷
  public readonly rawDataUploadBucket: s3.Bucket;
  public readonly snsTopicRawUpload: sns.Topic;
  public readonly snsTopicCalculatorSummary: sns.Topic;

  constructor(scope: cdk.App, id: string, props: SharedResourcesStackProps) {
    // Call super constructor
    super(scope, id, props);

    // Create raw landing bucket for S3
    this.rawDataUploadBucket = new s3.Bucket(this, "RawDataUploadBucket", {
      removalPolicy: cdk.RemovalPolicy.DESTROY,
      autoDeleteObjects: true,
      lifecycleRules: [
        {
```

```
          expiration: cdk.Duration.days(1),
        },
      ],
    });
    // Create SNS Notification topic for raw data upload
    this.snsTopicRawUpload = new sns.Topic(this, "SnsTopicRawUpload", {
      displayName: "Home Energy Coach SNS Topic",
      emailAddress: props.adminEmailAddress,
    });

    // Add email subscription to SNS topic for raw upload
    this.snsTopicRawUpload.addSubscription(
      new subscriptions.EmailSubscription(props.adminEmailAddress)
    );

    // Create SNS Notification topic for calculator summary
    this.snsTopicCalculatorSummary = new sns.Topic(
      this,
      "SnsTopicCalculatorSummary",
      {
        displayName: "Home Energy Coach SNS Topic for calculator summary",
        emailAddress: props.adminEmailAddress,
      }
    );

    // Add email subscription to SNS topic for calculator summary
    this.snsTopicCalculatorSummary.addSubscription(
      new subscriptions.EmailSubscription(props.adminEmailAddress)
    );
  }
}
```

Let's break down what is going on here:

❶ We import the various necessary modules from the AWS CDK and Node.js core libraries, including the AWS S3, SNS, and SNS Subscriptions modules from the AWS CDK Library.

❷ We define an interface, SharedResourcesStackProps, that extends the default StackProps. This interface requires the inclusion of the adminEmailAddress property for our SNS topics. Remember, interfaces are a way to define the shape of an object. In this case, we are defining the shape of the props that will be passed to our SharedResourcesStack class. This is like saying, "All instances of SharedResourcesStack must have an adminEmailAddress property."

❸ We create a new class, SharedResourcesStack, which extends the base AWS CDK Stack class. Here's what happens inside. First, we declare three public read-only properties: rawDataUploadBucket, snsTopicRawUpload, and snsTopic

CalculatorSummary. In TypeScript, the public keyword indicates that a member can be accessed from outside the class. The readonly keyword ensures that the property cannot be reassigned after it's initialized. The this keyword in TypeScript refers to the current instance of the class. So, when we use this.raw DataUploadBucket, we're setting a property to the current instance of the Shared ResourcesStack class.

Inside the constructor, we call the constructor of the parent Stack class using the super method, initializing our stack. We create a new S3 bucket named RawData UploadBucket with specific configurations, and we assign it to the rawDataUpload Bucket property.

Next, we set up two SNS topics: one for raw data uploads (snsTopicRawUpload) and another for calculator summaries (snsTopicCalculatorSummary). Both topics utilize the adminEmailAddress provided in the props. Now we can subscribe both SNS topics to an email address using the addSubscription method. This ensures that the specified email address receives notifications for both raw uploads and calculator summaries.

This SharedResourcesStack class sets up the foundational AWS resources, like an S3 bucket and two SNS topics, supporting an application that handles raw data uploads and some calculator functionality. Email notifications regarding these functionalities are sent to the provided administrator's email address.

Build Your Data Pipeline Stack

Next, we are going to modify our previous hello-cdk stack, now called stack-data-pipeline, to create a serverless event-driven data pipeline. This will expand upon the functionality of our earlier stack by adding a Lambda function that transforms the raw data into JSON and saves it to an S3 bucket. We will also add a second Lambda function that calculates the total energy usage and sends a summary to an SNS topic. This stack will be triggered by an S3 event notification. In addition, we will add an SNS topic for the calculator summary (Figure 5-3).

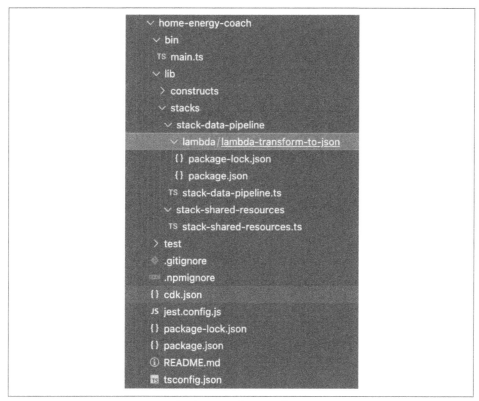

Figure 5-3. Directory structure for data pipeline stack

The code in Example 5-2 looks a lot like that in Example 5-1. This version has been rewritten, and we recommend you write everything in the example as if it were new. We think you will improve your CDK skills more quickly if you simply delete everything in your file and build from scratch. Our explanation will treat this as a brand-new stack.

In subsequent chapters, we will make more incremental changes to this stack, focusing only on the new code added. However, in this case, your new code will be the entire application.

Example 5-2. Data pipeline stack

```
import * as cdk from "aws-cdk-lib";
import { aws_s3 as s3 } from "aws-cdk-lib";
import { aws_lambda as lambda } from "aws-cdk-lib";
import { aws_s3_notifications as s3n } from "aws-cdk-lib";
import { aws_sns as sns } from "aws-cdk-lib";
import * as path from "path";
```

```
export interface DataPipelineStackProps extends cdk.StackProps {
  readonly rawDataLandingBucket: s3.Bucket;
  readonly snsTopicRawUpload: sns.Topic;
  readonly snsTopicCalculatorSummary: sns.Topic;
}

/**
 * The stack class extends the base CDK Stack
 */
export class DataPipelineStack extends cdk.Stack {
  /**
   * Constructor for the stack
   * @param {cdk.App} scope - The CDK application scope
   * @param {string} id - Stack ID
   * @param {DataPipelineStackProps} props - Data pipeline stack properties
   */
  constructor(scope: cdk.App, id: string, props: DataPipelineStackProps) {
    // Call super constructor
    super(scope, id, props);

    // Create S3 bucket to store transformed JSON
    const jsonTransformedBucket = new s3.Bucket(this, "JsonTransformedBucket", {
      versioned: true,
      removalPolicy: cdk.RemovalPolicy.DESTROY,
    });

    // Create Lambda function to transform CSV to JSON
    const transformToJsonLambdaFunction = new lambda.Function(
      this,
      "TransformToJsonLambdaFunction",
      {
        runtime: lambda.Runtime.NODEJS_18_X,
        handler: "index.main",
        code: lambda.Code.fromAsset(
          path.join(__dirname, "./lambda/lambda-transform-to-json")
        ),
        environment: {
          TRANSFORMED_BUCKET: jsonTransformedBucket.bucketName,
          AWS_REGION: cdk.Stack.of(this).region,
        },
        description:
          "Lambda function transforms CSV to JSON and saves to S3 bucket",
      }
    );

    // Create Lambda function to calculate energy usage and notify
    const calculateAndNotifyLambdaFunction = new lambda.Function(
      this,
      "CalculateAndNotifyLambdaFunction",
      {
        runtime: lambda.Runtime.NODEJS_18_X,
        handler: "index.main",
```

```
      code: lambda.Code.fromAsset(
        path.join(__dirname, "./lambda/lambda-calculate-notify")
      ),
      environment: {
        SNS_TOPIC_CALCULATOR_SUMMARY: props.snsTopicCalculatorSummary.topicArn,
        AWS_REGION: cdk.Stack.of(this).region,
      },
      description:
        ```Lambda function calculates
        total energy usage and sends
        a summary notification via SNS```,
    }
  );

  // Grant permissions for Lambda functions
  props.rawDataLandingBucket.grantRead(transformToJsonLambdaFunction);
  jsonTransformedBucket.grantWrite(transformToJsonLambdaFunction);
  jsonTransformedBucket.grantRead(calculateAndNotifyLambdaFunction);

  // Add event notification to trigger CSV transformation on .csv files
  props.rawDataLandingBucket.addEventNotification(
    s3.EventType.OBJECT_CREATED,
    new s3n.SnsNotification(props.snsTopicRawUpload, {
      suffix: ".csv",
    })
  );

  // Add event notification to trigger calculation on .json files
  props.rawDataLandingBucket.addEventNotification(
    s3.EventType.OBJECT_CREATED,
    new s3n.LambdaDestination(calculateAndNotifyLambdaFunction),
    { suffix: ".json" }
  );

  // Output S3 bucket names for reference
  new cdk.CfnOutput(this, "RawDataLandingBucketName", {
    value: props.rawDataLandingBucket.bucketName,
  });

  new cdk.CfnOutput(this, "JsonTransformedBucketName", {
    value: jsonTransformedBucket.bucketName,
  });

  }
}
```

Let's break down what's happening here. We start by importing the AWS CDK core library, alongside specific modules for S3, Lambda, and S3 Notifications. We also add an import for the AWS SNS module from the AWS CDK Library. Additionally, we import the Node.js `path` module to help manage and transform filepaths.
```

We define a new interface, called `DataPipelineStackProps`, which ensures that the following properties are present when creating an instance of our `DataPipeline Stack` class:

`rawDataLandingBucket`
Represents an S3 bucket meant for raw data uploads

`snsTopicRawUpload`
An SNS topic for notifications related to raw uploads

`snsTopicCalculatorSummary`
Another SNS topic but for notifications on calculator summaries

Next, we introduce the `DataPipelineStack` class, extending the basic CDK `Stack`. Within this class, three main elements are defined: an S3 bucket (`jsonTransformed Bucket`) meant for storing transformed JSON data, and two Lambda functions (`transformToJsonLambdaFunction` and `calculateAndNotifyLambdaFunction`). The former function transforms CSV data into JSON, while the latter does some form of calculation and notification. Both functions take environment variables to operate efficiently. Necessary permissions are set for the Lambda functions to interact with the S3 buckets.

Inside the constructor of the `DataPipelineStack` class, the call to the superclass's constructor initializes the stack. The S3 bucket event notifications are set up for specific events: notifying an SNS topic when a new *.csv* file is uploaded to the `rawData LandingBucket`, and triggering a Lambda function when a new *.json* file appears in the same bucket. Additionally, two CloudFormation outputs are created to display the names of the `rawDataLandingBucket` and `jsonTransformedBucket`.

AWS Lambda Insights can help with visibility into the performance and health of AWS Lambda functions. It automatically collects and analyzes data on Lambda function invocations, duration, errors, and throttling, offering insights and recommendations for optimizing your Lambda function's performance.

In summary, the `DataPipelineStack` class orchestrates the setup of AWS resources for the data pipeline. Its primary function is data processing: raw data in CSV format is uploaded to one S3 bucket, which triggers a Lambda function to convert this data into JSON format and save it into another bucket. Simultaneously, notifications are sent out for specific events, and another Lambda function performs a calculation and sends a notification based on the transformed data.

TypeScript features

We also introduced some new CDK features that we will use throughout the project. Take a look back at the code to see how these concepts are executed within the data pipeline:

Interface
> In TypeScript, the interface construct allows us to define the shape of an object without implementing any logic. It sets a contract for classes or objects to follow. For instance, `DataPipelineStackProps` defines what properties a `DataPipeline Stack` instance must receive.

`readonly`
> The `readonly` keyword, seen in the properties of the interface, ensures that the properties can't be changed after they're initialized. This is great for setting immutable configurations.

Class and constructor
> The class `DataPipelineStack` showcases TypeScript's class-based object-oriented programming. The constructor method is a special method used to create and initialize an object created from a class.

CDK features

We also introduced some new CDK features that we will use throughout the project. Take a look back at the code to see how these concepts are executed within the data pipeline:

Bucket events and notifications
> The CDK offers a streamlined way to add event notifications to S3 buckets using the `addEventNotification` method.

Lambda and environment variables
> The AWS Lambda service allows the execution of code in response to certain events without provisioning or managing servers. The CDK enables Lambda function creation, where you can specify runtime, handler, and even environment variables.

Permissions with `grantRead`/`grantWrite`
> Granting permissions between AWS resources is straightforward in CDK. For instance, `grantRead` and `grantWrite` are methods that give specified resources (like Lambda) read or write permissions on S3 buckets.

Remember to prioritize clarity and relevance, ensuring that descriptions are closely tied to the code's actions. "A lambda function for calc" is not as helpful as "Lambda function that calculates the total energy usage and sends a summary to an SNS topic."

Are you finished yet? No! We still need to define our Lambda functions. Let's do that in the next chapter.

Project Example: Build a Custom Resource for Amazon QuickSight Deployment

We can use this approach to build a custom resource for Amazon QuickSight for data visualization. To do this, we will need to define a custom resource that integrates with the Amazon QuickSight service using the `CustomResource` class. This class allows us to specify the properties and attributes of the resource, as well as the Lambda function that will function as the custom resource handler. You can define the input and output properties of the custom resource, which will be used to pass data between the CDK and the Lambda function.

You will need to write the Lambda function that acts as the custom resource handler. This function will be responsible for creating, updating, and deleting the Amazon QuickSight resources using the Amazon QuickSight service API. You can choose a programming language of your preference to implement the Lambda function (supported languages include Node.js, Python, Java, and others). The Lambda function will receive input from the CDK, which will contain the properties and attributes of the custom resource, and it will interact with the Amazon QuickSight service to perform the desired actions.

Once you have defined the custom resource and implemented the Lambda function, you can deploy it using the CDK. The CDK will synthesize a CloudFormation template that includes the custom resource and the associated Lambda function. You can then use the CDK, CLI, or SDK to deploy the CloudFormation stack, which will create the custom resource and the Lambda function in your AWS account.

After deploying the custom resource, you should test and validate its functionality to ensure that it works as expected. You can use the CDK and AWS, CLI, or SDK to interact with the custom resource and verify that it correctly creates, updates, and deletes the Amazon QuickSight resources. You should also test various scenarios and edge cases to confirm that the custom resource is robust and handles errors gracefully.

Check Your Work

After each deployment, it is important to review your work in AWS CloudFormation and then verify that each service has deployed as expected. In each chapter, we recommend following this approach.

Start by reviewing the resources deployed in AWS CloudFormation. Navigate to the AWS Console and ensure that you have selected the region where you chose to deploy. By default, this will be us-east-1 if you follow the default instructions in this book. Search for CloudFormation and select Stacks. Use the headings in this chapter as a guide. Can you see the resources you deployed listed there?

Next, visit each service in the AWS Console to double-check that all resources have been deployed. You should see several Lambda functions and S3 buckets. We recommend examining the code in those Lambda functions and verifying the names of the S3 buckets.

While you can rely on your local CLI outputs to confirm what has been deployed, for learning purposes, we strongly recommend that you explore the correspondence between your code and your infrastructure in the console. This hands-on approach is the best way to learn.

Here is a brief review of the resources you should be looking for:

- S3 bucket for raw data uploads
- S3 bucket for transformed JSON data
- SNS topic for raw data upload notifications
- SNS topic for calculator summary notifications
- Lambda function to transform CSV to JSON with S3 event notification
- Lambda function to calculate and notify with S3 event notification

Getting Unstuck

I've deployed my stack, but I don't see any EventBridge rules in the AWS Console. What could be the issue?

There are a few things to check. First, make sure you've actually added the EventBridge notification to your S3 bucket in your CDK code. Verify that you've deployed the latest version of your stack, and check for any error messages in the CloudFormation console or CDK deployment output. You should also make sure that the IAM role has the necessary permissions to create EventBridge rules. Finally, take a look in the S3 console to see if the event notifications are set up on the bucket.

My Lambda function isn't being triggered when I upload a file to the S3 bucket. How can I troubleshoot this?

We hate it when this happens! But don't despair—start by checking if the file you're uploading matches the suffix specified in the event notification (*.txt* in this case). Ensure that the Lambda function has the necessary permissions to be invoked by S3. You can check the CloudWatch Logs for your Lambda function for any error messages. In the S3 console, look at the properties of your bucket and check if the event notifications are correctly set up. Try uploading a file manually through the AWS Console to rule out any issues with your upload process. Make sure that your S3 bucket and Lambda function are in the same region, and check if there are any VPC configurations on your Lambda that might be preventing it from accessing S3 or EventBridge.

I'm getting a "circular dependency detected" error when I try to deploy my stack. What's causing this and how can I fix it?

Circular dependencies happen when two or more resources depend on each other. Review your code to identify where the circular dependency might be, and try creating the Lambda function first, then the S3 bucket, and finally add the event notification to the bucket. If the circular dependency continues, you might need to split your stack into multiple stacks. You can use `Fn.importValue()` to import values from one stack to another. You might want to consider using a custom resource to create the event notification after both the S3 bucket and the Lambda function have been created. You can use `DependsOn` to explicitly specify the order of resource creation. Finally, check if you're referencing the Lambda function's ARN in the S3 bucket configuration and vice versa.

My Lambda function is being triggered, but it's not reading the content of the uploaded file. What could be wrong?

In this case, ensure that you've granted the necessary permissions for the Lambda function to read from the S3 bucket. Check if your Lambda function code is correctly retrieving the S3 object. Next, verify that the Lambda function's execution role has the necessary IAM permissions to read from S3. You can use the CloudWatch Logs to inspect your Lambda function for any error messages related to reading the S3 object. Check that the S3 bucket name is correctly referenced in your Lambda function code (bucket names most be globally unique). If the file is large, try increasing the Lambda function's timeout, as it might be taking too long to read. Also, check if there are any encryption settings on the S3 bucket that could be preventing the Lambda function from accessing the file.

I've uploaded a file to the S3 bucket, but my Lambda function is being triggered multiple times. Why is this happening?

Several things could be causing this. First, check if you have multiple event notifications set up on the same bucket. Next, verify that you're not creating duplicate EventBridge rules in your CDK stack, and make sure your Lambda function is idempotent (able to handle being called multiple times with the same input). Check if S3 replication or versioning features are enabled, as they might be triggering multiple events. Review the CloudWatch Logs for any clues as to why the function is being triggered repeatedly. Also, verify that you're not manually invoking the Lambda function in addition to the S3 event. Finally, consider implementing a de-duplication mechanism using DynamoDB or another storage service.

My CDK deployment is failing with a resource handler returned message that reads:
"The specified bucket does not exist." What's going wrong?

This error occurs when you're trying to perform an operation on a bucket that doesn't exist. To troubleshoot, start by ensuring that you're not referencing the bucket before it's actually created in your CDK code. Next, confirm that you're operating in the correct AWS account and region where the bucket should exist. If you're updating an existing stack, make sure the bucket wasn't manually deleted outside of CDK. You should also verify that you're not trying to use a bucket name that's already taken (even if it's in a different account). Check if there are any IAM permission issues preventing the creation of the bucket, and ensure that your AWS CLI is configured with the correct credentials and region. Finally, you can destroy the stack completely (`cdk destroy`) and redeploy it from scratch.

Chapter Synth

In this chapter, you learned:

- How to modify the CDK application entry point
- How to structure a CDK application repository with multiple stacks
- How to pass the output of one stack to another as props
- How, when, and why to establish a shared resources stack
- How to use local context to deploy applications with constant parameters
- Terms and concepts, including CDK context, CDK entry point, shared resources stack, and CDK props

Coming up in the next chapters, you will learn to package Lambda functions and deploy them as application logic for your data pipeline.

Discussion

1. What are three ways that you can add context to a CDK application?
2. How do you deploy a single stack from an application?
3. What is the purpose of a shared resources stack? What is the purpose of putting items in this stack?
4. When is it appropriate to use a shared resources stack versus putting resources in an individual stack?
5. How can CDK context and props help manage complexity in larger CDK applications?

6. What are the benefits of using an event-driven architecture with Lambda functions instead of provisioned servers?

Extension Activities

In this chapter, you created a multistack AWS CDK application. You can extend the learning with the following optional activities:

1. Add SMS notifications to your SNS topic so that you receive SMS notifications when a file is uploaded to your S3 bucket.

2. Add a conditional clause to your calculator Lambda function that sends a warning notification if the energy usage is above a certain threshold.

3. Add a data quality check to your data pipeline that checks for empty files, missing records, or files that are not in the correct format. If the file is empty, missing records, or not in the correct format, send an SNS notification to the user.

4. Add user authentication to the data upload process using Cognito.

5. Visualize the pipeline data with Amazon QuickSight dashboards.

6. Send data to a time series database like Amazon Timestream for further analysis.

## CHAPTER 6

Packaging and Deploying Lambda Functions

In this chapter, you'll learn how to package and deploy Lambda functions using CDK. Your Lambda function will accept a transformed set of energy usage data and calculate the total energy usage in kilowatt hours (kWh). You will also have an opportunity to modify the function so that it performs some additional calculations. This is where you begin to think like an engineer and a product manager, making this application useful for your users. This is also a wonderful opportunity to experience the advantages that come with packaging Lambda functions in Node.js using CDK.

Project Architecture: Package and Deploy Lambda Functions with CDK

This project segment will focus on the two Lambda functions that will form the application logic for your serverless data pipeline. You will also learn how to pass environment variables to your Lambda functions. Please note that while our current pipeline is built by chaining Lambda functions together with S3 events, this is not the only way to build a data pipeline. We will cover using AWS Step Functions to build a data pipeline in a later chapter.

Figure 6-1 shows how we are building on the concepts we covered in the preceding chapters and adding in Lambda functions. Lambda is a very versatile tool, and we can use it to connect with a wide range of AWS services.

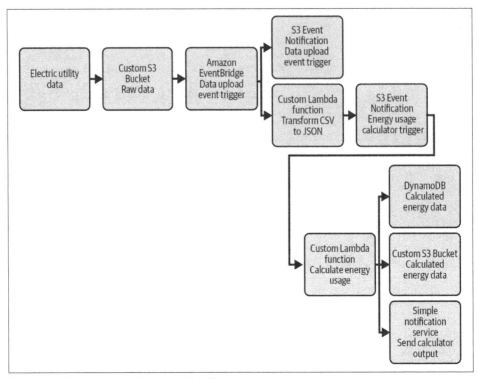

Figure 6-1. Energy calculator Lambda function

Now that you've set up the structure for your multistack application, it's time to implement the core logic of your data pipeline using AWS Lambda. The application is orchestrating the following AWS services:

- S3 bucket (raw data)
- Eventbridge notification
- Lambda function (transform to JSON)
- S3 bucket (transformed data)
- Eventbridge notification
- Lambda function (calculate energy use)
- DynamoDB table (energy use)
- S3 bucket (energy use)
- SNS notifications

Create a Lambda Function to Transform CSV to JSON

For our project, the initial electric utility comes to us in CSV format. We need to convert that to JSON format for our application to use the data. Let's set up the file structure for the conversion process:

1. Create a directory in the *./lib/stacks/stack-data-pipeline/lambda* directory and call it *lambda-transform-to-json*.

2. In the *./lib/stacks/stack-data-pipeline/lambda/lambda-transform-to-json* directory, create a file called *index.ts*.

We will now create a Lambda function that transforms CSV data to JSON. This simple function takes a CSV file as input and returns a JSON file. We will use this function to transform the raw data that is uploaded to our S3 bucket. We will also demonstrate how to pass environment variables to a Lambda function. Again, we *could* just modify our previous Lambda function, and you will see how they are very similar. But since we are learning, we will build this from scratch.

To get started, we are going to do something a little different. One of the great benefits of developing with CDK is that it allows us to work with our infrastructure definition and our application logic in the same place. In some organizations or teams, this may still mean different people writing that code, but they are still tightly integrated. In this case, you will be doing both (by the way, we think this is a fantastic way to develop).

CDK Lambda bundling is nice—like, really, really nice. There is a lot that happens behind the scenes for you when you deploy a Lambda function that you don't necessarily have to worry about. In this case, CDK takes care of bundling, zipping, validating, and uploading your Lambda. In most cases, it will also help check that your Lambda has the right permissions to do what you need it to do. Just note that the validation is not always perfect, so you should always test your Lambda functions before deploying them to production. We will cover testing in more detail in a later chapter.

Start by initializing a new Node.js project in the *./lib/stacks/stack-data-pipeline/lambda/lambda-transform-to-json* directory by running `npm init -y`. This will create a *package.json* file in your directory. This file defines your project and its dependencies. You can open the file and see that it contains some basic information about your project, along with a `dependencies` section. This is where you will define the dependencies for your project. You can also see that it has a `scripts` section. This is where you will define scripts that you can run from the command line. We will use this later to test our Lambda function.

Next, install the `aws-sdk` and `csvtojson` packages by running `npm install aws-sdk csvtojson`. This will install the packages and add them to your *package.json* file. You can see that the `dependencies` section has been updated with the packages you just installed.

 One advantage of working with JavaScript for AWS Lambda functions is that packaging of dependencies is seriously simplified. If we were to do the same thing with a Lambda function writing in Python, we would have to create a virtual environment, install the packages, and then zip the virtual environment and the code together. This isn't a huge deal, but it does require a little more work. In this case, we just install the packages, and CDK takes care of the rest.

We start with code for a Lambda function that transforms a CSV file stored in an S3 bucket to a JSON file and stores the transformed file in a different S3 bucket (Example 6-1). The code imports the `S3Client`, `GetObjectCommand`, and `PutObjectCommand` from the `@aws-sdk/client-s3` package. It also imports the `csvtojson` package, which is a dependency required for the transformation process. The code creates a new `S3Client` instance, which is used to interact with the S3 service. The region for the S3 client is set using the `AWS_REGION` environment variable. The code defines the `DESTINATION_BUCKET` variable, which holds the name of the S3 bucket where the transformed JSON file will be stored. The bucket name is read from the `transformed ToJsonBucket` environment variable.

Example 6-1. Lambda function to transform CSV to JSON

```
const {
  S3Client,
  GetObjectCommand,
  PutObjectCommand,
} = require("@aws-sdk/client-s3");
const csv = require("csvtojson"); // This package is required

const client = new S3Client({ region: process.env.AWS_REGION });
const DESTINATION_BUCKET = process.env.jsonTransformedBucket
```

Now we can add what we just created to the main function of the Lambda function in Example 6-1. In the next code block, we define the `main` function as an asynchronous function, which allows it to use the `await` keyword to handle asynchronous operations. The code extracts the `bucket` name and key (the filename) from the `event` object, which is passed to the Lambda function:

```
const main = async (event) => {
  const bucket = event.Records[0].s3.bucket.name;
  const key = event.Records[0].s3.object.key;

  console.log(
    `Event passed to Lambda including:\n Bucket: ${bucket} Key: ${key}`
  );

  const input = {
    Bucket: bucket,
    Key: key,
  };
```

This information is typically provided by the S3 event trigger that invoked the Lambda function. The code logs the extracted bucket and key information to the console, which can be useful for debugging and monitoring purposes. It's always a good idea to include logs. Finally, the code creates an input object, which contains the Bucket and Key properties. This object will be used in subsequent steps to interact with the S3 service:

```
  try {
    const command = new GetObjectCommand(input);
    const response = await client.send(command);

    const chunks = [];
    for await (const chunk of response.Body) {
      chunks.push(chunk);
    }
    const fileContents = Buffer.concat(chunks).toString("utf8");

    // Convert CSV to JSON
    const jsonArray = await csv().fromString(fileContents);

    // Upload JSON data to the destination bucket
    const putCommand = new PutObjectCommand({
      Bucket: DESTINATION_BUCKET,
      Key: key.replace(".csv", ".json"), // Assume the key had a .csv extension
      Body: JSON.stringify(jsonArray),
      ContentType: "application/json",
    });

    await client.send(putCommand);

    console.log(
      `File transformed and uploaded to: ${DESTINATION_BUCKET}/${key.replace(
        ".csv",
        ".json"
      )}`
    );

    return {
      statusCode: 200,
```

```
        body: JSON.stringify({
          message:
            ```CSV successfully transformed
            to JSON and uploaded to
            destination bucket```,
        }),
      };
    } catch (err) {
      console.error(err);
      return {
        statusCode: 500,
        body: JSON.stringify({
          message: "Error processing the operation.",
        }),
      };
    }
  }
};

module.exports = { main };
```

Let's break down the workings of this Lambda function:

Imports and dependencies

We use AWS SDK for JavaScript to interact with S3. Specifically, we use S3Client to establish a connection with S3 and GetObjectCommand and PutObjectCommand to interact with S3. The csvtojson module converts CSV data to JSON.

Lambda initialization

An S3Client named client is instantiated, with the region being read from the environment variable AWS_REGION. A constant DESTINATION_BUCKET is set up to read the destination S3 bucket name from the environment.

The core logic is encapsulated in the main function, which is triggered by an event. The event source is captured and unpacked to retrieve the bucket name and key of the S3 object triggering the Lambda. A command to fetch this object (GetObject Command) is created and sent to the S3 client, fetching the CSV content. Using the csvtojson library, the CSV data is converted to a JSON array. This transformed data is then uploaded back to S3 using the PutObjectCommand but with a *.json* extension instead of *.csv*. The function returns a success message if all operations complete successfully; otherwise, it handles errors and logs them.

The main function is exported for external usage, likely to be used as the entry point when the Lambda is triggered.

To relate this with the previously provided code, the Lambda function serves as the logic for the TransformToJsonLambdaFunction. When a *.csv* file is uploaded to the rawDataLandingBucket, this Lambda is designed to fetch the uploaded file, transform
```

it into JSON format, and then upload the JSON data to `jsonTransformedBucket`. This aligns with the description provided in the CDK stack definition.

JavaScript features

For this part of the project, we are introducing some new JavaScript features. These features come out of the box with JavaScript so we can use them to help make the code more readable, efficient, and easier to work with when handling asynchronous data processing and working with raw file content:

Destructuring
> The use of {...} in the `require` statement at the beginning is a destructuring assignment, a feature that lets you unpack values from arrays or properties from objects into distinct variables.

`Async/Await`
> The `async` and `await` keywords allow functions to pause and wait for a `Promise` to resolve or reject, providing a cleaner syntax over callbacks for working with asynchronous operations. For example, `await client.send(command)` waits for the S3 client to fetch the object.

`Buffer`
> `Buffer` is a built-in Node.js object that provides methods to perform raw data operations. Here, it's used to collate and convert data chunks from the CSV file into a readable string format.

AWS SDK features

Now let's take a look at the AWS SDK features introduced in this section. These components allow your Lambda functions to interact with S3 by sending commands through a client object. As always, we want to follow a consistent and modular pattern for working with AWS services:

`S3Client`
> This is a client object representing the S3 service in the AWS SDK. It is the primary entry point for interacting with S3.

`GetObjectCommand` *and* `PutObjectCommand`
> These commands represent the `get` and `put` operations on S3, respectively. They encapsulate details of the respective operations and are part of the AWS SDK's command pattern.

The Lambda function is a good representation of how AWS services can be interacted with programmatically using the AWS SDK. It shows the flow of data from one AWS service (S3), through a transformation process, and back to another AWS service (S3 again, but a different bucket).

Create a Lambda Function to Calculate Energy Use and Notify

We have one more Lambda function to add so that our data pipeline functionality is complete. This next function will calculate the total energy usage and send a notification to an SNS topic. We will use this function to demonstrate how to pass environment variables to a Lambda function. We *could* just modify our previous Lambda function, and you will see how they are very similar. But since we are learning, we will build this from scratch.

In this case, we do not need to add additional dependencies beyond what is defined in the default JavaScript environment for CDK, but just in case we want to add dependencies in the future, we will start, again, by running npm init -y to create our Node.js project. The latest JavaScript runtimes for Lambda functions require you to include the AWS SDKs as dependencies within a *package.json* file now. This keeps Lambda function packages smaller, so you only need to bring the dependencies you use, rather than having every AWS service represented in your package. Example 6-2 breaks down what we're doing in our Lambda functions, but we recommend you review the sample code (*https://oreil.ly/XnYIC*) and also look specifically within the Lambda directory to see the final code.

Example 6-2. Lambda function to calculate energy use and notify

```
/_
 * @module LambdaFunction
 * @description This module processes a JSON file from an S3 bucket, calculates
 * energy statistics, and then sends the results via an SNS notification.
 */

const { S3Client, GetObjectCommand } = require("@aws-sdk/client-s3");
const { SNSClient, PublishCommand } = require("@aws-sdk/client-sns");
const { DynamoDBClient, PutItemCommand } = require("@aws-sdk/client-dynamodb");

// Clients Initialization
const s3Client = new S3Client({ region: process.env.AWS_REGION });
const snsClient = new SNSClient({ region: process.env.AWS_REGION });
const dynamoClient = new DynamoDBClient({ region: process.env.AWS_REGION });

const snsTopic = process.env.snsTopicRawUpload;
```

In the preceding code, we use S3Client and GetObjectCommand from the AWS SDK for JavaScript. We use SNSClient and PublishCommand from the AWS SNS side for notifications.

We initialize the AWS services with s3Client and the snsClient and programmatically call the region we've set in our environment variable AWS_REGION. We have defined our snsTopic by fetching the topic ARN from the snsTopicRawUpload environment variable.

We need to set up AWS service clients to use environment variables and define the main Lambda handler. This code extracts the S3 bucket and object key from the event trigger and sets up the input needed to interact with the uploaded file:

```
/_
 * The main Lambda function handler.
 *
 * @param {Object} event - The Lambda event object.
 * @returns {Promise<Object>} The response object containing status and body.
 */
const main = async (event) => {
  /_
   * Extract the S3 bucket name and object key from the Lambda event.
   * @type {string}
   */
  const bucket = event.Records[0].s3.bucket.name;
  const key = event.Records[0].s3.object.key;

  console.log(`Received event for Bucket: ${bucket}, Key: ${key}`);

  const input = {
    Bucket: bucket,
    Key: key,
  };
```

When the main Lambda function gets triggered by an event (likely an S3 put object event), it first pulls out the bucket name and key of the triggering S3 object from the provided event. We use the AWS SDK to fetch this JSON object.

Once the data is retrieved, we perform a series of computations on it. First, we calculate the daily kWh consumption and augment our data with these daily totals. Then, we tabulate the usage of various equipment (like electric vehicle charging, hot water heaters, etc.) and compute the respective percentages. After completing the computations, we compose an email summarizing these statistics and send it using an SNS notification to the specified snsTopic. Pretty cool, right? Here's the code:

```
  try {
    /_ Retrieve and parse the JSON data from S3 */
    const response = await s3Client.send(new GetObjectCommand(input));
    const rawData = await response.Body.text();
    const data = JSON.parse(rawData);
    console.log('Successfully retrieved and parsed data from S3.');

    let totalKWH = 0;
    let counts = {
      electricVehicleCharging: { true: 0, false: 0 },
      hotWaterHeater: { true: 0, false: 0 },
      poolPump: { true: 0, false: 0 },
      heatPump: { true: 0, false: 0 },
    };
```

```
/_
 * Calculate energy statistics from the provided data.
 */
data.forEach((row) => {
  const dailyKWH = row["6am"] + row["12pm"] + row["6pm"] + row["12am"];
  totalKWH += dailyKWH;
  row["totalKWH"] = dailyKWH;

  for (let key in counts) {
    counts[key][row[key] ? "true" : "false"]++;
  }
});

/_
 * Calculate percentage counts for each energy source.
 * @type {Object}
 */
const percentageCounts = {
  electricVehicleCharging: {
    true: (counts.electricVehicleCharging.true / data.length) * 100,
    false: (counts.electricVehicleCharging.false / data.length) * 100,
  },
  hotWaterHeater: {
    true: (counts.hotWaterHeater.true / data.length) * 100,
    false: (counts.hotWaterHeater.false / data.length) * 100,
  },
  poolPump: {
    true: (counts.poolPump.true / data.length) * 100,
    false: (counts.poolPump.false / data.length) * 100,
  },
  heatPump: {
    true: (counts.heatPump.true / data.length) * 100,
    false: (counts.heatPump.false / data.length) * 100,
  },
};

/_
 * DynamoDB item preparation.
 */
const currentTimestamp = new Date().toISOString();
const dynamoItem = {
  TableName: process.env.CALCULATED_ENERGY_TABLE_NAME,
  Item: {
    primaryKey: { S: "1" },
    timestamp: { S: currentTimestamp },
    data: { S: JSON.stringify({ totalKWH, counts, percentageCounts, data }) }
  }
};

try {
  await dynamoClient.send(new PutItemCommand(dynamoItem));
  console.log('Successfully stored processed data in DynamoDB.');
```

```
  } catch (dynamoError) {
    console.error('Error storing data in DynamoDB:', dynamoError);
    throw new Error('DynamoDB storage error.');
  }

  /_
   * Prepare and send the SNS notification.
   */
  const emailContent =
  ```Total KWH: ${totalKWH}\n
  Electric Vehicle Charging - True: ${counts.electricVehicleCharging.true}
  (${percentageCounts.electricVehicleCharging.true.toFixed(2)}%),
  False: ${counts.electricVehicleCharging.false}
  (${percentageCounts.electricVehicleCharging.false.toFixed(2)}%) ...```;

  const snsParams = {
    Message: emailContent,
    Subject: "Processed JSON Results",
    TopicArn: snsTopic,
  };

  try {
    await snsClient.send(new PublishCommand(snsParams));
    console.log('Successfully sent notification via SNS.');
  } catch (snsError) {
    console.error('Error sending SNS notification:', snsError);
    throw new Error('SNS sending error.');
  }

  return {
    statusCode: 200,
    body: JSON.stringify({
      totalKWH,
      counts,
      percentageCounts,
      data,
    }),
  };

  } catch (err) {
    console.error('Main processing error:', err);
    return {
      statusCode: 500,
      body: JSON.stringify({
        message: "Error processing the S3 object.",
      }),
    };
  }
};

module.exports = { main };
```
```

This module provides us with a Lambda function designed to process energy statistics from a JSON file found in an S3 bucket. After processing, the results are sent out through an SNS notification.

If any of these steps fail, an error is logged, and a response is sent back indicating this failure.

The `module.exports` function exports the main function so that it is accessible for external invocation, primarily as the Lambda's entry point.

JavaScript features

We introduce a few JavaScript features that make the Lambda function code cleaner and more readable. These language features are common in CDK projects and help simplify asynchronous operations and object handling:

Arrow functions
> We're using ES6 arrow functions (e.g., `const main = async (event) => { ... }`) for a concise way to write functions.

`async/await`
> This feature makes our asynchronous code (like fetching an S3 object or publishing an SNS message) look and behave a bit more like synchronous code, making our code tidier and easier to understand.

Destructuring
> In our imports at the beginning, we use this ES6 feature to extract multiple properties from objects into distinct variables.

AWS SDK features

The code uses some new AWS SDK features to set up the interaction between S3 and SNS in our Lambda functions. They follow a client-command pattern that keeps the code modular and easy to extend:

`S3Client`
> This is our primary mechanism for talking to S3.

`GetObjectCommand`
> With this command, we instruct our `s3Client` to fetch a specific object from S3.

`SNSClient`
> This client allows us to interact with the SNS service.

`PublishCommand`
> This command is the vehicle for sending our SNS notifications.

Lambda can invoke these constructs to bridge between AWS's S3 and SNS. This simple data pipeline is a powerful combo for processing and communicating data insights and products. In this example, we use the pipeline to process energy data, but this pattern can be applied to any kind of data.

As a final step, we need to integrate all of these stacks with our application entry point, ensuring that we pass the output of one stack to another as props. This marks the final step in the project for this chapter.

Test, Deploy, Modify, and Destroy

It's time to check that your infrastructure deployed as expected. This time, you have several additional services to review, including Lambda functions, SNS topics and subscriptions, buckets to store outputs, and even a database. Let's go step by step to review each of these services.

Start by subscribing yourself to the SNS topic that was created. You can do this by going to the AWS Console, navigating to the SNS service, and selecting the topic that was created. You should see a subscription for your email address. If you do not see a subscription, you can create one by clicking the "Create subscription" button and entering your email address.

Next, check that your Lambda functions are deployed and have the correct environment variables set. You can do this by going to the AWS Console, navigating to the Lambda service, and checking the functions that were deployed. You can also check the environment variables that were set for each function.

Then, verify that your SNS topic and subscription are set up correctly. You can do this by going to the AWS Console, navigating to the SNS service, and checking the topic and subscription that were created.

Next, check that your DynamoDB table is set up correctly. You can do this by going to the AWS Console, navigating to the DynamoDB service, and checking the table that was created.

After that, confirm that your S3 buckets are set up correctly. You can do this by going to the AWS Console, navigating to the S3 service, and checking the buckets that were created.

Now that you have checked that all of your services are set up correctly, you can test your application by uploading a *.csv* file to the rawDataLandingBucket. You should see the file get transformed to JSON, followed by the energy usage being calculated and a notification sent to the SNS topic. You can also check the DynamoDB table to see the data that was stored there. Best of all, you can check your email to see the notification that was sent. You should have an email with the processed JSON results.

Getting Unstuck

I'm getting a "Module not found" error when my Lambda function runs. What could be causing this?

This error typically occurs when a required module is missing. Here are some steps to troubleshoot. Start by checking that all required packages are listed in your *package.json* file. Run `npm install` in your Lambda function's directory and check that you're using the correct runtime for your Lambda function (e.g., `lambda.Runtime.NODEJS_18_X`). Verify that the *node_modules* folder is included when you package your Lambda function. If using CDK to deploy, make sure your `lambda.Function` construct is pointing to the correct directory. Finally, you can try clearing your CDK build cache and redeploying.

My Lambda function is timing out when processing large CSV files. How can I fix this?

Lambda functions have a maximum execution time. If your function is timing out, increase the timeout setting for your Lambda function in the CDK stack. We recommend breaking down large files into smaller chunks and processing them in parallel. Use AWS Step Functions to orchestrate multiple Lambda functions for larger workloads. You might consider using a streaming approach to process the CSV data instead of loading it all at once. If the file is consistently too large for Lambda, consider using a different service, like AWS Batch.

I'm not receiving SNS notifications even though my Lambda function is running successfully. What should I check?

Start by verifying that the SNS topic ARN in your Lambda function's environment variables is correct. Check that your Lambda function has the necessary IAM permissions to publish to the SNS topic. You can look at the CloudWatch Logs for your Lambda function to see if there are any errors when trying to publish to SNS. Next, ensure that you've subscribed to the SNS topic with a valid email address and confirmed the subscription. You can try manually publishing a message to the SNS topic to see if it's working correctly and check if there are any SNS delivery status logs indicating issues with message delivery.

My transformed JSON data isn't saving to the destination S3 bucket. What should I do?

Start by reviewing your Lambda function and making sure it has the necessary permissions to write to the destination S3 bucket. Verify that the destination bucket name in your Lambda function's environment variables is correct. Check the CloudWatch Logs for your Lambda function for any errors during the S3 put operation. Make sure your Lambda function is being triggered by the S3 event from the source bucket. You can also try increasing the Lambda function's timeout if the transformation process is taking longer than expected. Finally, verify that the transformed data is valid JSON before attempting to save it.

The data in my DynamoDB table doesn't match what I expect from my Lambda function. How can I debug this?

Start by checking that you're using the correct data types when saving items to DynamoDB (e.g., S for string, N for number). Verify that your DynamoDB table has the correct primary key structure. You can add more detailed logging in your Lambda function to see exactly what data is being sent to DynamoDB. Ensure that your Lambda function has the necessary permissions to write to the DynamoDB table. Try writing a test item to DynamoDB directly (not through Lambda) to ensure that the table is set up correctly. Finally, check if there are any error messages in the CloudWatch Logs related to DynamoDB operations.

My CDK stack deploys successfully, but the Lambda functions aren't being triggered by S3 events. How can I correct this?

First, verify that you've added the S3 event notification to your bucket in your CDK stack. Ensure that the event type (e.g., `s3.EventType.OBJECT_CREATED`) matches what you're expecting to trigger the function, and check that the S3 bucket and Lambda function are in the same AWS region. Verify that the S3 bucket name in your stack matches the actual bucket name in your AWS account. Take a look at the bucket properties in the S3 console to ensure that the event notification is set up correctly. You can try manually invoking the Lambda function to ensure that it's deployed and functioning correctly. Finally, check the IAM roles and policies to ensure that S3 has permission to invoke the Lambda function.

Chapter Synth

In this chapter, you learned:

- How to package and deploy Lambda functions with CDK
- How to add application logic and compute statistics within Lambda functions
- How to connect Lambda functions to other AWS services like S3, DynamoDB, and SNS for building serverless data pipelines

Discussion

1. What are some benefits of using CDK for deploying Lambda functions versus manually creating them?
2. How can Lambda functions help build resilient and scalable data pipelines?
3. What are some use cases where a serverless architecture with Lambda may be more suitable than traditional servers?

Extension Activities

Here are some additional activities to consider now that you have completed this chapter:

1. Add validation logic in the Lambda functions to check data formats and field values.

2. Send processed summaries from Lambda to an email subscription list via SNS.

3. Visualize the processed statistics in a dashboard using Amazon QuickSight.

## CHAPTER 7

Extending CDK Constructs

In this chapter, you will build custom L3 CDK constructs for an S3 bucket and a Lambda function by extending existing L3 constructs. In the next chapter, you will build on this knowledge by creating your own custom construct from scratch. Custom L3 constructs are useful when teams of developers need to adhere to a common standard for cost, performance, security, compliance, or compatibility purposes. In our case, we will be creating a custom construct for an S3 bucket that has access logging enabled and public access blocked for security and compliance purposes. It will also have a lifecycle policy enabled to reduce the cost of storing data that is accessed less frequently.

We will also create a custom Lambda function construct that enables logging for security purposes and that uses the Graviton2 compute instance to optimize cost and reduce the carbon footprint of our data processing compute. You might use custom constructs for similar purposes, or to meet some other goal for your team or your individual project. The goal of a custom construct is to standardize a repeatable configuration so that you don't have to code it from scratch every time or copy/paste it from a template. Now you and your team can update the code in a central place. In this case, our custom constructs will live within our project, but teams often choose to maintain their own private repositories of custom constructs in a central npm repository.

Project Architecture: Custom S3 and Lambda Constructs

In this project segment, you will extend the functionality of two existing CDK constructs to create a custom Lambda configuration and a custom S3 bucket configuration.

A *construct* in AWS CDK is a reusable piece of cloud infrastructure code that represents a single unit of deployment. It could be a cloud resource, such as an Amazon S3 bucket or an AWS Lambda function, or it could be a higher-level abstraction that represents a collection of resources or a complete architecture.

A construct can be defined in CDK using a programming language of your choice, such as Python, TypeScript, or Java. When defining a construct, you can explicitly specify the resources that should be created as part of the construct. These are known as *explicit resources* in CDK.

Explicit resources are defined within the construct class using CDK's language-specific libraries or modules. For example, in TypeScript, you can use the `aws-cdk-lib` library to define explicit resources.

Figure 7-1 shows where the S3 buckets fit in with our overall project and includes the key components of our custom S3 bucket construct: S3 bucket, access log bucket, IAM permissions, versioning, and encryption.

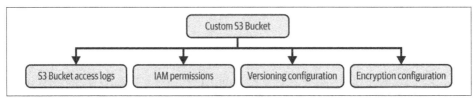

Figure 7-1. High-level architecture for the S3 customer bucket constructs that we will use in this chapter

In this chapter, we are also adding a custom Lambda function construct. Figure 7-2 shows where the new Lambda function fits in with our project.

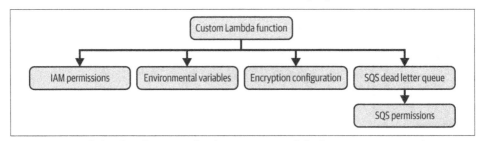

Figure 7-2. High-level architecture for the custom Lambda function construct that we will build in this chapter

The diagram illustrates the components of our custom Lambda function construct. The construct manages security with IAM permissions and encryption. It sets the environmental variables we will need for the application and creates a dead letter queue for failed executions.

Create a Custom Lambda Function

Let's start by making a new Lambda function (Example 7-1). We need to put the function into a specific folder so that CDK can find it:

1. Create a directory in the *./lib/constructs* directory called *construct-hec-lambda*.

2. Create a file called *construct-hec-lambda.ts* in the *./lib/constructs/construct-hec-lambda* directory.

3. Create a file called *README.md* in the *./lib/constructs/construct-hec-lambda* directory.

 README files are important for constructs so that they can be easily repackaged and reused. Our goal is to keep the code "DRY" and be kind to future users of the code (which may be our future selves). DRY is an acronym that stands for "do not repeat yourself." If you find that you are repeating the same code, then you should probably consider making a function to simplify your code.

Example 7-1. Home Energy Coach custom Lambda construct

```
import { Duration } from "aws-cdk-lib"; ❶
import { aws_lambda as lambda } from "aws-cdk-lib";
import { Construct } from "constructs";
import { Integer } from "aws-sdk/clients/apigateway";
import { aws_sqs as sqs } from "aws-cdk-lib";
import { IRole } from "aws-cdk-lib/aws-iam";
import { NagSuppressions } from "cdk-nag";

interface HecLambdaProps { ❷
  readonly lambdaName?: string;
  readonly concurrencyLimit?: Integer;
  readonly timeout?: Duration;
  readonly runtime: lambda.Runtime;
  readonly role?: IRole;
  readonly description?: string;
  readonly handler: string;
  readonly code: lambda.Code;
  readonly layers?: Array<lambda.ILayerVersion>;
  readonly environment?: Record<string, string>;
}

export class HecNodeLambdaConstruct extends lambda.Function { ❸
  public readonly lambdaFunction: lambda.Function;
  public readonly lambdaDlq: sqs.Queue;

  constructor(scope: Construct, id: string, props: HecLambdaProps) { ❹
    const dlq = new sqs.Queue(scope, `${id}DLQ`, {
```

```
    queueName: `${id}dlq.fifo`,
    deliveryDelay: Duration.millis(0),
    contentBasedDeduplication: true,
    enforceSSL: true,
    retentionPeriod: Duration.days(14),
  });
  super(scope, id, {
    ...props,
    runtime: props.runtime,
    code: props.code,
    handler: props.handler,
    layers: props.layers,
    description: props.description,
    role: props.role,
    timeout: props.timeout ? props.timeout : Duration.minutes(5),
    environment: props.environment || undefined,
    architecture: lambda.Architecture.ARM_64,
    deadLetterQueueEnabled: true,
    deadLetterQueue: dlq,
    tracing: lambda.Tracing.ACTIVE,
  });
  this.lambdaFunction = this;
  this.lambdaDlq = dlq;
  }
}
```

Let's break down this CDK construct:

❶ We start by importing the modules we will need.

❷ Now we will set up the Lambda function. There are lots of arguments here, but we can break it down step by step. We provide a name and set the concurrency limit (default is 100). We can choose to change the timeout duration (default is 15 minutes). We also set the Lambda runtime. Sometimes we need to grant the Lambda function additional privileges, and we can have Lambda assume a specific role. All functions should have descriptions and have clear path instructions. Finally, we have the option to set environment variables—these are always encrypted by default.

❸ This construct provides a preconfigured default Node Lambda function that meets the cdk_nag AWS specifications for security and well-architected infrastructure.

❹ Now we create a Node Lambda function that enables cdk_nag compliance through defaults. This function includes a first in, first out (FIFO) dead letter queue, AWS X-Ray tracing enabled by default, and x86 architecture with which we can use Graviton2 instances to improve performance and reduce electricity consumption. We also pass in some parameters.

 As a reminder, all code in this book is available on Git-Hub (*https://github.com/hands-on-aws-cdk-book/hands-on-aws-cdk-book-projects*) with additional comments and notes.

In this section of code, we introduce the `cdk-nag` construct as a helper function. CDK-Nag is an open source tool used in AWS CDK projects to identify and prevent common security and best practice violations. It helps developers identify potential security risks and misconfigurations in their CDK applications before deployment. The tool comes with a set of predefined rules that are written in YAML format. These rules define the best practices and security checks that `cdk-nag` performs on the CDK code. For example, rules can check for the usage of insecure protocols, open permissions, and other security vulnerabilities in CDK constructs.

The `cdk-nag` tool provides a CLI that developers can use to run the tool on their CDK codebase. The CLI takes the YAML rules file as input and scans the CDK code to identify violations of the defined rules. It provides detailed output with information about the violations found, including the line numbers and code snippets where the issues are detected.

The `cdk-nag` tool can also be integrated into GitHub Actions, which allows for automated scanning of CDK code during the development process. Developers can configure `cdk-nag` as a GitHub Action in their CDK projects to automatically run the tool on code changes, pull requests, and other events in the GitHub repository. This helps catch potential security issues early in the development lifecycle.

There are lots of use cases for `cdk-nag`. CDK-Nag helps identify and prevent security best practice violations in CDK code, such as the usage of insecure protocols, overly permissive permissions, or other configurations that may expose vulnerabilities in the deployed infrastructure.

CDK-Nag can be used to ensure that CDK code complies with regulatory and compliance requirements, such as the AWS Well-Architected Framework, CIS AWS Foundations Benchmark, and other industry-specific standards. CDK-Nag can enforce coding standards and consistency across a CDK codebase, helping to maintain code quality and reduce technical debt. It can catch issues like unused resources, missing tags, and other inconsistencies in the CDK code.

We like that CDK-Nag integrates into automated build and deployment pipelines, such as GitHub Actions or other CI/CD tools, to automatically scan CDK code for security issues as part of the development and deployment process.

In short, cdk nag helps us (and hopefully you) improve the security and compliance posture of our CDK applications by identifying and preventing common security and best practice violations. It can be used as part of the development workflow to catch potential issues early and ensure that CDK code meets security and compliance requirements.

Understand the CDK Features

The most important part here is that we are using the construct class to build a new constructor. In the context of the AWS CDK, a construct class is a fundamental building block used to define cloud resources and their properties in an object-oriented manner. It represents a reusable piece of cloud infrastructure code that can be composed to create more complex AWS architectures. The construct class in CDK consists of several key components:

Construct constructor
> This is the entry point for creating a new instance of a construct. It typically takes two arguments: the parent construct (i.e., the construct that contains this construct as a child) and a unique ID that identifies this construct within the scope of the parent construct.

Properties
> These are the configurable attributes or parameters that define the behavior of the construct. Properties are set during the construction of the construct and can be used to customize the behavior of the cloud resource that the construct represents.

Methods
> These are functions or operations that can be performed on the construct. Methods allow you to define the behavior and interactions of the construct, such as adding child constructs, setting up event triggers, or defining access controls.

Lifecycle hooks
> These are optional callback functions that can be implemented in the construct to perform actions at different stages of the construct's lifecycle. For example, the onCreate hook is called after the construct is created, and the onUpdate hook is called when the construct is updated.

Child constructs
> Constructs can be composed hierarchically to form a treelike structure, where child constructs are nested within a parent construct. Child constructs can be added to a parent construct using methods such as addChild or by passing them as arguments to the parent construct's constructor. This allows for easy organization and composition of complex cloud architectures.

Events and notifications

> Constructs can emit events or notifications, which can be used to trigger actions or workflows in other parts of your CDK application. For example, a construct representing an S3 bucket could emit an event when a new object is created, and other constructs could listen for that event and perform additional actions in response.

CDK metadata

> Constructs can also define metadata, which provides additional information about the construct, such as version numbers, licensing information, or documentation URLs. This metadata can be used for documentation generation, version tracking, or other purposes.

Define Props

In CDK, *props* is short for *properties*. In CDK, props are the configurable attributes or parameters that define the behavior of a construct.

When you create a new instance of a construct by invoking its constructor, you can pass in props as arguments to customize the behavior of the construct. Props are used to set the initial state and configuration of the construct, such as setting the name, size, or other properties of a cloud resource that the construct represents.

Props are defined as parameters in the construct's constructor, and their values are passed in when the construct is instantiated. Props can be simple data types such as strings, numbers, and booleans, or more complex objects, depending on the requirements of the construct.

For example, if you have a construct that represents an Amazon S3 bucket, you might define props such as the bucket name, access control lists, encryption settings, or versioning configuration as parameters in the construct's constructor. When you create an instance of that construct, you can pass in the desired values for those props as arguments to customize the behavior of the S3 bucket resource created by the construct.

Props allow you to parameterize your constructs and make them reusable in different contexts, enabling you to create dynamic and customizable cloud architectures using the CDK.

Define Your Construct

A *construct* is a reusable piece of cloud infrastructure code that represents a single unit of deployment. It could be a cloud resource, such as an Amazon S3 bucket or an AWS Lambda function, or a higher-level abstraction that represents a collection of resources or a complete architecture.

A construct can be defined in CDK using a programming language of your choice, such as Python, TypeScript, or Java (we are going to continue using TypeScript). When defining a construct, you can explicitly specify the resources that should be created as part of the construct. These are known as *explicit resources* in CDK.

Explicit resources are defined within the construct class using CDK's language-specific libraries or modules. For example, in TypeScript, you can use the `aws-cdk-lib` library to define explicit resources. Here's an example of how you might define a simple S3 bucket construct with explicit resources using TypeScript:

```
import { Construct } from 'constructs';
import { Bucket } from 'aws-cdk-lib/aws-s3';
export class MyS3BucketConstruct extends Construct
 { constructor(scope: Construct, id: string) {
  super(scope, id); // Define explicit S3 bucket resource

  new Bucket(this, 'MyBucket', {
   bucketName: 'my-bucket-name', // other bucket configuration options });
  }
 }
```

In this example, the `MyS3BucketConstruct` class extends the `Construct` class and defines an S3 bucket resource using the `Bucket` class from the `aws-cdk-lib/aws-s3` module. The `Bucket` class is instantiated with the desired configuration options, such as the bucket name, and is created as part of the construct.

By defining explicit resources within a construct, you have fine-grained control over the configuration and behavior of the cloud resources that are created as part of your CDK application. You can specify the exact properties and settings of the resources, and you can also leverage CDK's features for managing the lifecycle, dependencies, and updates of those resources as part of your application's deployment and management workflow.

Document Your Construct

Documenting a construct for reuse in the AWS CDK is an important practice to provide clear documentation and usage instructions for your construct to other developers who may want to reuse it. JSDoc comments are special comments that can be added to your construct's code to provide documentation in a standardized format that can be easily parsed and understood by code editors, IDEs, and documentation generators.

Using JSDoc comments in your CDK construct's code helps provide self-contained documentation that can be easily understood by other developers who may want to use your construct. It enables them to quickly understand how to instantiate and configure your construct, making it easier for them to reuse it in their own CDK applications. Let's look at Example 7-2.

Example 7-2. Home Energy Coach documentation

Home Energy Coach Custom Lambda Infrastructure Construct

This construct `HecNodeLambdaConstruct` extends the default
AWS CDK Lambda function construct by incorporating well-architected
principles and default configurations to ensure compliance with `cdk_nag`
AWS specifications.

What it does

`HecNodeLambdaConstruct` offers a pre-configured default Lambda Function
that is optimized for security and well-architected infrastructure.
Features include:

1. X-Ray tracing enabled by default.
2. Usage of the x86 architecture, specifically targeting Graviton2
instances for improved performance and reduced electricity consumption.
3. An integrated FIFO dead letter queue (DLQ) for addressing failed lambda
executions.

How To Use

To make use of the `HecNodeLambdaConstruct`, you'll need to import it and
pass in the necessary properties:

```typescript
import { HecNodeLambdaConstruct } from "path-to-construct";

const myLambda = new HecNodeLambdaConstruct(this, "MyLambdaID", {
  lambdaName: "MyLambda",
  runtime: lambda.Runtime.NODEJS_14_X,
  code: lambda.Code.fromAsset("path-to-lambda-code"),
  handler: "index.handler",
  concurrencyLimit: 50,
  timeout: Duration.minutes(10),
  role: myIAMRole,
  description: "My awesome lambda function",
  layers: [myLayer1, myLayer2],
  environment: {
    KEY1: "Value1",
    KEY2: "Value2",
  },
});
```

⚙ Configuration Details

Here are the configurations you can specify for the construct:

- lambdaName: (Optional) Name of the lambda function.
- concurrencyLimit: (Optional) Concurrency limit for the lambda, default is 100.

```
- timeout: (Optional) Timeout duration, default is 15 minutes.
- runtime: (Required) Lambda runtime environment.
- role: (Optional) Specific IAM role for the lambda function.
- description: (Optional) Description for the lambda function.
- handler: (Required) The handler function in your lambda code.
- code: (Required) Directory path or asset for the lambda code.
- layers: (Optional) Lambda layers.
- environment: (Optional) Environment variables for the lambda. Note: These are
  encrypted by default.

## Additional Features

Included by default in the construct:

- FIFO DLQ: A dead letter queue is created to handle messages not processed by the
  Lambda function.
- Graviton2 Based Architecture: Uses x86_64 architecture to harness the efficiency of
  Graviton2.
- X-Ray Tracing: All functions enabled with this construct come with X-Ray tracing
  for enhanced observability.

Keep on building!
```

Let's talk a bit about what's going on in this documentation.

We use JSDocs to help with self-documenting TypeScript for AWS CDK. JSDocs helps provide clear and comprehensive documentation for your code, making it more readable and understandable to others, as well as to your future self.

JSDoc is a popular documentation syntax used in JavaScript and TypeScript to provide inline comments that describe the purpose, usage, and behavior of functions, classes, properties, and other code elements. When used effectively, JSDoc comments can serve as self-documentation, helping developers understand how to use your code correctly without needing to dig into the implementation details.

JSDocs isn't magic. It relies on the comments within the code. To get the best out of JSDocs, begin by always including the purpose, inputs, outputs, and behavior of your functions, classes, and other code elements in clear and concise comments. Use descriptive names for your code elements, and explain their purpose and usage in plain English.

JSDoc is looking for docstrings with defined parameters and return types, so be sure that all your functions include comments for function parameters, specifying their type, purpose, and any constraints. Also, document the return type of functions, indicating what the function returns and any associated information.

In addition to parameters, you also want to document properties and methods. You can use JSDocs to describe the purpose, usage, and behavior of properties and methods in classes. Document their parameters, return types, and any side effects they may have.

Documentation, like all things, is only useful if it is kept current. Update your JSDoc comments as your code evolves to ensure that the documentation remains accurate and relevant.

By following these practices, you can create self-documenting TypeScript code for CDK that is easier to understand, use, and maintain, making your codebase more robust and developer friendly.

Use Your Construct

Integrating a CDK construct within a stack or as a separate construct is a common practice in AWS CDK applications. Constructs are the building blocks for our applications.

Create a Custom S3 Bucket Construct

Like we did for the Lambda function, we need to create a specific structure for our S3 bucket. Note that in the code in Example 7-3, *S3* is written as *s3*.

1. Create a directory in the *./lib/constructs* directory and call it *construct-hec-s3*.

2. Create a file called *construct-hec-s3.ts* in the *./lib/constructs/construct-hec-s3* directory.

3. Create a file called *README.md* in the *./lib/constructs/construct-hec-s3* directory.

Our goal is to reuse the code we create. We do this by creating our code as modular components that can be assembled in multiple ways. We need the *README.md* files so that we know what task a given module was supposed to complete. You may think that you will remember, but trust us, you want to write this down. Be kind to your (future) self.

Example 7-3. Home Energy Coach custom S3 construct

```
import { Construct } from "constructs";
import { RemovalPolicy, Duration, PhysicalName } from "aws-cdk-lib";
import { aws_s3 as s3 } from "aws-cdk-lib";
// Removed: import { LifecyclePolicy } from "aws-cdk-lib/aws-efs";
import { NagSuppressions } from "cdk-nag";

interface HecS3Props extends s3.BucketProps {
  /**
   * Optional: set bucket name manually if required
```

```
   * @default PhysicalName.GENERATE_IF_NEEDED
   */
  readonly bucketName?: string;

  /**
   * Optional: Array of lifecycle rules to be applied to the bucket.
   * @default "Standard lifecycle policy."
   */
  readonly bucketLifeCyclePolicyArray?: Array<s3.LifecycleRule>;

  /**
   * Optional: set bucket storage class (currently not used).
   * @default "S3 standard"
   */
  readonly bucketStorageClass?: boolean;
}

export class HecS3Construct extends s3.Bucket { ❶
  /**
   * S3 bucket object to be passed to other functions
   */
  public readonly s3Bucket: s3.Bucket;
  /**
   * Optional: Access log bucket (if implemented)
   */
  public readonly accessLogBucket?: s3.Bucket;

  constructor(scope: Construct, id: string, props: HecS3Props) { ❷
    super(scope, id, {
      ...props,
      bucketName: props.bucketName
        ? props.bucketName
        : PhysicalName.GENERATE_IF_NEEDED,
      encryption: s3.BucketEncryption.S3_MANAGED,
      cors: props.cors,
      enforceSSL: true,
      blockPublicAccess: s3.BlockPublicAccess.BLOCK_ALL,
      versioned: props.versioned !== undefined ? props.versioned : true,
      removalPolicy: RemovalPolicy.DESTROY,
      autoDeleteObjects: true,
      serverAccessLogsPrefix: id,
    });

    // Assign the created bucket reference for clarity
    this.s3Bucket = this;

    const costOptimizedLifecycleRule = [❸
      {
        transitions: [
          {
            storageClass: s3.StorageClass.INFREQUENT_ACCESS,
            transitionAfter: Duration.days(30),
```

```
        },
        {
          storageClass: s3.StorageClass.GLACIER_INSTANT_RETRIEVAL,
          transitionAfter: Duration.days(90),
        },
      ],
    },
  ];

  if (props.bucketLifeCyclePolicyArray) { ❹
    console.log("Lifecycle policy option enabled");
    props.bucketLifeCyclePolicyArray.forEach((policy) => {
      this.addLifecycleRule(policy);
    });
  }
  }
 }
}
```

Let's break down this CDK construct:

❶ This construct provides a preconfigured S3 bucket that meets AWS security and Well-Architected specifications through cdk-nag compliance. It deploys an S3 bucket with an associated access log bucket and includes AWS-managed encryption, blocked public access, versioning, and automatic object deletion by default.

❷ The constructor creates an S3 bucket with security-focused defaults that satisfy cdk-nag requirements, including AWS-managed encryption, public access blocking, versioning, and automatic object deletion.

❸ This section of the code creates a standard opinionated, cost-optimized lifecycle policy. When we created our S3 bucket, it used S3 standard storage. We are going to change it so that if an object is not accessed within 30 days, it automatically moves to S3 infrequent access. Objects move to S3 Glacier Instant Retrieval if they haven't been accessed in the past 90 days. This lifecycle policy will save us money without requiring us to delete objects.

❹ Here we create an option so that if the bucketLifeCyclePolicyArray is defined as a prop, it will loop through an array of policies and add each to the S3 bucket. This allows standard S3 policy to be default and the user can define any additional policies to override this default. Most of the time, this is what you want to use, and with the policy, you don't have to spend time thinking about it anymore.

Deploy Your Custom Constructs

Follow the steps from previous chapters to deploy your custom constructs and test them out. You can test your constructs using the AWS Console or using the AWS CLI. We recommend trying both to build your comfort and familiarity.

Modify Your Application to Use the New Constructs

Now that you have successfully built and deployed these custom constructs you are ready to use them in your application. You can modify your existing CDK application to use these new constructs by importing them and passing in the necessary properties. Give it a try on your own first. You will need to modify your import statements as well as the instantiation of the S3 and Lambda classes in your application. If you get stuck, take a look at the examples in the project repo for guidance.

Test Your New Application

Once you have modified your application to use the new constructs, you can test it to ensure that everything is working as expected. You can use the AWS Console or the AWS CLI to verify that the S3 bucket and Lambda function are created with the correct configurations and settings. You can also test the functionality of the Lambda function by invoking it with test data and verifying that it behaves as expected. What is different about these constructs as compared to the others? Go back in the chapter and see if you can identify the key differences to look for. Do you see those differences reflected in the deployed resources?

Getting Unstuck

I'm getting a "Type X is not assignable to type Y" error when trying to use my custom construct. What's wrong?

This error often occurs when there's a mismatch between the properties you're passing and what the construct expects. Start by double-checking the interface definition for your construct's props. Next, ensure that all required props are being passed when instantiating the construct, and verify that the types of the props you're passing match the interface definition. If you're extending an existing construct, make sure you're including all required props from the parent construct. You can use TypeScript's type checking features (like as const) to ensure that type inference is working correctly.

My custom S3 construct is being created, but the lifecycle rules aren't being applied. What could be the issue?

If your lifecycle rules aren't being applied, start by verifying that you are passing the lifecycle rules correctly in the props when creating the construct. Next, check that the `bucketLifeCyclePolicyArray` property is defined and contains valid lifecycle rules. The `addLifecycleRule` method needs to be called for each policy in the array. You can try applying a simple lifecycle rule directly in the construct definition to test if it works. You can also check the AWS S3 Console to see if the rules are visible there, as sometimes it can take a few minutes for them to appear. Finally, check that the CloudFormation template generated by CDK included the lifecycle rules as you had expected.

I've created a custom Lambda construct, but the X-Ray tracing isn't working. How can I fix this?

If X-Ray tracing isn't working for your custom Lambda construct, it could be a problem with the construct's properties. Start by checking that `tracing: lambda.Tracing.ACTIVE` is set and that the IAM role associated with your Lambda function has the necessary permissions for X-Ray. If you are using a region outside `us-east-1`, make sure that X-Ray is enabled in the AWS region you're using. You can try invoking the Lambda function and check the X-Ray console for any traces. You can also look at the Lambda function configuration in the AWS Console to confirm tracing is enabled. Finally, if you are using Lambda layers or custom runtimes, ensure that they're compatible with X-Ray tracing.

My custom construct is throwing a "circular dependency detected" error during synthesis. How do I resolve this?

Ugh, these errors are the worst! For starters, review your construct to identify any resources that might be referencing each other. Try to break the circular dependency by restructuring your resources. You might consider using `Fn.importValue()` to import values from one part of your construct to another. If the circular dependency is between two separate constructs, you might need to refactor them. We like to use the `DependsOn` attribute to explicitly specify the order of resource creation. As a last resort, you can use custom resources to break circular dependencies, but this should be done carefully (in other words— danger!).

I've extended the S3 bucket construct, but my custom properties aren't being applied. What am I missing?

If your custom properties aren't being applied, then ensure that you're calling `super()` in your construct's constructor with the spread operator: `super(scope, id, {...props})`. Verify that you're setting your custom properties after the `super()` call. Next, check that your custom properties are being correctly passed when instantiating the construct. You can use `console.log` statements to debug and see what properties are being received by the construct. You also need to ensure that your custom properties are not conflicting with any built-in properties of the S3 bucket construct. Finally, if you are overriding methods, make sure you're calling the parent method using `super.methodName()`.

My custom construct is deployed successfully, but I can't see the README documentation in the AWS Console. Where is it?

The README documentation for custom constructs is not automatically displayed in the AWS Console. README files are typically used for documentation within your codebase, not in the AWS Console. To make your documentation accessible, consider adding it to your team's internal documentation system. You can include important information as descriptions or tags on the AWS resources themselves. You can use CDK annotations or aspects to add metadata to your constructs that can be viewed in the CDK Toolkit output. You might consider generating CloudFormation template descriptions that include key information from your README. Finally, remember: the README is primarily for developers using your construct, not for runtime documentation in AWS.

Chapter Synth

In this chapter, you learned:

- How to extend existing CDK constructs to create custom constructs that adhere to organizational standards or meet specific goals around cost, performance, security, and so on
- The process for building custom S3 and Lambda function constructs, including defining the construct interface and props, setting defaults, and incorporating well-architected principles
- How to properly document constructs using JSDoc and README files so that they can be easily reused by other developers

Discussion

1. In what situations might you want to create a custom CDK construct versus using the default construct? What are some key drivers behind that decision?

2. How can custom constructs help improve things such as consistency, security posture, and cost management across large development teams? What benefits have you seen from standardizing constructs?

3. What best practices should be followed when creating reusable custom constructs to ensure that they interoperate nicely with other CDK codebases?

Extension Activities

Here are some additional activities to consider now that you have completed this chapter:

1. Create custom constructs for other resource types, like DynamoDB tables and API Gateway.

2. Publish your custom constructs to your team's/organization's private construct library for reuse.

3. Refactor an existing CDK app to use custom constructs, and evaluate the benefits.

## CHAPTER 8

Creating New Custom CDK Constructs

In the previous chapter, you learned about extending existing L3 constructs by creating custom constructs with configurations specifically tailored to your business requirements. In this chapter, you will build on that knowledge by creating a new CDK construct that combines existing L2 constructs into a "sane default" configuration. In our case, we will create a custom L3 construct to represent a Lambda Integrated RESTful API that uses Cognito authorization. We will take this a step further in the next chapter when we create a custom construct from existing L1 constructs.

Project Architecture: Package and Deploy a Serverless API

In this project segment, you will create a RESTful API using Amazon API Gateway and AWS Lambda. The API will be used to query and mutate data in a DynamoDB table. The DynamoDB table will be used to store data about the energy usage of a home. This API will be authenticated using Amazon Cognito.

Let's examine how the energy calculator Lambda function integrates with our custom API Gateway construct. Figure 8-1 shows the complete architecture and how these components work together.

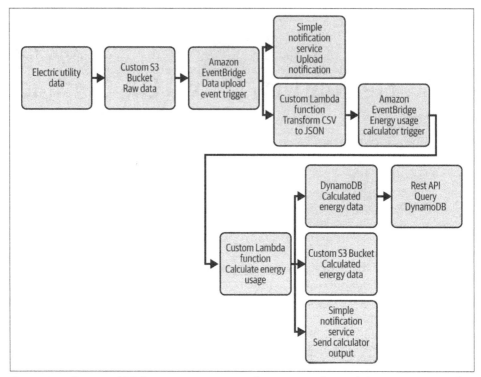

Figure 8-1. Custom API Gateway construct architecture with Lambda integration and Cognito authentication

Our application is becoming more sophisticated by building on the components we have already made. We are setting up an API gateway and Cognito to allow the application to run on any server and still be accessed by authorized users. These are the components of our serverless API architecture:

- S3 bucket (raw data)
- S3 Event Notification
- Lambda function (transform to JSON)
- S3 bucket (transformed data)
- S3 Event Notification
- Lambda function (calculate energy use)
- DynamoDB table (energy use)
- SNS notifications
- Custom API Gateway construct

Why REST API and Why Serverless?

Why build a GraphQL API anyway? APIs are a simple programmatic way to perform CRUD (create, read, update, delete) operations on data that is in a database. If you have gotten this far in the book, you probably know a little something about that. But our architecture is a little different from your granddad's REST API. Read the following case study to find out how it's different.

Case Study

When the engineering team at a major utility in North America were looking to build a consumer energy use dashboard and mobile app for consumers, they wanted to get the full benefits of building a solution in the cloud first. They didn't want to manage servers and infrastructure, and they wanted to be able to scale up with major weather events without needing to have developers and site reliability engineers on call. They also wanted to be able to minimize the number of queries to their databases and the number of individual calls to their APIs to reduce costs and improve the performance of their application for consumers.

They chose AWS API Gateway because it allowed them to front their applications with an AWS service that could handle the scaling and security of their application. They chose a serverless architecture backed by Lambda functions because they could scale up and down with demand and not have to worry about managing servers. They chose a RESTful API because it was a simple way to perform CRUD operations on their data. By switching from managing their own API logic to using API Gateway and a serverless architecture, they were able to reduce the number of queries to their databases and the number of individual calls to their APIs. This reduced costs and improved the performance of their application for consumers.

You are going to deploy a similar architecture in this project segment. You will use a serverless architecture backed by Lambda functions and a RESTful API to perform CRUD operations on a DynamoDB table. You will also use Amazon Cognito to authenticate users and secure your API. The team in the case study did run into one pain point: manually defining and updating all of their API endpoints and operations in CDK became a challenge because they had to synchronize their API Gateway configuration with their Lambda functions and their Cognito user pool. To make this easier they have asked their AWS developer to create a custom CDK construct that would allow them to define their API Gateway, Lambda functions, and Cognito user pool in a single construct. Your task is to build it.

Go Build!

In the previous project segments, we allowed for some interactivity, but it was limited. Adding GraphQL lets us access and use data from databases that will make our application much more interesting.

CDK construct libraries are collections of pre-built, reusable components that provide abstraction layers for provisioning and managing AWS resources in an IaC manner. They are designed to simplify the development of cloud applications using CDK and offer a wide range of functionalities across various AWS services. Here are some common uses of CDK construct libraries:

Infrastructure provisioning

CDK construct libraries offer pre-built constructs for provisioning and managing various AWS resources such as EC2 instances, S3 buckets, Lambda functions, RDS databases, API Gateway, and CloudFront distributions. These constructs encapsulate the underlying AWS CloudFormation templates, making it easier to define, configure, and deploy complex infrastructure components in a declarative manner.

Application components

CDK construct libraries provide higher-level constructs for building application components such as serverless applications, containerized applications, messaging systems, and data pipelines. These constructs encapsulate the configuration and integration of multiple AWS resources into a cohesive application component, making it easier to define, manage, and deploy complex applications.

Custom abstractions

CDK construct libraries allow developers to create their own custom abstractions on top of AWS resources, encapsulating common patterns or best practices in reusable constructs. These custom constructs can be used across multiple projects or teams, promoting consistency and standardization in infrastructure provisioning and management.

Extensions and plug-ins

CDK construct libraries provide extensibility points for adding custom functionality or integrating with third-party tools or services. These extensions and plug-ins can be used to augment the capabilities of CDK, add new features, or integrate with existing infrastructure or deployment workflows.

CDK construct libraries offer a wide range of functionalities and abstractions for provisioning, managing, and integrating AWS resources in a CDK application. They allow developers to encapsulate complex infrastructure components into reusable constructs, promote consistency and standardization, and extend the capabilities of CDK through custom abstractions, extensions, and plug-ins.

When creating custom CDK constructs, it's important to properly document them to make it easy for others (and your future self) to understand their purpose, usage, and configuration options. Here are some guidelines for documenting your constructs:

README

Create a clear and comprehensive README file that provides an overview of the construct, its purpose, and how to use it. Include installation instructions, usage examples, and any other relevant information. Make sure to update the README as needed to keep it current with any changes to the construct.

JSDocs

Include inline comments in your construct's code using the JSDoc format to provide documentation directly in the code. This can help other developers understand the purpose and usage of the construct while reading the code. Include descriptions of class properties, methods, and their parameters, as well as any return values or other relevant information.

Create a Blank Construct

Let's start by creating a placeholder for our construct. Even if the *README.md* is blank, it is good practice to set these things up:

1. Create a directory in the *./lib/constructs* directory and call it *api*.
2. Create a file called *api-construct.ts* in this directory.
3. Create a *README.md* file within this directory so that you can document your construct for others who might use it.

 We like to set up these files as reminders to document our code even if they are blank to begin with.

You can copy the code in Example 8-1 or find all the code in the GitHub repository. For a more detailed look at this construct, we recommend going to the GitHub repository where you can see additional documentation and usage examples.

Example 8-1. Home Energy Coach serverless API construct

```
import * as cdk from "aws-cdk-lib";
import * as apigateway from "aws-cdk-lib/aws-apigateway";
import * as lambda from "aws-cdk-lib/aws-lambda";
import * as dynamodb from "aws-cdk-lib/aws-dynamodb";
import * as cognito from "aws-cdk-lib/aws-cognito";
import { Construct } from "constructs";
```

```
import * as path from "path";


/** Configuration for a single API operation */
interface ApiOperation {
 /** HTTP method (GET, POST, etc.) */
 method: string;
 /** API path (/energy-data, /customers, etc.) */
 path: string;
 /** Operation name (used for Lambda function naming) */
 name: string;
 /** Lambda handler file name (without .ts extension) */
 handlerFile: string;
 /** Optional Lambda environment variables */
 environment?: Record<string, string>;
 /** Optional request validator */
 requestValidator?: {
   /** Request body JSON schema */
   bodySchema?: { [key: string]: any };
   /** Required query string parameters */
   requiredQueryParams?: string[];
   /** Required request headers */
   requiredHeaders?: string[];
 };
}


/** Configuration for the REST API construct */
export interface RestApiConstructProps {
 /** DynamoDB table for data access */
 readonly table: dynamodb.Table;
 /** List of API operations to create */
 readonly operations: ApiOperation[];
 /** Optional API name */
 readonly apiName?: string;
 /** Optional API description */
 readonly description?: string;
 /** Base directory for Lambda handlers */
 readonly handlersPath: string;
 /** Optional CORS configuration */
 readonly cors?: {
   allowOrigins: string[];
   allowMethods?: string[];
   allowHeaders?: string[];
 };
 auth?: {
   cognitoUserPool?: cognito.IUserPool;
   apiKey?: boolean;
 };
}
```

```typescript
/** Creates a REST API with Lambda integrations for each operation */
export class RestApiConstruct extends Construct {
  /** The underlying API Gateway REST API */
  public readonly api: apigateway.RestApi;
  /** Map of operation names to their Lambda functions */
  public readonly lambdas: { [key: string]: lambda.Function } = {};


  constructor(scope: Construct, id: string, props: RestApiConstructProps) {
    super(scope, id);


    // Create the REST API
    this.api = new apigateway.RestApi(this, "RestApi", {
      restApiName: props.apiName ?? "EnergyUsageApi",
      description: props.description ?? "API for energy usage data",
      defaultCorsPreflightOptions: props.cors
        ? {
            allowOrigins: props.cors.allowOrigins,
            allowMethods: props.cors.allowMethods ?? [
              "GET",
              "POST",
              "PUT",
              "DELETE",
            ],
            allowHeaders: props.cors.allowHeaders ?? ["*"],
          }
        : undefined,
    });


    // Create Cognito authorizer if provided
    let authorizer: apigateway.IAuthorizer | undefined;
    if (props.auth?.cognitoUserPool) {
      authorizer = new apigateway.CognitoUserPoolsAuthorizer(
        this,
        "CognitoAuthorizer",
        {
          cognitoUserPools: [props.auth.cognitoUserPool],
        }
      );
    }


    // Create models for request validation
    const models: { [key: string]: apigateway.Model } = {};


    // Create each operation
    props.operations.forEach((operation) => {
      // Create the Lambda function
      const lambdaFunction = new lambda.Function(
```

```
      this,
      `${operation.name}Function`,
      {
        runtime: lambda.Runtime.NODEJS_18_X,
        handler: "index.handler",
        code: lambda.Code.fromAsset(
          path.join(props.handlersPath, operation.handlerFile)
        ),
        environment: {
          TABLE_NAME: props.table.tableName,
          ...operation.environment,
        },
      }
    );


    // Grant table permissions to Lambda
    props.table.grantReadWriteData(lambdaFunction);


    // Store Lambda reference
    this.lambdas[operation.name] = lambdaFunction;


    // Create request validator if needed
    let validator: apigateway.RequestValidator | undefined;
    if (operation.requestValidator) {
      // Create model for body validation
      if (operation.requestValidator.bodySchema) {
        models[operation.name] = this.api.addModel(`${operation.name}Model`, {
          contentType: "application/json",
          modelName: `${operation.name}Model`,
          schema: {
            type: apigateway.JsonSchemaType.OBJECT,
            properties: operation.requestValidator.bodySchema,
          },
        });
      }


      validator = new apigateway.RequestValidator(
        this,
        `${operation.name}Validator`,
        {
          restApi: this.api,
          validateRequestBody: !!operation.requestValidator.bodySchema,
          validateRequestParameters: !!(
            operation.requestValidator.requiredQueryParams?.length ||
            operation.requestValidator.requiredHeaders?.length
          ),
        }
      );
```

```
    }

    const resource = this.api.root.resourceForPath(operation.path);
    const methodOptions: apigateway.MethodOptions = {
      apiKeyRequired: props.auth?.apiKey,
      authorizer: authorizer,
      authorizationType: authorizer
        ? apigateway.AuthorizationType.COGNITO
        : props.auth?.apiKey
        ? apigateway.AuthorizationType.IAM
        : apigateway.AuthorizationType.NONE,
      requestValidator: validator,
      requestModels: operation.requestValidator?.bodySchema
        ? { "application/json": models[operation.name] }
        : undefined,
      requestParameters: {
        ...operation.requestValidator?.requiredQueryParams?.reduce(
          (acc, param) => ({
            ...acc,
            [`method.request.querystring.${param}`]: true,
          }),
          {}
        ),
        ...operation.requestValidator?.requiredHeaders?.reduce(
          (acc, header) => ({
            ...acc,
            [`method.request.header.${header}`]: true,
          }),
          {}
        ),
      },
    };


    resource.addMethod(
      operation.method,
      new apigateway.LambdaIntegration(lambdaFunction),
      methodOptions
    );
  });
 }
}
```

This construct simplifies the creation of REST APIs in AWS by handling all the complex setup for you. Instead of individually configuring API Gateway endpoints, Lambda functions, and permissions, you just tell it what endpoints you want and what code should handle them. It automatically creates the API Gateway resources, sets up Lambda functions with the right permissions, and connects everything together. You can easily add authentication with API keys or Cognito user pools, enable CORS for web applications, and validate incoming requests. This makes it much faster to build APIs and reduces the chance of configuration errors, letting you focus on writing your application code instead of infrastructure setup.

Like many abstractions in software development, writing and perfecting this initial construct may be a bit more work than simply writing out all of the routes in a stack. But what is special about this construct is that it can be extended for several routes, and used as a standard way to construct all your APIs. This becomes especially useful when you want to centrally change the way you manage APIs or authentication. Instead of having to go into every stack for every API in your organization, you can simply change a central construct and it will allow you to propagate that change across multiple applications. We have written a lot of serverless API infrastructure as code routes, and we thought this saved a lot of time and ensured consistency in a big way.

As always, consult the GitHub sample code and *README* file for more information about using and extending this construct, and to ensure that you are working with the most updated version.

Now that we have a construct ready to go, we need to integrate this into a stack and eventually into our main application. Begin by creating a directory for your stack, and a file for your stack. Within this stack directory, we will also need a directory for Lambda functions. Now review the documentation for the construct. Test your knowledge by attempting to build out the stack using this construct on your own. You can use the Lambda function code taken from the project repository. We encourage you to read line by line and understand what you are copying and pasting into your application. There are a few custom environmental variables you will need to bring to the API—specifically, you will need the identifier for your Amazon Q Business stack, which we implement later in the book. For now, we will build a route to query data and a route to summarize data. Eventually you will add a route for chat. Review the sample code for the stack (*https://oreil.ly/V1TOW*) and the sample code for integrating this into the main application (*https://oreil.ly/xFbQv*) to complete this section of your project.

The API abstracts away from the CDK you are building now and gives you flexibility to change how the API is served in the future. This construct allows the user to create an API in a single configuration, and it allows the maintainer to keep an opinion about how the API is set up and how authentication is handled. Go ahead and try adding your own endpoints if you would like to.

Test Your Custom Serverless API Construct

Now that you have made your API, it is time to test it to make sure that it returns the results you are expecting. Follow these steps to verify your infrastructure deployed as expected:

1. Navigate to the AWS Console and search for *CloudFormation*.
2. Select Stacks and look for a stack called `HecRestApi` with appended values at the end (something like `HecRestApi1234abcd`).
3. Search for *API Gateway*.
4. Verify that you have an API called `HecRestApi` available in the console with endpoints available as expected.

Now let's test this resource out. There are a few additional steps you will need to take to set up API keys. For more details on how to test your API, code samples, and different methods for authentication, please consult the README for the API Stack in the sample code repository (*https://oreil.ly/CqJ4R*).

1. Navigate to the API Gateway console.
2. Select the API you created.
3. Select the API Keys tab.
4. Create a new API key.
5. Select the Usage Plans tab.
6. Create a new usage plan.
7. Add the API key to the usage plan.
8. Add the usage plan to the API stage.
9. Deploy the API by selecting the stage and clicking the Deploy button.
10. Test the API using the invoke URL, which is available in the API Gateway console.

You can also test the API using the AWS CLI. Here is an example of how you can test the API using the AWS CLI:

```
aws apigateway test-invoke-method --rest-api-id '<API_ID>' --resource-id
'<RESOURCE_ID>'
--http-method '<HTTP_METHOD>' --path-with-query-string '<PATH>'
```

If you don't like using the AWS CLI, you can instead use curl. Note that the syntax is different:

```
curl -X '<HTTP_METHOD> <INVOKE_URL>/<PATH>'
```

Notice that we didn't just give you the command to run. That's because your API will be somewhat unique to you. You will need to replace the placeholders with the values that are specific to your API. This is another great opportunity to develop your skills in reading the documentation and understanding how to interpret the use of AWS tooling.

Next up, we will put this to use by integrating it with a web application.

Getting Unstuck

I'm getting a "Cannot find module" error when trying to import my custom construct. What's wrong?

This error usually occurs when the module path is incorrect or the construct hasn't been exported properly. To fix it, begin by checking that the filepath in your import statement is correct and that you've exported your construct class using export class or module.exports. If you are using npm packages, make sure you've run npm install. If using TypeScript, make sure your *tsconfig.json* is set up correctly for module resolution. If these things don't work, try clearing your TypeScript compilation cache and rebuilding your project.

My API Gateway endpoints aren't being created as expected. What could be the issue?

If your API Gateway endpoints aren't showing up, start by double-checking that you're passing the correct ApiEndpointConfig array to your construct. Each endpoint configuration needs the correct path, httpMethod, and lambdaFunction Props. Check that the Lambda functions referenced in your endpoints exist and are correctly configured. You can check the CloudFormation template generated by CDK to see if the resources are being created and look for any error messages in the CDK synthesis output or CloudFormation stack events. Finally, try creating a simple endpoint directly in the construct (not through props) to isolate the issue.

I'm having trouble integrating Cognito with my API Gateway. How can I debug this?

Integrating Cognito with API Gateway gives us trouble sometimes too. When this isn't working for you, start by verifying that the Cognito User Pool is being created correctly in your construct and ensure that the Cognito Authorizer is properly attached to your API Gateway methods. Check that you're passing the correct Cognito User Pool to the Authorizer and verify that your API Gateway deployment stage is set up correctly. Next, test your API with and without authentication to isolate the issue. You can look at the CloudWatch Logs for your API Gateway and Cognito to see any error messages.

My custom construct is created, but the Lambda functions aren't being triggered. What's wrong?

If your Lambda functions aren't being triggered, start by verifying that the Lambda function code is being correctly bundled and uploaded. Next, take a look at the handler specified in `lambdaFunctionProps` and make sure it matches your actual function name. Nothing will work as expected if the IAM roles and permissions aren't set up correctly for your Lambda functions. You can test the Lambda functions directly from the AWS Console to ensure that they're working, and then check the API Gateway settings to ensure that the integration with Lambda is correct. CloudWatch logs everything, so review the logs for both API Gateway and Lambda for error messages. Finally, you can try invoking the API endpoint manually (using curl or Postman) to see if it reaches the Lambda function.

I'm getting a "Circular dependency detected" error when using my custom construct. How do I resolve this?

Circular dependencies can be tricky. If you find yourself going in circles, start by reviewing your construct to identify any resources that might be referencing each other, and try to break the circular dependency by restructuring your resources. Consider using `Fn.importValue()` to import values from one part of your construct to another. If the circular dependency is between two separate constructs, you might need to refactor them. We've found that the `DependsOn` attribute can be a huge help to explicitly specify the order of resource creation. As a last resort, you can use custom resources to break circular dependencies, but this should be done carefully.

How can I add custom domain names and SSL certificates to my API Gateway construct?

Use the `aws-route53` and `aws-certificatemanager` modules to add custom domain names and SSL certificates in your CDK code. You can create a new `DomainName` construct for your API Gateway and create or import an SSL certificate using AWS Certificate Manager. Make sure to associate the domain name with your API Gateway stage and create a Route 53 record to point your custom domain to the API Gateway domain. Also, you need to ensure that your account has the necessary permissions to manage certificates and domains. Finally, remember to validate the certificate if you're creating a new one, which might require manual steps.

Chapter Synth

In this chapter, you learned:

- How to create a new custom CDK construct that combines existing constructs into a reusable component
- The process for building a Lambda-integrated RESTful API using API Gateway and Cognito authorization
- Best practices for documenting custom CDK constructs like updating the README and using JSDocs

Discussion

1. What are some other use cases where you could create a custom CDK construct? When is it better to use premade constructs?
2. How does creating higher-level abstractions with custom constructs improve productivity?
3. What other AWS services could be integrated into this REST API construct?

Extension Activities

Here are some activities to consider now that you have completed this chapter:

1. Extend the custom construct to support additional API Gateway features like usage plans.
2. Create a frontend application that consumes the REST API.
3. Add monitoring and analytics to track API usage and performance.
4. Integrate your API with Lambda authorizers or Cognito to authenticate usage.

## CHAPTER 9

Working with CDK Custom Resources

Sometimes there are no published L2 or L3 CDK constructs that meet your needs. One alternative to working with L1 constructs is to use something called a *CDK custom resource*. CDK custom resources are essentially AWS Lambda functions that deploy temporarily, launch some resources using an SDK, and then clean up, saving their state so that you can make modifications. This allows you to use the CDK to deploy resources that are not yet supported with L2 or L3 constructs but are supported by the AWS SDKs.

For our project, we will deploy an Amazon Q Business application using a CDK custom resource. Amazon Q Business lets you point foundational large language models at your private data, keeping it private while gaining the power of a fully managed generative AI (GenAI) chatbot for your own business use. In our case, we will use Amazon Q to summarize, identify patterns in, and make recommendations about our electric utility consumption data. Using custom resources really allows you to build quickly and bring the support of the SDKs to the CDK. At the time of writing this book, Amazon Q was not yet supported as an L2 or L3 construct in the CDK. At the time of reading this book, it may be supported, but you can still deploy the custom resource to learn how to do it. Think of a custom resource as a way to extend the CDK to support any AWS service that has an SDK until it is available as an L2 or L3 constructs either because someone else contributed it or because you built it!

Project Architecture: Deploy Amazon Q Business Application

In this project segment, you will deploy an Amazon Q Business application using a CDK custom resource. Your Amazon Q application will retrieve data from your electric utility outputs in S3 and then use the Amazon Q API to summarize, identify patterns in, and make recommendations about your electric utility consumption data. Figure 9-1 shows the logical architecture for this segment of the project. We are adding several components of Amazon Q which will access our S3 bucket.

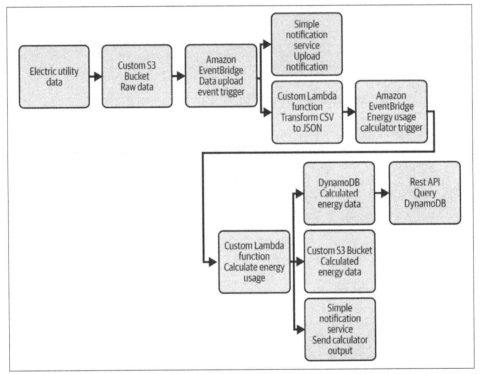

Figure 9-1. Our architecture is developing and becoming more complex. In this chapter, we add in generative AI using Amazon Q.

We will use Amazon Q (a custom resource) to analyze utility data stored in S3 and generate insights using GenAI. Our application is reusing components we built in previous chapters and adding GenAI with Amazon Q:

- S3 bucket (raw data)
- EventBridge notification
- Lambda function (transform to JSON)

- S3 bucket (transformed data)
- EventBridge notification
- Lambda function (calculate energy use)
- DynamoDB table (energy use)
- SNS notifications
- Custom API Gateway construct
- Amazon Q custom resource

CDK Custom Resources

A CDK custom resource is a generic mechanism to extend the functionality of CloudFormation by integrating custom logic that can be executed during stack creation, update, or deletion. This custom logic is typically implemented using AWS Lambda functions.

You define a custom resource by creating an AWS Lambda function that handles the lifecycle events (create, update, delete) of the custom resource. You then create a custom resource in your CDK stack that triggers this Lambda function. CDK custom resources are useful for tasks that cannot be natively handled by CloudFormation, such as interacting with external systems, performing complex conditional logic, or managing resources not directly supported by CloudFormation.

Here is an example of a CDK custom resource:

```
import * as cdk from 'aws-cdk-lib';
import * as lambda from 'aws-cdk-lib/aws-lambda';
import * as cr from 'aws-cdk-lib/custom-resources';

const fn = new lambda.Function(this, 'MyFunction', {
  runtime: lambda.Runtime.NODEJS_20_X,
  code: lambda.Code.fromAsset('lambda'),
  handler: 'index.handler',
});

const myProvider = new cr.Provider(this, 'MyProvider', {
  onEventHandler: fn,
});

new cdk.CustomResource(this, 'MyResource', {
  serviceToken: myProvider.serviceToken,
});
```

Note that this provides a bit more flexibility, as you are essentially wrapping a Lambda function to run ephemerally with your CDK deployments. But with that comes the need to manage the lifecycle of the Lambda function, write all of the commands it runs, and manage all the dependencies. A more "out-of-the-box" option is the AWS custom resource.

AWS Custom Resources

An AWS custom resource is a specific type of custom resource provided by the AWS CDK, which simplifies the process of invoking AWS SDK calls directly within a CloudFormation stack. It is built on top of Lambda and allows you to make SDK calls without writing the Lambda function code yourself.

AWS custom resources use AWS Lambda to make SDK calls to other AWS services. The Lambda function code is abstracted away, and you define the SDK calls you want to make directly in your CDK stack. AWS custom resources are useful for directly interacting with AWS services, such as making API calls to modify resources, retrieve information, or trigger specific actions that are not directly supported by CloudFormation resources.

Here's an example of using an AWS custom resource to create a custom resource that invokes an AWS SDK call:

```
import * as cdk from 'aws-cdk-lib';
import * as cr from 'aws-cdk-lib/custom-resources';

const awsCustom = new cr.AwsCustomResource(this, 'MyAwsCustomResource', {
  onCreate: {
    service: 'S3',
    action: 'putBucketNotificationConfiguration',
    parameters: {
      Bucket: 'my-bucket',
      NotificationConfiguration: {
        LambdaFunctionConfigurations: [{
          Events: ['s3:ObjectCreated:*'],
          LambdaFunctionArn:
            'arn:aws:lambda:region:account-id:function:my-function',
        }],
      },
    },
    physicalResourceId: cr.PhysicalResourceId.of('MyAwsCustomResourcePhysicalId'),
  },
  policy: cr.AwsCustomResourcePolicy.fromSdkCalls({
    resources: cr.AwsCustomResourcePolicy.ANY_RESOURCE,
  }),
});
```

Choosing the Right Custom Resource Type

When deciding between a CDK custom resource and an AWS custom resource, consider factors such as flexibility versus simplicity. A CDK custom resource offers greater flexibility since you can write any custom logic in the Lambda function. An AWS custom resource simplifies making AWS SDK calls without needing to write and manage Lambda code.

Also consider control versus abstraction. A CDK custom resource gives you full control over the custom resource lifecycle, while an AWS custom resource abstracts away the Lambda function and provides a higher-level interface for making SDK calls.

A final thought is balancing complexity with ease of use. A CDK custom resource requires writing and managing the Lambda function code, which can be more complex. An AWS custom resource simplifies the process by allowing you to define SDK calls directly in your CDK stack.

Go Build!

In this section, we are going to give you a bit more independence to follow the project sample code, but also to review the AWS CDK documentation and the AWS SDK documentation. Since AWS Custom Resources are a way to take action with the SDK, we need to get familiar with the SDK. In this project, we will build a new construct called chatbot, implement that in a chatbot stack, and integrate that with our main stack to deploy with our application. This chatbot will allow us to index, search, query, and summarize basic insights about our data in S3, and even DynamoDB if we choose to extend it.

There are a few prerequisites to start this project. To begin, you will need to enable AWS IAM Identity Center, since you will use IAM Identity Center to authenticate into your business application. Follow the directions outlined in the Amazon Q user guide to set that up for your Amazon Q Business Application (*https://oreil.ly/1IjEe*).

Next, you will need to create directories and files for your construct and the stack that deploys your construct. Remember we create the construct so that we can reuse it in other parts of our application or even other applications across our business or teams. Inside of your construct directory, create a directory called *chatbot* and a file within that directory called *chatbot-construct.ts*. Inside of your stack directory, create a directory called *chatbot* and a file within that directory called *chatbot-stack.ts*. You can also name them something else if you think it makes more sense. This is your application.

Now that you have these directories set up, we are going to build our construct, integrate it with our stack, and then define it within our main application. Our construct will have several inputs from other components of our application, including the S3 bucket where our data is stored and our DynamoDB table. It will output key data and information that will let us integrate with our API. Please review the full construct, stack, and main implementation at the following locations within the sample project code:

- Chatbot Construct (*https://oreil.ly/vN5Cj*)
- Chatbot Stack (*https://oreil.ly/r9Qs6*)
- Chatbot Integration with Main (*https://oreil.ly/BnNZx*)

Make sure you include the AWS IAM Identity Center ARN as an input to the chatbot stack in order for it to work. Please use the code samples in the GitHub repository as your "source of truth" for this project. Since Amazon Q is developing rapidly, we want to make sure that your example is as current as possible. Read the comments and README in the GitHub repository for a line-by-line breakdown of the code.

To review the Custom Construct for the Amazon Q Business chatbot, please visit the code sample in the previous link provided.

Let's break down what is happening in the AWS Custom Resource Construct:

1. The construct accepts several inputs as props, including S3 bucket for our processes utility data, the ARN for the AWS IAM Identity Center instance that you created following the documented link previously provided, the application name, and the DynamoDB table for our calculated energy usage data.
2. We establish IAM policies and permissions to allow Amazon Q Business necessary access to data and resources for the application.
3. We create an application, an index, and an application data source using the existing S3 bucket, and we sync the data and index of the data. This effectively makes our available data searchable and schedules indexing of the data on a regular basis so that we can easily find what we need with search and then summarize insights from it.

It's important to note what is going on behind the scenes with an AWS Custom Resource. The Custom Resource is a simple way of defining Lambdas that create, modify, and delete resources using standard SDK calls. This is an elegant way of taking action that cannot yet be taken directly through infrastructure as code. In our case, we are deploying several Lambda functions that make AWS SDK calls via JavaScript to create, modify, and delete the Amazon Q Business resources. This opens up a whole set of possibilities beyond what is already supported with CloudFormation. Use this functionality of CDK to build with new AWS services, or even do more complex things that extend the capabilities of of existing AWS services. We challenge you to get creative and try some new things.

Now, navigate back to the sample code repository and follow the examples to integrate the custom construct into your chatbot stack, and then into the *main.ts* file and stack. We challenge you to extend, or reuse this construct, perhaps for another use case. The power of constructs is in their flexibility and reusability. Make it your own and test your knowledge by applying it in a new context.

Test, Deploy, Modify, and Destroy

Let's test this new construct out!

1. Start by deploying the stack containing your ChatbotStack by using the cdk deploy ChatbotStack command in the CLI. This will provision all the necessary resources, including the Amazon Q Business application.

2. After deployment, you can verify that the Amazon Q Business application has been created successfully. Use the AWS Management Console or CLI to inspect the resources.

3. If you need to make changes to the application (e.g., update the data source), modify the stack and redeploy using cdk deploy. The CDK will automatically detect changes and update the resources accordingly.

4. Once you're done, clean up all resources by destroying the stack: cdk destroy ChatbotStack. This will delete all resources created by the stack, ensuring no lingering costs.

Don't worry if you delete everything. You have created IaC, so you can reinstantiate it easily! Now you can deploy your full application using cdk deploy -all when you are ready.

> Remember to document your code. Check out Chapter 3 for instructions on how to document using JSDocs.

Now that we have the stack, let's look at our API pipeline.

Test Your API

Consult the API documentation located within the API stack sample code (*https://oreil.ly/4-ZF_*). Using the documentation provided, do the following three things to test the entire end-to-end data pipeline and API:

Upload data

Upload your utility data to the S3 bucket. This will trigger the Lambda functions to transform and calculate energy use.

Query the API

Use the API Gateway endpoint provided by the stack to query the transformed data. You can test various queries to ensure that Amazon Q is summarizing and identifying patterns correctly.

Verify responses

Ensure the responses from the API are accurate and reflect the processed data.

You can use tools like Postman or the AWS CLI to test the API endpoints.

Getting Unstuck

I'm getting an "Access Denied" error when my custom resource tries to create the Amazon Q application. What could be wrong?

This error usually indicates an IAM permissions issue. To start, check that the IAM role associated with your Lambda function has the necessary permissions to create and manage Amazon Q resources. Verify that you've granted the correct permissions to the custom resource's execution role. You need to make sure that your AWS account has been enabled for Amazon Q Business. Next, double-check the region you're deploying to, as Amazon Q might not be available in all regions. Finally, try running the AWS CLI command to create an Amazon Q application manually to see if you encounter the same error.

My custom resource is timing out during creation. How can I resolve this?

custom resource timeouts can occur for several reasons. To start, increase the timeout setting for your Lambda function in the CDK stack. Then, check if the Amazon Q API is experiencing any delays or issues. You might consider breaking down the creation process into smaller steps if it's a complex setup. Finally, verify that all the dependencies and configurations required for Amazon Q are correctly set up beforehand.

The Amazon Q application has been created, but it's not connecting to my S3 data. What should I check?

If the Amazon Q application isn't accessing your S3 data, start by verifying that the S3 bucket permissions allow access from the Amazon Q application. Check that the S3 bucket name and path are correctly specified in your custom resource code. S3 lets you store data in any format, so check to make sure that the data format in S3 is compatible with what Amazon Q expects. You can look for any error messages in the Amazon Q application logs. You can also try accessing the S3 data manually using the AWS CLI to ensure that it's available and readable.

I'm having trouble updating my custom resource. The update operation seems to have no effect. What could be the issue?

This is one of those tricky things when working with custom resources. But don't worry, you can resolve it. To start, ensure that your custom resource handler properly implements the update event and check that the physical ID of the resource hasn't changed (if it has, CloudFormation treats it as a replacement instead of an update). Next, look at whether the properties you're trying to update are actually configurable for the Amazon Q application. You can use the `PhysicalResourceId.of()` method to explicitly control the physical ID of your resource.

My CDK synthesis is failing with a "Cannot find module" error related to the AWS SDK. How do I fix this?

Receiving this error usually indicates a problem with dependencies. To start, ensure that you've installed the necessary AWS SDK modules, particularly for Amazon Q. Check your *package.json* file to verify that all required dependencies are listed, and run `npm install` or `yarn install` to ensure that all dependencies are properly installed. If you're using TypeScript, make sure your *tsconfig.json* is correctly configured for module resolution. Finally, consider using `aws-sdk-v3` instead of `aws-sdk-v2` if you're not already, as it has better modular imports.

After destroying my stack, some Amazon Q resources seem to still exist. How can I ensure a complete cleanup?

Incomplete resource cleanup happens for a few reasons. Check if you've set any `RemovalPolicy` options that might be preventing resource deletion. You can manually check the AWS Console for any lingering resources and delete them if necessary. Consider implementing a custom retention policy or cleanup Lambda function as part of your stack and using AWS Config rules or custom scripts to periodically check for and clean up any orphaned resources.

Chapter Synth

In this chapter, you learned:

- How to create custom CDK constructs to deploy resources not natively supported by CDK
- The process for defining, implementing, and deploying a custom resource handler using Lambda
- How to document and publish custom CDK constructs to make them reusable across projects

Now you have a deeper understanding of how to extend the capabilities of the CDK using custom resources. This knowledge enables you to work with AWS services that are not yet supported by L2 or L3 constructs.

Discussion

1. What are some use cases where a custom resource would be useful compared to using existing CDK constructs?

2. What are some challenges or downsides to using custom resources instead of native CDK constructs?

3. How could you optimize the performance and cost of a custom resource handler implemented with Lambda?

Extension Activities

Here are some additional activities to consider now that you have completed this chapter:

1. Try creating a custom resource to deploy a service not yet supported by CDK, and document the process.

2. Publish your custom construct to npm or another package manager for reuse.

3. Analyze the performance and cost profile of your custom resource handler in different usage scenarios.

## CHAPTER 10

Working with Third-Party CDK Constructs

Sometimes you need to use a CDK construct that is not available in the AWS Construct Library. You might be working with an open source construct or a construct published by somebody in your company, or you might be testing out a construct in development. In this chapter, you will learn how to use constructs available on GitHub and available via npm. You will round out your Project 1 web application by adding an Amplify Web Application frontend and adding a retrieval-augmented generation chatbot that uses a combination of search and a large language model to generate summaries of energy usage and some recommendations for how to save energy and money.

Both of these resources are available as CDK constructs on GitHub and npm, one published by AWS (disclosure: our team worked on this, but it's free and open source) and another published for this project. You will learn how to use these constructs in your CDK project and how to modify them to suit your needs.

Project Architecture: Extend Functionality of CDK Constructs

In this project segment, you will extend the functionality of two existing CDK constructs to create a custom Lambda configuration and a custom S3 bucket configuration. Figure 10-1 shows how you start using other CDK constructs to augment things you have made yourself.

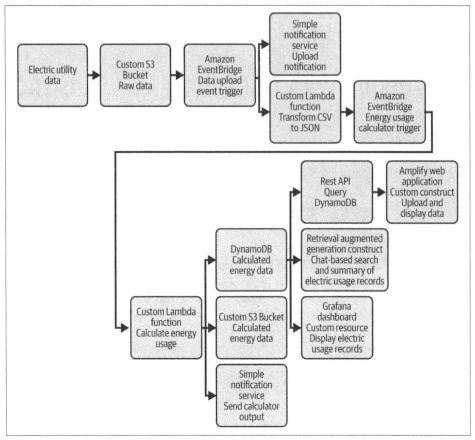

Figure 10-1. We don't always have to create our own CDK constructs. Thankfully, we can use constructs made by others (third parties) to accelerate our development.

In this project section, we create an AWS Amplify Web Application that integrates with our API using environmental variables. This web application has some basic functionalities that allow users to sign in, access data, interact with their calculated data, and perform some basic analysis. Our architecture provides a repository to host the code, a frontend integrated with your API, and a cognito user pool to handle authentication in the application:

CodeCommit repository
> This is where we store our CDK code for the Amplify Web Application and the Lambda function that powers the chatbot.

Amplify Web Application
> This is a frontend application that will be used to interact with the chatbot. It will be hosted on S3 and served via CloudFront.

Cognito User Pool
> This is a managed service that provides user authentication for our Amplify Web Application.

Best Practices for Observability

In addition to AWS-provided services, you can also implement custom logging and monitoring solutions using third-party tools and services, such as log aggregators, performance monitoring tools, and application performance monitoring (APM) solutions, to gain additional insights into your AWS resources, services, and applications. Other good things to do include the following:

- Set up detailed CloudWatch alarms to monitor critical metrics and receive alerts when thresholds are breached.

- Enable AWS CloudTrail to capture detailed logs of API calls and changes to resources for auditing and troubleshooting purposes.

- Use AWS X-Ray to trace requests and responses across distributed applications to gain insights into performance and troubleshoot issues.

- Implement centralized logging and analysis of logs using services like Amazon S3, Amazon Elasticsearch, or third-party log aggregators.

- Use AWS CloudFormation StackSets to ensure consistent deployment and configuration of observability resources across multiple AWS accounts and regions.

- Follow the AWS Well-Architected Framework best practices for designing, building, and operating observability in your AWS architectures. More on this in Chapter 13.

Go Build!

Now we are starting to pull all the threads together. But our application is missing a frontend. We will use the Amplify Web Application construct to add a frontend to our application. This will give us an interface to do things like:

- Upload files to S3.
- Interact with the chatbot.
- View the chatbot's responses.
- Enter our data through an alternate means in a form.
- Read documentation about the application.
- Visualize our data in a dashboard.

Do Your Research

Before you actually build the Amplify Web Application, you need to do some research. Even though we created this construct for you, it's extremely important to make sure you understand what you are building and how it works. It's also important when using third-party software, even from trusted sources, to assess how well maintained the software is and if there are any ongoing issues:

1. Go to the Amplify Web Application construct's GitHub repository (*https:// oreil.ly/mYYzB*).

2. Read the *README.md* file to understand how the construct works.

3. Look at the Issues tab to see if there are any ongoing issues or bugs. How quickly are they generally addressed? When was the last commit? When was the last release? When was the last response to an issue?

4. If there are any open issues, read through them to see if they are relevant to your use case. If you have any questions, ask them in the Issues tab.

5. Look at the code to see if you understand how it works. If you don't, spend a bit of time stepping through it.

Is this a bit tedious? Yes. But it's a lot easier to carefully vet third-party software and tools before they become a dependency for your project. Third-party software can be a huge time saver, but it can also be a huge time sink if it doesn't work as expected. We would consider external dependencies as a "one-way door" in many ways. It's easy to add them, but it's hard to remove them without doing a lot more work.

OK, but we did build this one for you, and we are going to use it. We'll break down what this construct does and how it works, but before we begin, install the custom amplify construct from npm: `npm install @hands-on-aws-cdk-book/ custom-amplify-construct`. This installs the construct from a public npm repository and makes it available for use as a dependency in your project.

Use the Amplify Web Application Construct

Now that we've set up the file structure, it's time to use the Amplify Web Application Construct we've provided. This construct simplifies the deployment of your frontend application using AWS Amplify. CDK will handle the setup so you can focus on building features. Let's take a look at how it works:

1. Create a directory in your *lib/stacks* directory called *web*.

2. Create a file within it called *web-stack.ts*, or choose something different that works for you.

See Example 10-1 for an example of usage, and consult the online documentation for the construct and the sample application for further clarification and examples.

Example 10-1. Home Energy Coach Amplify Web Application construct

```
import * as cdk from "aws-cdk-lib";
import { Construct } from "constructs";
import { CustomAmplifyConstruct } from
      "@hands-on-aws-cdk-book/custom-amplify-construct";
interface WebStackProps extends cdk.StackProps {
 githubRepositoryUrl: string;
 githubBranch: string;
 userPoolId: string;
 userPoolClientId: string;
 apiEndpointUrl: string;
}
export class WebStack extends cdk.Stack {
 public readonly amplifyApp: CustomAmplifyConstruct;
 constructor(
scope: Construct,
id: string,
props: WebStackProps) {
   super(scope, id, props);


   // Create Amplify app using the custom construct
   this.amplifyApp =
new CustomAmplifyConstruct(this, "AmplifyApp", {
     appName: "MyWebApp",
     githubRepositoryUrl: props.githubRepositoryUrl,
     githubTokenSecretName: props.githubTokenSecretName,
     branch: props.githubBranch,
     environmentVariables: {
       VITE_USER_POOL_ID: props.userPoolId,
       VITE_USER_POOL_CLIENT_ID: props.userPoolClientId,
       VITE_REGION: props.region,
       VITE_API_ENDPOINT: props.apiEndpointUrl,
     },
   });
 }
}
```

Take a look at this stack and visit the documentation for a detailed breakdown of what's happening. Our stack accepts props for the GitHub repository URL, the branch to use for deployment, the Cognito user pool that we created in previous chapters, and the endpoint of our API, which we will authenticate through our web app with Cognito.

In our stack, we translate the user pool ID and API endpoints into variables that can be used in our frontend application. If you'd like to understand this better, please review the README for the frontend application (*https://oreil.ly/kZSA7*). This construct allows us to deploy a hosted Amplify application with just a few inputs, and integrate with other resources within our application. This construct will tie together all the components of our application into a frontend user experience.

Now that you've created your stack, it's your turn to integrate this stack with your *main.ts* file and deploy into your main application. We have created a frontend application for you that will wrap all of this together, as long as everything else in your application is correct. You can find this and all necessary documentation in the GitHub repository (*https://oreil.ly/Y9UVF*). Try integrating and deploying this stack on your own before you consult the project sample code to verify and check your work.

Test, Deploy, Modify, and Destroy

Now that you have an outside construct integrated into your application, it's time to test the construct, stack, and application to ensure that it deploys correctly. Use your knowledge of deployment to go through this process on your own. What do you think you will see when deployment is successful? Go to the CloudFormation console and eventually to the Amplify section of the console to see that your application has deployed. Review the example in the frontend sample code. Your application should look like and behave like this.

Getting Unstuck

How do I know if a third-party CDK construct is secure and reliable?
> To assess the security and reliability of a third-party CDK construct, start with the project's GitHub repository for recent activity, open issues, and how quickly they're addressed. You can look at the number of stars, forks, and contributors as indicators of community support. You can also review the code for best practices and security considerations and check if the construct has been audited or reviewed by reputable sources. It is always a good idea to test the construct thoroughly in a nonproduction environment before using it in production to avoid surprises.

I'm getting a "Module not found" error when trying to use a third-party construct. How can I fix this?
> This error usually occurs when the module isn't properly installed or imported. To get started, ensure that you've installed the package using npm or yarn (e.g., `npm install <my-construct>`). Check that the package name in your import statement matches the installed package name, and verify that the package is listed in your *package.json* file. Run `npm install` to ensure that all dependencies are properly installed, and check for any peer dependencies that might be required. If you are using TypeScript, ensure that your *tsconfig.json* is configured correctly for module resolution.

The Amplify Web Application construct isn't deploying correctly. What should I check?

If you're having issues deploying the Amplify Web Application, start by checking that you have the necessary permissions to create all required resources. Check the CloudFormation events in the AWS Console for any specific error messages. Ensure that your AWS account is properly configured for Amplify (e.g., service quotas), and verify that all required props are correctly passed to the construct. Check if there are any region-specific requirements or limitations, and try deploying a simple Amplify app manually to isolate the problem to determine whether it's a construct issue or an account/permission issue. Finally, review the construct's documentation for any known issues or required configurations.

I've modified a third-party construct, but my changes aren't reflected when I deploy. What's going on?

When modifying third-party constructs, start by ensuring that you're modifying the correct file—some packages use *dist* folders for compiled code. If you've modified the package in *node_modules*, remember that these changes can be overwritten—consider forking the repository instead. Make sure you're importing your modified version of the construct, not the original. At this point, you should consider clearing your CDK build cache (*cdk.out* directory) and try synthesizing again. If you're using TypeScript, ensure that you've recompiled the code after making changes, and then check if the construct uses any caching mechanisms that might be preventing updates. Finally, consider creating a patch file or using npm's `patch-package` for tracking and applying your modifications.

The chatbot integration isn't working as expected. How can I troubleshoot this?

To troubleshoot chatbot integration issues, start by checking the Lambda function logs in CloudWatch for any error messages. Verify that the necessary permissions are in place for the Lambda function to access other resources (e.g., S3, DynamoDB). Ensure that API Gateway is correctly configured to trigger the Lambda function, and test the chatbot Lambda function directly using the AWS Console to isolate any issues. You also need to verify that the input format from the Amplify application matches what the chatbot Lambda expects, and check if there are any resource constraints (e.g., Lambda timeout, memory) affecting the chatbot's performance. Finally, you can review the integration between the Amplify frontend and the backend services to ensure proper configuration.

Chapter Synth

In this chapter, you learned:

- How to work with third-party CDK constructs published on GitHub and npm
- How to extend existing CDK constructs to customize configurations for your needs
- How to build your own custom CDK constructs to encapsulate infrastructure code

Discussion

1. When is it better to build your own custom construct versus using an existing third-party construct? What are the trade-offs?
2. How can you make sure third-party constructs you use are secure and reliable?
3. What best practices should you follow when publishing your own custom constructs for others to use?

Extension Activities

Now that you have completed this chapter, here are some additional activities to consider:

1. Publish your custom construct from this chapter to GitHub or npm for others to use.
2. Find an open source CDK construct and contribute code or documentation back to the project.
3. Build a custom construct for another type of resource not covered in the book, like a message queue or search index.

## CHAPTER 11

Testing CDK Applications

Writing tests for your CDK application is a topic worthy of its own book. There are some great books out there on writing tests, test-driven development, and testing infrastructure. For this chapter, we will focus specifically on testing CDK applications and infrastructure using some of the unique tools that come with CDK. There is a big debate about the best way to incorporate tests into your development process. Some people say that all development should be test driven, meaning that you write your tests before you even write your application logic. While this is a good fit for some development teams, we have chosen to build our logic first and write tests second. We will leave it up to you to decide what works best for your team.

In this case, we will write two kinds of tests: infrastructure tests and end-to-end tests. Infrastructure tests will test the infrastructure that we have built using CDK—basically, we want to make sure that we are deploying the things we intended to deploy before we start creating resources. End-to-end tests will test the entire application from the frontend to the backend—we want to make sure that the inputs or user interactions with our application produce a predictable and accurate output. We will not be writing tests for our frontend application, but in the notes at the end of the chapter, we recommend some books and resources for testing frontend applications.

In this project, we will write some infrastructure tests for our S3 buckets and APIs to make sure that we have the proper permissions in place. We wouldn't want to deploy an application that has been modified to prevent the flow of data through our pipeline. We will also write a single end-to-end test that uploads some data to our application, waits for the pipeline to run, and then queries our API to make sure that the data is available and the calculations are accurate. We will use Jest to write our infrastructure tests and Cypress to write our end-to-end tests. In Chapter 12, we will use GitHub Actions to automate our testing and deployment process, but for now we will run this locally.

Project Architecture: Extend Functionality of CDK Constructs

So far, we've been scrappy. We have been doing things manually that we should automate. Let's turn our focus to using tools that improve code quality, enforce standards, and support automated testing. As shown in Figure 11-1, these additions elevate our project and ensure maintainability, security, and testing are built into all aspects of the application.

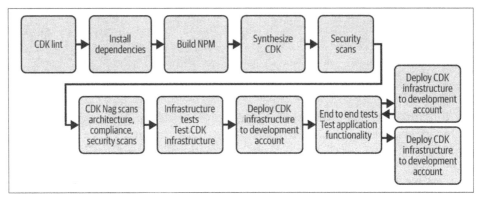

Figure 11-1. Testing architecture for CDK applications using Jest, Cypress, and `cdk-nag`

We will use several tools to make our code easier to manage and maintain. We will use Precommit Hooks for Git Secrets, TSLint, and Prettier. We will use Jest for infrastructure tests, Cypress for end-to-end tests, and Artillery for load tests. CDK-nag will help with security and architecture analysis.

Like with application code, you can write two main types of tests for your infrastructure code: unit tests and integration tests.

Unit tests focus on testing individual components or pieces of your CDK code. In this case, you're not deploying any cloud resources; instead, you're testing the logical structure of your CDK constructs. This could involve verifying that a particular resource, such as an S3 bucket or a Lambda function, is defined correctly.

Why should you bother with unit tests? They are fast to execute because they don't interact with AWS services. They help ensure that your code is logically correct before actual deployment.

Integration tests are a little different. While unit tests check the logical structure of your CDK code, integration tests verify that the cloud resources you defined are being deployed and configured correctly in your AWS environment. This means that your code will interact with real AWS services, and you will need to handle actual resources such as EC2 instances, S3 buckets, or Lambda functions.

In summary, integration tests ensure that your cloud infrastructure behaves as expected in a real environment. Integration tests catch issues that unit tests can't, such as permission problems or deployment failures.

 Integration tests are slower and more resource intensive than unit tests because they interact with real AWS services. It's also essential to clean up any resources (such as S3 buckets or EC2 instances) after the tests are complete.

Precommit Hooks

Precommit hooks are scripts that run automatically before each commit in version control systems, such as Git (which we are using), to perform tasks like linting, formatting, or running tests, ensuring that code quality and standards are maintained. For AWS CDK projects, precommit hooks are particularly useful because they can enforce best practices, validate AWS CloudFormation templates, and ensure that the IaC adheres to security and compliance standards before changes are committed.

There are several ways to implement precommit hooks, and we will be using a tool called Husky.

To set up precommit hooks in an AWS CDK project with Husky, you first need to install Husky in your project by running `npm install husky --save-dev`. Then, configure Husky in your *package.json* by adding a husky section where you define your hooks, such as precommit, and specify the commands you want to run, like linting or testing your CDK code. This automation helps maintain code quality and prevent potential issues in your AWS infrastructure deployments.

Here are the steps to set up Husky:

1. Run `npm install husky --save-dev` at the root of your project.

2. Add the code from Example 11-1 underneath your `dev-dependencies` section in *package.json*.

Example 11-1. Husky precommit hook setup

```
...your dependencies
"husky": {
    "hooks": {
      "pre-commit": "npm run build && cdk synth"
    }
  }
```

This precommit hook ensures that you always build and synthesize your code before committing. In future sections, we can add other steps to this to run custom linters or tools like git-secrets.

Handle Secrets and Sensitive Data

Handling secrets and sensitive data securely is an important aspect of building secure applications. Here are some recommended best practices for handling secrets in the context of an AWS CDK application in addition to using git-secrets:

Use AWS Secrets Manager or AWS Parameter Store
  AWS provides services like AWS Secrets Manager and AWS Systems Manager Parameter Store that are designed to securely store and manage secrets such as passwords, API keys, and certificates. You can store secrets in these services and securely retrieve them in your CDK application using AWS SDKs or CDK constructs.

Avoid hardcoding secrets in code
  Avoid hardcoding secrets directly in your CDK application code or configuration files, as this can expose them to potential risks, such as accidental exposure in logs or version control. Instead, store them in a secure location like AWS Secrets Manager or AWS Parameter Store, and retrieve them dynamically during runtime.

Use CDK context or environment variables
  You can use CDK context or environment variables to pass sensitive data to your CDK application during deployment. For example, you can define context values or environment variables for secrets like API keys or passwords, and retrieve them in your CDK code using this.node.tryGetContext() or process.env, respectively. Be sure to encrypt and securely manage the context or environment variables to prevent unauthorized access.

Follow the principle of least privilege
  When using secrets in your CDK application, follow the principle of least privilege. Limit the permissions and access of secrets to only the necessary resources and users. Avoid using overly permissive IAM policies or sharing secrets with unnecessary resources or users.

Encrypt secrets in transit and at rest
  Ensure that secrets are encrypted in transit and at rest. For example, use HTTPS when transferring secrets over the network, and enable encryption options like AWS KMS encryption for secrets stored in AWS Secrets Manager or AWS Parameter Store.

Monitor and audit secret access

Set up logging and monitoring for secret access to detect and respond to any unauthorized access attempts. Regularly review and audit the access to secrets to ensure that only authorized users and resources are accessing them.

Secrets are secret only if you handle them securely. Following these tips will help you effectively handle secrets and sensitive data in your CDK application and ensure the security of your AWS resources and applications.

Prettier, TSLint, and Other Formatting Tools

Prettier and TSLint are popular tools used for formatting and linting code to ensure consistency and maintainability. Here's how you can use them to ensure neatly and consistently formatted CDK code.

Prettier

Prettier is a code formatting tool that automatically formats your code based on a predefined set of rules. To use Prettier with CDK code, install Prettier as a development dependency in your CDK project: `npm install prettier --save-dev` or `yarn add prettier --dev`.

Create a *.prettierrc* or *prettier.config.js* file in the root of your project to configure Prettier options, such as indentation, line width, and other formatting rules.

Run Prettier on your CDK code using a script in your *package.json* file, like "format": `prettier --write 'lib/**/*.js'`, where `lib/**/*.js` is the glob pattern for your CDK code files.

You can also configure your code editor to automatically format your CDK code with Prettier on save, for seamless integration with your development workflow.

TSLint

TSLint is a popular linter for TypeScript code that helps catch potential issues and enforce coding standards. To use TSLint with CDK code, start by installing TSLint as a development dependency in your CDK project: `npm install tslint --save-dev` or `yarn add tslint --dev`.

Create a *tslint.json* file in the root of your project to configure TSLint options, such as coding rules, formatting rules, and other linting rules.

Run TSLint on your CDK code using a script in your *package.json* file, like "lint": `tslint --project .` or "lint": `tslint -c tslint.json 'lib/**/*.ts'`, where `lib/**/*.ts` is the glob pattern for your CDK TypeScript files.

You can also configure your code editor to show TSLint warnings and errors in real time, so you can fix them as you write your CDK code.

Prettier and TSLint help ensure that your CDK code is neatly and consistently formatted, follows coding standards, and is free from potential issues, resulting in clean, maintainable, and error-free CDK applications.

Infrastructure Tests with Jest

Jest is a popular JavaScript testing framework designed to ensure correctness of any JavaScript codebase. It allows developers to write tests with a rich set of features like mock functions, test suites, and coverage reports. Jest is well suited for testing frontend applications, Node.js services, and IaC. Typically, CDK testing with Jest involves:

Unit testing
> This involves writing tests for individual constructs or smaller units of your infrastructure to validate that they behave as expected. This might include testing the properties of a resource, such as an S3 bucket or an IAM role, ensuring that they're set up with the correct configurations.

Snapshot testing
> This is particularly useful in infrastructure testing. It allows you to take a *snapshot* of your AWS CDK stack's CloudFormation template and compare it against future versions. This ensures that changes to your infrastructure are intentional and correctly implemented.

Mocking AWS services
> By mocking AWS SDK calls that your CDK app might make, you can simulate the behavior of AWS services without actually making any real API calls. This is useful for testing how your infrastructure reacts to different responses from AWS services.

In this chapter, we will focus on writing Jest code for unit testing of CDK resources. Basically, this helps you test your infrastructure before it deploys to make sure it produces the outcome you expect. This is especially important when you start introducing changes to your infrastructure.

For a simplified example, let's look at Example 11-2, a Jest test that checks your app to verify that you have three S3 buckets, all with public access turned off and all with versioning turned on.

Example 11-2. Jest S3 check

```
import { App } from 'aws-cdk-lib';
import { Template, Match } from '@aws-cdk/assertions';
import { MyCdkStack } from './MyCdkStack';

test('3 S3 Buckets with Public Access Blocked and Versioning Enabled', () => {
  const app = new App();
  const stack = new MyCdkStack(app, 'MyTestStack');
  const template = Template.fromStack(stack);

  // Assert that there are exactly 3 S3 Bucket resources
  template.resourceCountIs('AWS::S3::Bucket', 3);

  // Assert that each S3 bucket has public access blocked and versioning enabled
  template.hasResourceProperties('AWS::S3::Bucket', {
    PublicAccessBlockConfiguration: {
      BlockPublicAcls: true,
      BlockPublicPolicy: true,
      IgnorePublicAcls: true,
      RestrictPublicBuckets: true
    },
    VersioningConfiguration: {
      Status: 'Enabled'
    }
  });
});
```

Let's go ahead and add this test to our repository. CDK already comes with Jest installed, and there is even an existing directory for scripts like this. Go to *./tests* and add a file called *stack-shared-resources.test.ts*. This creates a test file that corresponds with your shared resources stack. You can group tests in any way you choose, but to create a clear 1:1 correspondence we will name the test to match the stack.

Try modifying this to match the expected pattern in our shared resources stack. Take a look at the architecture diagrams to see what the expected infrastructure is. This is a good opportunity to reread some of the previous chapters to verify which resources you are deploying.

Write Your Own Jest Tests

Now it's your turn to try writing some Jest tests. Remember: these are static tests, so you are checking that the things you are deploying really are the things that will deploy. You can check this chapter's repository for several examples. But we challenge you to write a few more tests of your own. Here are some suggestions:

1. Write a test to check that your API deploys successfully and that you have authentication attached to the API.

2. Write a test to check that you have deployed the correct number of Lambda functions and that all Lambdas are running with Node.js V20.

Custom Commands

You can write your own test commands that can help you automate testing processes in your CDK project. Here's how you can create custom test commands:

1. Define test scripts in your *package.json* file: You can define custom test scripts in the `scripts` section of your *package.json* file. For example:

```
"scripts": { "test:unit": jest --config jest.config.js
"test:integration": jest --config jest.integration.config.js
"test:functional": jest --config jest.functional.config.js }
```

In this example, we have defined three test scripts for running unit, integration, and functional tests using Jest.

1. Create Jest configuration files. For each test script, you can create a separate Jest configuration file that specifies the testing options and settings. For example, you can create *jest.config.js*, *jest.integration.config.js*, and *jest.functional.config.js* files for unit, integration, and functional tests, respectively.

2. Customize test command options. You can customize your test command options based on your specific testing requirements. For example, you can specify test files or directories to run, enable, or disable specific test reporters, configure code coverage settings, and more. Jest provides a wide range of configuration options that you can use to tailor your test commands to your needs.

3. Run custom test commands. Once you have defined your test scripts and Jest configuration files, you can run them using `npm run` or `yarn run` commands. For example:

```
npm run test:unit` // Runs unit tests
npm run test:integration // Runs integration tests
npm run test:functional // Runs functional tests
```

These custom test commands allow you to run specific types of tests in your CDK project based on your testing requirements, and they provide a convenient way to automate your testing processes.

Getting Started with CDK-Nag

CDK-Nag is a popular open source tool used in AWS CDK projects to identify and prevent common security and best practice violations. It helps developers identify potential security risks and misconfigurations in their CDK applications before deployment. CDK-Nag includes:

---

cdk-nag *rules*

A set of predefined rules that are written in YAML format. These rules define the best practices and security checks that CDK-Nag performs on the CDK code. For example, rules can check for the usage of insecure protocols, open permissions, and other security vulnerabilities in CDK constructs.

cdk-nag *CLI*

A CLI that developers can use to run the tool on their CDK codebase. The CLI takes the YAML rules file as input and scans the CDK code to identify violations of the defined rules. It provides detailed output with information about the violations found, including the line numbers and code snippets where the issues are detected.

cdk-nag *GitHub Actions*

Allows for automated scanning of CDK code during the development process. Developers can configure CDK-Nag as a GitHub Action in their CDK projects to automatically run the tool on code changes, pull requests, and other events in the GitHub repository. This helps catch potential security issues early in the development lifecycle.

 We talked about the value and use cases of cdk-nag back in Chapter 7.

Integrating CDK-Nag with Your Manual Tests

Integrating cdk-nag into manual tests can help ensure that CDK code is continuously scanned for security and best practice violations during the development process. Start by installing cdk-nag as a development dependency in the CDK project. This can be done using npm with the following command: npm install cdk-nag --save-dev. This installs CDK-Nag as a development dependency in the project.

Now we can create cdk-nag rules to define the best practices and security checks to be performed on the CDK code. These rules are written in YAML format and can be created or customized according to project requirements. For example, rules can be defined to check for insecure protocols, open permissions, and other security vulnerabilities in CDK constructs.

Once we have the rules, we can create shell scripts to automate the execution of cdk-nag on the CDK codebase. These scripts can be written to run cdk-nag with the installed rules against the CDK code and generate reports with the violations found. For example, a shell script can use the cdk-nag CLI to run CDK-Nag with the defined rules against the CDK codebase.

We can also integrate cdk-nag with manual tests. The shell scripts can be integrated into manual testing processes as part of the overall testing workflow. For example, the scripts can be executed as a precheck before code reviews, or as a step in the manual testing process to verify that CDK code complies with the defined rules and does not have any security or best practice violations.

As we already discussed, we can automate cdk-nag with npm commands to simplify the execution of the shell scripts. For example, npm scripts can be defined in the project's *package.json* file to run the shell scripts with a single command. This makes it easier for developers to integrate cdk-nag into their manual testing workflow using npm commands.

Integrating cdk-nag into manual tests using shell scripts and npm commands helps ensure that CDK code is continuously scanned for security and best practice violations during the development process. This helps you catch potential issues early and maintain a higher level of security and compliance in CDK applications.

Integrating CDK-Nag with Your CI/CD Pipelines and GitHub Actions

Integrating cdk-nag with your CI/CD pipelines and GitHub Actions can help automate the scanning of CDK code for security and best practice violations as part of the deployment process. Just like in the testing stage, we need to make sure that cdk-nag is installed as a development dependency in the CDK project using npm install cdk-nag --save-dev.

Now we define specific cdk-nag jobs in a CI/CD pipeline configuration to run cdk-nag with the installed rules against the CDK codebase. For example, you can configure a separate job in your CI/CD pipeline that runs cdk-nag as part of the build or test process.

We can also use GitHub Actions to create custom GitHub Actions workflows that include cdk-nag jobs. GitHub Actions allows you to define custom workflows in YAML format, and you can use the cdk-nag CLI to run CDK-Nag with the defined rules against the CDK codebase.

Sometimes things won't work the first time and we will need to correct and remediate cdk-nag errors. When cdk-nag identifies errors or warnings in the CDK code, it provides detailed information on the violations. Developers can then use this information to correct and remediate the issues in the codebase. This may involve building custom CDK constructs or aspects that address the specific violations identified by CDK-Nag. For example, if CDK-Nag flags a security vulnerability in the use of an insecure protocol, developers can create a custom CDK construct that uses a secure alternative.

Once we fix an issue, we can validate `cdk-nag` remediation through the CI/CD pipeline and GitHub Actions to ensure that the issues identified by `cdk-nag` have been successfully addressed.

GitHub Actions and `cdk-nag` are great together. They help us build custom constructs or aspects to correct and remediate any `cdk-nag` errors or warnings, and you can automate the process of ensuring that your CDK code complies with security and best practice standards. This helps maintain a higher level of security and compliance in your CDK applications throughout the development and deployment process.

Remediating cdk-nag Errors and Warnings

When using `cdk-nag` to scan your CDK codebase, you may encounter errors and warnings that need to be addressed. There are two main approaches to handling these issues: creating custom constructs to fix violations and using suppressions to document accepted risks.

Using custom constructs

If `cdk-nag` identifies violations that need to be addressed, you can create custom CDK constructs that implement the necessary changes. For example, if `cdk-nag` flags a violation related to an insecure protocol, you can create a custom construct that uses a secure alternative.

Using suppressions

Sometimes fixing a violation isn't practical or necessary. In these cases, `cdk-nag` provides a *suppressions* feature that allows you to ignore specific violations while documenting why. Here's how to use suppressions effectively: . Add the suppression using comments in your code. You can annotate the CDK construct with suppression metadata using the `NagSuppressions.addResourceSuppressions()` method. For example:

```
import { NagSuppressions } from 'cdk-nag';

const bucket = new s3.Bucket(this, 'MyBucket', {
  encryption: s3.BucketEncryption.S3_MANAGED,
});

NagSuppressions.addResourceSuppressions(bucket, [
  {
    id: 'AwsSolutions-S1',
    reason: 'This bucket only stores non-sensitive
                temporary data and does not
                require access logging.',
  },
]);
```

In this example, the `AwsSolutions-S1` rule is suppressed with a clear, documented reason:

Provide a detailed justification

Always explain why you are suppressing a rule. This ensures that future developers (including future-you) understand the rationale. A good justification should include context, such as business constraints, architectural decisions, or compensating controls that mitigate the risk. Hint: if you don't have a clear justification you probably shouldn't be suppressing!

Suppress specific rules only

Avoid using broad or catch-all suppressions. Instead, target individual rule IDs for specific resources. This helps keep your suppressions focused and auditable. Do suppress a specific bucket like above. DO NOT suppress access logging for ALL buckets.

Avoid using suppressions as a workaround

Suppressions are not a substitute for secure or well-architected infrastructure. Use them only when there's a valid reason that the rule does not apply to your use case. If you find yourself using suppressions in every section of your repository consider using a different CDK-nag compliance pack or creating your own.

Track and review suppressions regularly

As your codebase evolves, some suppressions may become obsolete or unnecessary. Some may also become overused, which should trigger you to modify standard rules. Periodically audit your suppressions to ensure they're still valid and still meet your team's security and compliance requirements. Also remember that you can create custom constructs within your own construct library so that all your resources are compliant. It's always best to do a little extra work to meet compliance requirements.

Suppressions should be used thoughtfully and sparingly

If you are spending significant time writing suppressions or notice they are in every file and showing up regularly in blocks of code you should make adjustments either to the CDK-nag package you're using, to your custom constructs, or to your overall application architecture. Also note that sometimes meeting compliance standards can lead to higher costs. As you work to improve your security and compliance posture you should also be sure to monitor cost and ensure you don't end up with any surprise bills.

Documenting Your CDK-Nag Remediations and DevOps Integrations

When using CDK-Nag to scan and remediate errors in your CDK codebase, it's important to document your remediation efforts for future use and scalability.

Create detailed documentation for the specific errors identified by CDK-Nag and the corresponding remediation steps taken. Include the rule ID, the affected resource, the justification for the remediation, and any other relevant information. This documentation should be clear, concise, and easily understandable by future developers.

We like to use a centralized documentation repository, such as a wiki or a documentation website, to store all our CDK-Nag remediation documentation. This allows for easy access and reference by future developers and ensures that the documentation remains up-to-date and organized. Remember to review and update your CDK-Nag remediation documentation regularly to ensure that it remains accurate and up-to-date. As your CDK codebase evolves and requirements change, some remediations may need to be revised or updated. Make sure to keep the documentation current and reflective of the current state of your CDK codebase.

The value of cdk-nag is that you can easily include it with your DevOps integrations or automation implemented as part of your CDK-Nag remediation efforts. For example, if you have integrated CDK-Nag into your CI/CD pipelines or GitHub Actions, document the steps taken to set up the integration, including any configuration files, scripts, or commands used.

It is always a good idea to share the CDK-Nag remediation documentation with your development team and other relevant stakeholders. This helps ensure that the documentation is easily accessible and available to everyone involved in the CDK development process, promoting consistency and standardization in your CDK codebase.

By documenting your CDK-Nag remediation efforts and DevOps integrations, you can provide valuable guidance and knowledge for future developers, ensuring that your CDK codebase remains compliant with security and best practice standards, as well as enabling scalability and maintainability of your CDK applications.

Develop Your Security Checklist and Requirements

The cdk-nag tool can help you with security, but nothing beats a solid security checklist aligned with application and business requirements. Here are some things to think about to ensure that your cloud infrastructure and applications are protected against potential security threats:

Identify application and business requirements

Begin by understanding the specific security requirements of your application and business. This may include compliance regulations, data sensitivity, access controls, authentication and authorization, logging and monitoring, and disaster recovery, among others.

Assess threats and risks

Identify potential security threats and risks that could impact your application and business. This may include external threats such as hackers, malware, and denial-of-service (DoS) attacks, as well as internal threats such as unauthorized access, data breaches, and misconfigurations.

Define security controls

Based on the identified threats and risks, define a set of security controls that are necessary to mitigate those risks. This may include implementing strong authentication and authorization mechanisms, encrypting sensitive data, setting up monitoring and logging, establishing backup and disaster recovery procedures, and regularly patching and updating software and systems.

Review AWS security best practices

Familiarize yourself with AWS security best practices, which provide guidance on how to secure different AWS services and resources. This may include setting up appropriate IAM policies, configuring network security, implementing encryption, enabling logging and monitoring, and following AWS security best practices for specific services such as S3, RDS, and EC2.

Implement security controls

Based on the identified security controls and AWS security best practices, implement the necessary security measures in your cloud infrastructure and applications. This may involve using AWS security services, such as AWS IAM, AWS CloudTrail, AWS Config, and AWS GuardDuty, as well as custom configurations and scripts to enforce security policies and settings.

Regularly review and update

Security is an ongoing process, so regularly review and update your security controls to adapt to changing threats and requirements. This may involve conducting regular security audits, vulnerability assessments, and penetration testing, as well as staying updated with the latest security patches, updates, and best practices from AWS and other security sources.

Document and train

Document your security controls, configurations, and procedures, and provide training to your team members on how to follow them. This ensures that everyone involved in managing your cloud infrastructure and applications is aware of the security requirements and best practices and follows them consistently.

Getting Unstuck

My Jest tests are failing, but I can't figure out why. How can I debug this?

We've been there. This is super frustrating. When Jest tests fail, start by looking at the log statements from your tests. You can print out the test values and see what is happening with `console.log()`. Try rerunning Jest with the `--verbose` flag so that it prints more detailed output. If you need to narrow things down, try `describe.only()` or `it.only()` to focus on specific test suites or cases. Check that your test is importing the correct modules and constructs and verify that your CDK construct is being instantiated correctly in the test. If things still aren't working, use Jest's `expect().toMatchSnapshot()` to see how your construct's CloudFormation template has changed. Finally, run Jest with the `--detectOpenHandles` flag if tests are hanging.

I'm getting a "Cannot find module" error when running my tests. What's wrong?

This error usually indicates a problem with module resolution. Begin by validating that all the dependencies are installed (`npm install`). Look at the output to make sure that the import statements in your test files are correct. Verify that the *tsconfig.json* file is configured correctly for your project structure. Sometimes there are gremlins in the system—you can vanquish them by clearing Jest's cache with `jest --clearCache`. If things still aren't working, check that your *jest.config.js* is set up correctly for TypeScript and that the module you're trying to import is listed in your *package.json*. If the module is a local file, make sure the path is correct relative to the test file.

My Cypress tests are not interacting with elements on the page as expected. How can I fix this?

Sometimes Cypress tests don't interact correctly with page elements. If you are having trouble with Cypress, start with Cypress's `.debug()` command to pause execution and inspect the state of the application. Ensure that the elements are visible and not covered by other elements when Cypress tries to interact with them, and check that you're using the correct selectors for your elements (IDs, classes, data attributes). The `.should('be.visible')` or `.should('exist')` assertions will help when interacting with elements. Sometimes Cypress gets bogged down if there are lots of network requests or animations. You may need to increase the default timeout if elements are taking longer to appear than expected, or you may need to use Cypress's `.wait()` command to wait for specific conditions before proceeding.

The `cdk-nag` checks are failing, but I'm not sure how to fix the issues. What should I do?

Sadly, sometimes CDK-Nag checks fail. When that happens, start by reviewing the CDK-Nag output to understand which specific rules are being violated. Sometimes you need to look up the rule documentation to understand the rationale behind each rule. Sometimes things are flagged as "violations" but aren't really that important. So, you should consider whether it's a genuine issue that needs fixing or whether it can be suppressed with justification using `NagSuppressions.addResourceSuppressions()`. Otherwise, you need to fix the issue (e.g., adding encryption, tightening IAM policies). For complex issues, consult AWS documentation or the CDK community for best practices. We recommend creating custom constructs that enforce CDK-Nag rules by default for commonly used resources because this will save you time in future projects.

My precommit hooks are not running when I try to commit changes. How can I troubleshoot this?

If precommit hooks aren't running, start by verifying that Husky is correctly installed and configured in your *package.json* and that the precommit script in your *package.json* is correctly defined. Try running the precommit hook manually to see if there are any errors. Sometimes Git ignores hooks, so check this with `git config core.hooksPath`. You can also check that the hook files have execute permissions (`chmod +x .husky/pre-commit`). If you are using Windows, you also need to check that you are using the correct shell to run the hooks. If those steps don't work, try reinstalling Husky and reconfiguring the hooks. (Yep, we are recommending that you turn it off and back on again. The *IT Crowd* was spot-on with that recommendation.)

I've added new tests, but they're not being picked up by Jest. What could be the issue?

There are a few things that can cause Jest to miss new tests. Start by checking that your test files follow Jest's naming conventions (e.g., *.test.ts* or *.spec.ts*). Also check that Jest is configured to look in the directory where the test files are stored in the *jest.config.js* file. With TypeScript, you need to ensure that your test files are being compiled before running Jest. You can clear Jest's cache with `jest --clearCache` and then try running the tests again. You can use the `--detectOpenHandles` flag to see if there are any hanging processes. Finally, check if you've accidentally used `describe.skip()` or `it.skip()` in your new tests. If so, delete those commands.

Chapter Synth

In this chapter, you learned:

- How to write infrastructure tests using Jest to validate CDK infrastructure before deployment to prevent errors or security issues
- How to write end-to-end tests with Cypress that test the full application flow from front to back to validate that the entire system works as expected
- How GitHub Actions can automate running tests on every code change to validate quality and security before deploying updates as part of the CI/CD process

Discussion

1. How do Jest and Cypress compare to other testing frameworks you have used?

2. What are some examples of bugs or issues that tests could have caught in your previous projects?

3. How much time and effort should be spent on writing tests versus writing application code? What is the right balance?

Extension Activities

Now that you have completed this chapter, here are some additional activities to consider:

1. Add more infrastructure and integration tests for other parts of the CDK application.

2. Research frontend testing frameworks like the React Testing Library and write some basic frontend tests.

3. Set up GitHub Actions to automatically run all tests on every pull request before allowing a merge to the main branch.

## CHAPTER 12

Automating DevSecOps for CDK

Deploying your application locally is fine for development, but even small projects can benefit from automation and pipelines that let you build, test, and deploy an application in a repeatable way. In this chapter, you will learn how to automate your CDK application deployments using GitHub Actions. We will build a multistep GitHub Actions workflow that will build, audit, and test your application and will deploy only if all tests pass. This will be a CDK-specific intro or refresher on CI/CD and developer and security operations (DevSecOps) concepts.

This chapter gives you some important tools to help you build and deploy your CDK applications in a secure and repeatable way. Getting your GitHub Actions workflows down is awesome because it will save you time, effort, and headaches—letting you speed up your development velocity and focus on building.

Project Architecture: Automating Testing and Deployment

We are continuing to refine the processes around our application. We have improved the code, and now, we want to improve the DevSecOps pipeline using GitHub Actions. Figure 12-1 shows the architecture for this pipeline, which will help ensure that every change you make is automatically validated and safely deployed.

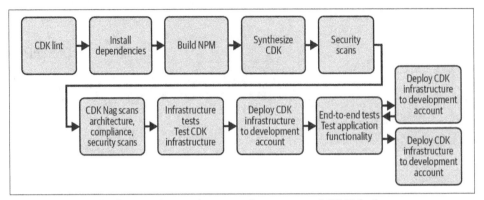

Figure 12-1. DevSecOps pipeline architecture for automated CDK deployment

We have been running tests manually. Now we are going to use GitHub Actions to automate the workflow. It will do the same tasks that we did manually, but now in a streamlined and automated process. The diagram shows the components of our automated deployment pipeline:

- Precommit hooks: Git secrets, ESLint, Prettier
- GitHub Actions workflow:
  — Build and lint
  — CDK synthesize
  — Security scanning
  — cdk-nag audit
  — Automated tests
  — Deployment

Precommit Hooks

Precommit hooks are a great way to ensure that your code is always in a good state before you commit it to your repository. They can be used to run tests, linting, and other checks on your code before you commit it to your repository. This helps catch errors early in the development process and ensures that your code is always in a good state. In this chapter, you will learn how to set up precommit hooks for your CDK applications using Husky and lint-staged.

Install Husky

Husky is a tool that allows you to set up precommit hooks for your CDK applications. It is easy to set up and use, and it integrates well with other tools such as lint-staged.

In this chapter, you will learn how to set up Husky for your CDK applications, and how to use it to automate your deployments.

The following code will install Husky and add a precommit hook that will run the `npm run lint` command before committing your code to your repository:

```
npm install husky --save-dev
npx husky install
npx husky add .husky/pre-commit "npm run lint"
```

You can change this to run any command that you want, such as `npm run test` or `npm run build`. Let's add a few more.

Navigate to *.husky/pre-commit* and add the following code:

```
# Lint
npm run lint
# Build
npm run build
# Synthesize
cdk synth
```

Now that your code will be thoroughly checked before you commit it to your repository, you can be more confident that it is in a good state before it even gets to GitHub. You should not, however, rely on precommit hooks alone to ensure that your code is always in a good state. So, we will also set up GitHub Actions to run our tests and other checks before deploying our application. Let's get started with that now.

GitHub Actions for CDK

GitHub Actions is a CI/CD tool that allows you to automate your development workflows. It is a great tool for automating your CDK application deployments because it is easy to set up and use and allows you to keep your testing and DevOps infrastructure separate from your application (this can get very messy, trust us). In this section, you will learn how to set up GitHub Actions for your CDK applications and how to use it to automate your deployments.

Create Your Workflow

GitHub Actions use a unit of automation called a *workflow*, which is a set of steps that are executed in a specific order to perform a task or automate a process. Workflows can be triggered by events such as pushes to a repository, pull requests, or scheduled events. You can define workflows using YAML files, which are stored in the *.github/workflows* directory of your repository:

```
mkdir .github/workflows
touch .github/workflows/cdk.yml
```

Provide Secure Permissions

When setting up GitHub Actions for your CDK applications, it is important to ensure that your workflows have the appropriate permissions to access your AWS resources. You can do this by configuring AWS credentials in your workflow file, through either environment variables or GitHub Secrets. This allows your workflows to authenticate with AWS services and perform actions on your behalf.

The most secure way to do this is to use OpenID Connect (OIDC) tokens, which are short-lived credentials that can be used to authenticate with AWS services. You can generate OIDC tokens using the AWS CLI or AWS SDKs, and pass them to your workflow as environment variables or GitHub Secrets. This allows your workflows to authenticate with AWS services using OIDC tokens, which can be revoked at any time.

We have put together a tool that makes it easy to generate OIDC tokens for your GitHub Actions workflows. Either you can deploy this using the CDK (follow the docs) or you can just use the one-click CloudFormation deployment link to add it to your account.

Create Your GitHub Actions Workflow

Get started with your *.github/workflows/cdk.yml* file that you just created (see Example 12-1).

Example 12-1. Home Energy Coach GitHub Actions workflow simple

```
name: CDK CI/CD

on:
  push:
    branches:
      - main

jobs:
  build:
    runs-on: ubuntu-latest

    steps:
      - name: Checkout code
        uses: actions/checkout@v2

      - name: Install dependencies
        run: npm install

      - name: Build
        run: npm run build

  lint:
```

```
      runs-on: ubuntu-latest

    steps:
      - name: Checkout code
        uses: actions/checkout@v2

      - name: Install dependencies
        run: npm install

      - name: ESLint
        run: npm run lint

  synthesize:
    runs-on: ubuntu-latest

    steps:
      - name: Checkout code
        uses: actions/checkout@v2

      - name: Install dependencies
        run: npm install

      - name: CDK Synthesize
        run: npx cdk synth

  secrets-check:
    runs-on: ubuntu-latest

    steps:
      - name: Checkout code
        uses: actions/checkout@v2

      - name: Install dependencies
        run: npm install

      - name: Check for secrets
        run: git secrets --scan

  nag:
    runs-on: ubuntu-latest

    steps:
      - name: Checkout code
        uses: actions/checkout@v2

      - name: Install dependencies
        run: npm install

      - name: CDK Nag
        run: npx cdk-nag

  jest-tests:
```

```
    runs-on: ubuntu-latest

    steps:
      - name: Checkout code
        uses: actions/checkout@v2

      - name: Install dependencies
        run: npm install

      - name: Run Jest tests
        run: npm run test

  cypress-tests:
    runs-on: ubuntu-latest

    steps:
      - name: Checkout code
        uses: actions/checkout@v2

      - name: Install dependencies
        run: npm install

      - name: Run Cypress E2E tests
        run: npm run cypress

  deploy:
    needs: [build, lint, synthesize, secrets-check, nag, jest-tests, cypress-tests]
    runs-on: ubuntu-latest

    steps:
      - name: Checkout code
        uses: actions/checkout@v2

      - name: Install dependencies
        run: npm install

      - name: CDK Deploy
        run: npx cdk deploy --all
```

Now let's add some additional tools to our workflow to make it a bit more advanced. In Example 12-2, you will incorporate some of the tests you just wrote, add some static code audit tools, and check for the presence of secrets in your files.

Example 12-2. Home Energy Coach GitHub Actions workflow advanced

```
  lint:
    runs-on: ubuntu-latest

    steps:
      - name: Checkout code
        uses: actions/checkout@v2
```

```yaml
    - name: Install dependencies
      run: npm install

    - name: ESLint
      run: npm run lint

secrets-check:
  runs-on: ubuntu-latest

  steps:
    - name: Checkout code
      uses: actions/checkout@v2

    - name: Install dependencies
      run: npm install

    - name: Check for secrets
      run: git secrets --scan

nag:
  runs-on: ubuntu-latest

  steps:
    - name: Checkout code
      uses: actions/checkout@v2

    - name: Install dependencies
      run: npm install

    - name: CDK Nag
      run: npx cdk-nag

jest-tests:
  runs-on: ubuntu-latest

  steps:
    - name: Checkout code
      uses: actions/checkout@v2

    - name: Install dependencies
      run: npm install

    - name: Run Jest tests
      run: npm run test

cypress-tests:
  runs-on: ubuntu-latest

  steps:
    - name: Checkout code
      uses: actions/checkout@v2
```

```
- name: Install dependencies
  run: npm install

- name: Run Cypress E2E tests
  run: npm run cypress
```

We can do a lot more advanced work with CDK and GitHub Actions workflows. For our project repository, you will actually see that we run something called a "reusable workflow" that is triggered by a workflow "orchestrator." This basically means we have a central workflow that triggers other workflows. This becomes especially useful when we are deploying infrastructure sequentially across sandbox, dev, staging, and production accounts. If you would like to engage with a more advanced version of the GitHub Actions workflow setup, take a look at the main branch of the project repository.

Deploy to Test

Now we will deploy our application to a test environment. This is the first time we will actually deploy our application. We will deploy to a test environment to ensure that our application is working as expected before deploying to production. We use a specific test environment, which is different from development or staging because the test environment stays completely clean—meaning that with every pipeline, we build and deploy the entire application in a fresh environment. This ensures that we are not relying on any existing resources or configurations that may have been created in previous deployments. This is important because it helps us ensure that our application is working as expected and that we are not relying on any existing resources or configurations that may have been created in previous deployments.

To deploy to a test environment, we will add a step to our GitHub Actions workflow.

Test

Now that our application is deployed to test, let's actually run our tests, since that is the whole point! We will use the npm run test command to run our tests. Good thing we created that in the previous chapter. This will run all of the tests in our application and will output the results to the console. In our case, we will simply stop here because we want this application to stay available for testing, sharing, and learning. But if you were deploying to production, you would want to add a step to your GitHub Actions workflow that would run your tests and then deploy to staging if all tests pass, and then eventually to production through a manual approval process or timed release. You can do fancy stuff like canary tests, blue/green deployments, and other cool stuff. But we will keep it simple for now.

Deploy to Staging and Production

Next up, we would usually deploy to staging and eventually to production. We will skip staging for now, but if you wanted to add an additional staging environment, you would usually set up a new set of keys for an AWS account that is dedicated to staging. This is important because it helps ensure that your staging environment is completely isolated from your production environment, that your application is working as expected, and that you are not relying on any existing resources or configurations that may have been created in previous deployments.

Document Your Deployment

Documenting your testing and deployment process is essential to ensure that others can easily understand and replicate your deployment workflow. Here are some steps to document your testing and deployment process.

Provide a brief overview of your testing and deployment process, including the purpose and goals of the process. Document the setup of the testing and deployment environment, including the required tools, technologies, and configurations. Include any specific instructions for setting up AWS accounts, configuring access credentials, and installing necessary software.

Describe the testing process, including the different types of tests you perform (e.g., unit tests, integration tests, end-to-end tests) and their purpose. Document the steps to run tests, analyze test results, and interpret the outcomes. Outline the deployment process, including the steps to package and deploy your application to the target environment. Include any specific commands, scripts, or configurations used during the deployment process, and highlight any important considerations or best practices.

Document the process for rolling back deployments in case of issues or failures. Include steps to revert changes, restore previous configurations, and perform post-deployment verification to ensure that the application is back to a stable state. Provide troubleshooting guidance for common issues that may arise during testing or deployment, along with their solutions. Include any known limitations or known issues that may impact the testing and deployment process.

Include examples or sample commands, scripts, or configuration files to illustrate the testing and deployment process. Provide references to relevant documentation, tools, and resources that can further assist users in understanding and implementing the testing and deployment process.

We know that documentation is nobody's idea of a good time. But by documenting your testing and deployment process, you can ensure that others can easily follow and replicate your workflow, leading to efficient and reliable deployments of your application. We guarantee that you will be thankful when you return to the code in six months and don't have to puzzle out, "What was I thinking here?!"

CI/CD Concepts in CDK

CI/CD practices are essential for modern software development workflows, including those involving the CDK. Here's an overview of CI/CD concepts in CDK and AWS:

Continuous integration
CI is the practice of automatically building, testing, and integrating code changes into a shared repository. In the context of CDK, this typically involves using a version control system (such as Git) to store CDK code, and setting up automated build and test processes that are triggered whenever changes are pushed to the repository. This helps catch and fix issues early in the development process.

Continuous deployment
CD is the practice of automatically deploying code changes to production or other environments after passing through the CI pipeline. In the context of CDK, this typically involves automatically synthesizing and deploying CDK stacks using CI/CD tools such as AWS CodePipeline or Jenkins. CDK provides APIs and constructs for programmatically deploying and updating stacks, making it easy to integrate into CD pipelines.

Infrastructure as Code in CDK
CDK enables the use of IaC principles, where infrastructure is defined and managed as code. CDK code, written in a programming language such as TypeScript, Python, or Java, can be versioned, reviewed, and tested just like application code. This allows for automated build, test, and deployment processes, similar to application code, resulting in consistent and reproducible deployments.

Stack update and drift detection in CDK
CDK allows for updates to existing stacks, enabling easy management of infrastructure changes over time. CDK also provides built-in drift detection, which helps identify and manage configuration drifts between the desired and actual stack resources. This can be integrated into CI/CD pipelines to ensure that drifts are detected and addressed automatically.

Blue/green and canary deployments in CDK
CDK allows for blue/green and canary deployments, where new infrastructure stacks can be created alongside existing ones, tested, and gradually switched over to production traffic. This provides a safe and controlled way to deploy changes to infrastructure, minimizing the impact of potential issues on production environments. CDK constructs and APIs can be used to implement blue/green and canary deployment strategies in CD pipelines.

Automated testing and validation in CDK

CDK allows for automated testing and validation of infrastructure changes before deployment. CDK provides built-in testing and validation capabilities, such as the `aws-cdk-assume-role-credential-plugin` for testing stack updates with different IAM roles, and the `aws-cdk-lib` library for writing unit and integration tests for CDK applications. These automated testing and validation practices can be integrated into CI/CD pipelines to ensure the correctness and quality of CDK deployments.

Infrastructure deployment automation with AWS CloudFormation

CDK leverages AWS CloudFormation under the hood for deploying and managing infrastructure. CloudFormation provides a declarative way to define and manage AWS resources using templates, and CDK generates CloudFormation templates from CDK code. This allows for automated deployment and management of infrastructure using CloudFormation, which can be integrated into CI/CD pipelines for consistent and repeatable deployments.

You can achieve faster feedback loops, reduce manual errors, and improve the overall quality, reliability, and security of your infrastructure deployments by incorporating CI/CD practices into CDK and AWS workflows.

Writing Deployment Scripts

When it comes to deploying AWS CDK applications, you can use deployment scripts to automate the process and ensure consistent deployments across different environments.

You can use any scripting language that is supported by your development environment or CI/CD pipeline, such as Python, Shell, or PowerShell, to write your deployment scripts. You can determine the parameters that need to be passed to your CDK application during deployment, such as AWS region, stack name, and any custom configuration values. Define these parameters in your deployment script as variables or arguments that can be easily configured or passed during runtime.

When we write deployment scripts, we need to ensure that we set up AWS CLI and CDK dependencies. Ensure that you have the AWS CLI and CDK installed on the machine or environment where you will be running the deployment script. Set up any necessary authentication or credentials, such as AWS access keys, in the deployment script or via environment variables to authenticate with AWS services. Depending on your CDK application, you may need to build and package your code before deploying it. You can use CDK commands or you can custom-build scripts to compile, package, and generate artifacts for your CDK application, if required.

Use the CDK commands or SDKs in your chosen scripting language to deploy your CDK stacks. Pass the deployment parameters that you defined earlier as arguments or environment variables to configure your stacks during deployment. Include error handling in your deployment script to handle any deployment failures or errors that may occur during the process. Additionally, consider adding clean-up steps to remove any temporary artifacts or resources created during the deployment process to maintain a clean and efficient deployment environment.

You can run your deployment script locally to test it. Run it on your development machine or in a local development environment, and verify that your CDK stacks are deployed correctly and function as expected. Make necessary adjustments to your script or CDK application as needed.

A key value of CDK is portability. To make your deployment script portable, avoid hardcoding values that may change across environments, such as AWS region or stack names. Instead, use variables or arguments that can be easily configured during runtime. This allows for easy deployment to different environments, such as development, staging, or production, with minimal changes to the script.

Following these steps will help you write deployment scripts that automate the deployment process for your CDK applications, making it easier to ensure consistent deployments across different environments and facilitating local testing for smooth and efficient deployments.

Setting Up GitHub Actions

Setting up GitHub Actions involves creating workflows that define the automated tasks or actions that you want to perform in your GitHub repository. Here are the steps to set up and define GitHub Actions:

Create a directory
> Create a *.github/workflows* directory in the root of your GitHub repository. This directory will store your workflow files.

Define a workflow file
> Create a YAML file with a *.yml* extension in the *.github/workflows* directory. This file will define the configuration for your GitHub Actions workflow.

Define workflow triggers
> Specify the events that should trigger your workflow, such as push events, pull request events, or schedule events. You can also define custom event triggers based on your requirements.

Define workflow jobs
> Within your workflow file, define one or more jobs. Jobs are the individual tasks or actions that you want to perform as part of your workflow. Each job runs in a separate virtual environment or runner.

Define workflow steps

Within each job, define the steps that should be executed. Steps are the individual actions that are performed within a job. You can use predefined actions from the GitHub Marketplace, or you can create your own custom actions.

Configure workflow inputs and outputs

You can define inputs and outputs for your workflow, which allow you to pass data between different steps or jobs within the workflow.

Configure workflow environment

You can specify the environment in which your workflow runs, such as the operating system, version of programming language, or any other custom environment variables.

Set up secrets

If your workflow requires any sensitive information, such as API keys or credentials, you can store them as secrets in GitHub and reference them in your workflow file. Secrets are encrypted and can only be accessed by GitHub Actions.

Review and commit

Review your workflow file, make any necessary adjustments, and commit the file to your GitHub repository.

Monitor workflow runs

Once your workflow is set up, you can monitor its runs in the GitHub Actions tab of your repository. You can view the status, logs, and results of each workflow run to track the progress and troubleshoot any issues.

By following these steps, you can set up and define GitHub Actions in your repository to automate tasks, perform actions, and streamline your CI/CD processes, making your development workflow more efficient and automated.

Integrating GitHub Actions for Deployment

To integrate GitHub Actions with AWS accounts for automated deployment, you can set up a workflow in GitHub Actions that triggers on certain events, such as a push to a specific branch. Within the workflow, you can define steps that use AWS CLI or AWS SDKs to interact with your AWS resources, such as CloudFormation stacks or ECS services, to deploy your application.

To do this, you'll need to configure AWS credentials in the GitHub Actions workflow, through either environment variables or GitHub Secrets. You can then use these credentials to authenticate and interact with AWS services in your deployment scripts. Once the workflow is set up, it will automatically trigger on the defined events, allowing for automated deployments based on changes in your GitHub repository.

Deploying with Git

Deploying from the command line or on a schedule using Git is a common practice in many software development workflows. This involves using Git, a version control system, to manage the source code of your application, and leveraging Git hooks or scheduled tasks to trigger deployment scripts or commands.

To deploy from the command line, you can use Git commands to push changes to a specific branch or tag, and then configure your deployment scripts or commands to automatically build, test, and deploy your application based on these changes.

Alternatively, you can set up Git hooks, which are scripts that are triggered automatically by Git events such as commits or pushes, to execute deployment scripts or commands. This allows for automated deployments whenever changes are pushed to a specific branch or tag. Another approach is to use scheduled tasks or cron jobs to trigger deployment scripts at specific times or intervals, allowing for automated deployments on a schedule.

By leveraging Git for deployment, you can streamline your development workflow, automate deployments, and ensure that your application is always up-to-date with the latest changes in your Git repository.

Getting Unstuck

My precommit hooks aren't running when I try to commit changes. What could be wrong?

> If your precommit hooks aren't running, start by checking that Husky is correctly installed and correctly defined in your *package.json*. Make sure that the path to your precommit hook script is correct, and try running the precommit hook manually to see if there are any errors. You can check your permissions with `chmod +x .husky/pre-commit`. You can check if Git is ignoring your hooks with `git config core.hooksPath`. If you are using Windows, you should also check that the correct shell is being used to run the hooks. Finally, you can try reinstalling Husky and reconfiguring the hooks.

I'm getting an "Access Denied" error when my GitHub Actions workflow tries to deploy to AWS. How can I fix this?

> This error usually indicates an issue with AWS credentials or permissions. You should start by checking that you've correctly set up the AWS credentials in your GitHub repository secrets and verify that the IAM user or role associated with the credentials has the necessary permissions to deploy your CDK stacks. Next, you should double-check that you're using the correct AWS region in your workflow. If you are using OIDC, ensure that the trust relationship is correctly set up between GitHub and your AWS account. You can try using the AWS CLI to deploy manually with the same credentials for isolation to check if it's

a permissions issue or a workflow issue. Finally, check the IAM policy attached to your deployment role to ensure that it has the required permissions for all resources in your CDK stacks.

My GitHub Actions workflow is failing at the "CDK Synthesize" step. What could be causing this?

If the CDK synthesis is failing, start by checking the workflow logs for specific error messages. You want to make sure that all required dependencies are installed correctly in your workflow. Check your *cdk.json* file to make sure it is correctly configured. You can try running cdk synth locally to see if you can reproduce the error. Finally, if using context values, ensure that they're correctly set in the workflow environment.

The cdk-nag step in my workflow is failing, but I'm not sure how to address the issues. What should I do?

When cdk-nag fails, start by reviewing the cdk-nag output in the workflow logs to understand which rules are being violated. Then, you can consult the cdk-nag documentation to understand the rationale behind each failing rule. For each violation, decide if it needs to be fixed or if it can be suppressed with justification. If you decide to fix the issue, update your CDK code to address the issue (e.g., adding encryption, tightening IAM policies). If you decide to suppress the violation, use NagSuppressions.addResourceSuppressions() with a clear justification. You can also consider creating custom constructs that enforce cdk-nag rules by default for commonly used resources. If you're unsure about a specific rule, we recommend that you consult the AWS Well-Architected Framework or seek advice from the CDK community.

My Cypress tests are failing in the GitHub Actions workflow, but they pass locally. How can I debug this?

When Cypress tests fail in CI but not locally, start with Cypress's built-in video recording and screenshot features to see what's happening during the test run. You should check that your workflow is using the same Node.js version and dependencies as your local environment. Next, look at the environment-specific configurations and check that these match your CI environment. You can use cypress run --headed in your workflow to run tests in headed mode for debugging (if supported by your runner). Next, you can increase the test timeout in your Cypress configuration to account for potentially slower CI environments. Check to see if there are any network-related issues in the CI environment that might be affecting your tests. You can use Cypress's cy.wait() command to account for any timing issues in the CI environment.

My CDK deployment is successful, but some resources are not being created or updated. What could be the issue?

If some resources are not being deployed or updated correctly, check your CDK code to ensure that all resources are properly defined and included in the stack. Next, verify that your IAM permissions allow creation and modification of all resource types in your stack. Look for any conditional logic in your CDK code that might be preventing certain resources from being created. You should check the CloudFormation events in the AWS Console for any specific error messages or warnings. Next, you can check that you're not hitting any AWS service limits or quotas. If you decide to update existing resources, check if you're modifying any immutable properties, which would require replacement instead of updating. Finally, consider using the `--verbose` flag with `cdk deploy` to get more detailed information about the deployment process.

Chapter Synth

In this chapter, you learned:

- How to use precommit hooks using Husky and lint-staged to automatically run tests, linting, and other checks before code is committed to ensure that it meets quality standards

- How to set up GitHub Actions workflows to automate build, test, audit, and deployment processes for CDK apps using triggers like push events. Workflows provide CI/CD for IaC

- How to automate linting, building, synthesizing, security scanning, drift detection, and testing to improve deployment pipelines before releasing CDK applications

Discussion

1. What are some key benefits of implementing CI/CD practices for CDK applications? What challenges might arise, and how can they be addressed?

2. How does IaC with CDK enable greater automation and reproducibility in deployment workflows? What testing and validation practices are important for ensuring reliability?

3. What security considerations are important when setting up CI/CD pipelines and automating deployments for CDK applications? How can credentials and permissions be managed securely?

Extension Activities

Now that you have completed this chapter, here are some additional activities to consider:

1. Set up a CI/CD pipeline using GitHub Actions to automate building, testing, and deploying your CDK application.

2. Enable drift detection in your CDK stacks, and set up alerts to detect configuration drift over time and remediate any issues.

3. Implement canary deployments for your CDK applications using AWS CodeDeploy to test changes on a small subset before full deployment.

## CHAPTER 13

Contributing to CDK

CDK construct libraries are typically published as npm packages and can be installed and used in CDK applications using standard package management tools. They provide a convenient way to encapsulate and share reusable infrastructure components, making it easier for developers to provision and manage AWS resources in their CDK applications.

This chapter "zooms out" from a specific CDK project and covers how to package your solutions to share with others.

Anatomy of an npm Library

An npm library typically consists of several parts and functions that contribute to its overall functionality. Libraries are packages published to the npm registry and provide reusable components. Because others will be using this code, it is important that you include all the expected components:

package.json
> This is a mandatory file in any npm library and serves as the configuration file for the package. It includes metadata such as the package name, version, description, dependencies, scripts, and other information that defines the package's behavior and dependencies.

Source code
> These are the actual JavaScript or TypeScript source code files that implement the functionality of the library. These source files may be organized in directories or modules, depending on the library's structure and design.

Entry point

The entry point is the main file that gets executed when the library is imported or required in a Node.js or JavaScript application. It typically defines the public API of the library and exposes the functions, classes, or objects that users can interact with.

Tests

These include unit tests, integration tests, or other forms of tests that are written to ensure the correctness and reliability of the library. These tests are typically organized in a separate directory and can be executed as part of the library's development process to catch potential bugs or issues.

Documentation

Documentation is an important part of an npm library and typically includes README files, inline comments, or other forms of documentation that provide instructions on how to use the library, explain the library's features, and provide examples or usage patterns.

License

The license is a legal agreement that defines the terms under which the library can be used, modified, and distributed. It is important to include a license file in the npm library to specify the permissions and restrictions for users of the library.

Dependencies

The npm libraries may depend on other npm packages or external libraries to function correctly. These dependencies are typically listed in the *package.json* file and can be installed automatically when the library is installed, using npm or other package management tools.

Scripts

The npm libraries can include custom scripts that automate tasks such as building, testing, or generating documentation. These scripts are defined in the *package.json* file and can be executed using npm or other build tools.

Versioning

The npm libraries use semantic versioning (semver) to indicate the stability and compatibility of different versions of the library. Version numbers consist of major, minor, and patch numbers, and they are used to communicate changes in the library's API or behavior.

It may seem like a lot, but these parts and functions work together to define the functionality, behavior, and usage of the library, making it easy for developers to install, use, and integrate the library into their projects.

Document and Publish Your Constructs

In addition to npm libraries, you can publish your constructs for others to use. There are several ways to do this, but here is our recommended way to get started using GitHub and JSDocs. Remember, we also talked about this way back in Chapter 3:

Add inline comments

Within your construct code, add inline comments using JSDoc syntax to provide documentation for your constructs. Include descriptions, parameters, return values, and any other relevant information that can help users understand how to use your constructs.

Generate JSDocs

Use a JSDoc tool to automatically generate documentation from your inline comments. There are several popular tools available, such as JSDoc, TypeDoc, and `jsdoc-to-markdown`. Configure the tool to scan your construct codebase and generate documentation in a desired format, such as HTML, markdown, or other formats.

Include usage instructions

In addition to inline comments, provide clear and concise usage instructions in your documentation. This should include examples, code snippets, and step-by-step instructions on how to use your constructs in a real-world application.

Publish to GitHub

Create a GitHub repository to host your construct library. Commit your construct code and generated JSDoc documentation to the repository. You can also add a *README.md* file with additional information about your constructs, such as installation instructions, configuration details, and other relevant documentation.

Enable GitHub Pages

Enable GitHub Pages for your repository to make your documentation accessible as a website. Configure the GitHub Pages settings to use the generated JSDoc documentation as the source for your documentation website.

Update and version your constructs

Keep your constructs and documentation up-to-date with new features, bug fixes, and improvements. Use Git versioning to manage changes to your constructs and documentation, and follow semantic versioning principles to clearly communicate any changes to users.

Share and promote your constructs
> You made something useful (and cool!). Share your construct library with the community through social media, developer forums, and other relevant channels. Promote your constructs by providing examples, demonstrations, and tutorials to showcase their capabilities and benefits.

GitHub and JSDocs are helpful tools for creating clear documentation and usage instructions for users, making it easier for them to understand and utilize your constructs in their projects. By following best practices for documentation, versioning, and promotion, you can create a valuable resource for the community and foster adoption of your constructs.

Contributing to CDK

Contributing to the AWS CDK can be a rewarding way to contribute to the open source community and help improve the CDK ecosystem. The CDK is organized into different levels of constructs, including L1 constructs for low-level AWS service resources, L2 constructs for higher-level abstractions, and L3 constructs for custom abstractions built on top of L2 constructs. Here are some steps to contribute to CDK:

Familiarize yourself with CDK
> Before you contribute, you need a solid understanding of the CDK framework, its architecture, and the different levels of constructs (L1, L2, L3). Fortunately, if you have read the preceding chapters, then you already know how CDK works and have built a project. Check!

Identify areas of contribution
> There are many ways to contribute. We recommend you review the CDK GitHub repository for open issues or enhancement requests related to the L1, L2, or L3 constructs. Identify areas where you can contribute based on your expertise, interests, and the needs of the CDK community. This can include fixing bugs, adding new features, improving documentation, or providing test cases.

Fork the CDK repository
> Now that you know what you want to contribute, fork the CDK repository on GitHub to create your own copy of the CDK codebase so that you can make changes to the code and submit pull requests for review.

Develop and test changes
> Create a branch in your forked repository to develop your changes. Follow the CDK contribution guidelines, coding standards, and testing practices to ensure that your changes are of high quality. Test your changes thoroughly using the CDK testing framework and existing CDK constructs. Seriously, you don't want to skip this step and have your contribution rejected because it didn't pass the unit tests.

Submit a pull request

Once your changes are complete, submit a pull request to the CDK repository for review. Provide a clear description of the changes, the motivation behind them, and any relevant documentation or test cases. Be responsive to feedback from the CDK community and iterate on your changes as needed.

Follow the contribution process

This can change, so be sure to check the official GitHub instructions and follow the CDK contribution process, including signing the Contributor License Agreement (CLA) if required and adhering to the code of conduct. Be patient and respectful during the contribution process, as it may take time for your changes to be reviewed and merged.

Celebrate

You did it! Congrats!

Collaborate with the CDK community

If a construct is published but no one knows it is available, was it really made? Of course, but it is always nicer to give back to the community. Engage in discussions, reviews, and feedback loops with the CDK community. Be open to suggestions, learn from other contributors, and address any concerns or questions raised during the review process. Collaborate with the CDK maintainers and other contributors to ensure that your changes align with the overall goals and vision of the CDK project.

What About Terraform?

This is a book about CDK, and obviously we are big fans of using CDK for IaC. But it isn't the only solution. CDK is flexible, and you can use both AWS CDK and Terraform to provide a powerful approach to managing cloud infrastructure. Here are some things to consider when you are thinking about using Terraform IaC solutions with AWS CDK:

Understand the fundamentals

Gain a solid understanding of both AWS CDK and Terraform individually. Understand their respective concepts, syntax, and workflows. Familiarize yourself with AWS services, their configuration options, and the desired state of your infrastructure.

Define infrastructure requirements

Define your infrastructure requirements, including the desired architecture, resources, configurations, and dependencies. Consider the scalability, availability, and security aspects of your infrastructure.

Choose the right tool for the job

Evaluate whether AWS CDK or Terraform is the right tool for your specific use case. AWS CDK provides a higher-level, programmatic way of defining infrastructure using familiar programming languages like Python, TypeScript, or Java. Terraform, on the other hand, uses its own declarative language to define infrastructure configurations.

Leverage AWS CDK for infrastructure provisioning

If AWS CDK is the chosen tool, use it to provision AWS resources as part of your infrastructure. Define CDK constructs in your preferred programming language to set up AWS resources, their configurations, and dependencies. Use CDK's high-level abstractions to define infrastructure components, such as VPCs, EC2 instances, S3 buckets, and more.

Use CDK's deployment capabilities

CDK provides deployment capabilities to package and deploy your infrastructure as a CloudFormation stack, which can be managed using the AWS CloudFormation service. Leverage CDK's deployment capabilities to create, update, and delete your infrastructure in an idempotent and controlled manner.

Use Terraform for infrastructure management

If Terraform is the chosen tool, use it to manage the lifecycle of your infrastructure. Define Terraform configurations in HashiCorp Configuration Language (HCL) to define resources, providers, and configurations. Use Terraform's declarative syntax to specify the desired state of your infrastructure, and use Terraform commands to create, update, and delete resources accordingly.

Follow best practices

Regardless of the tool you choose, follow best practices for managing IaC, including version control, code review, automated testing, and documentation. Use Git or other version control systems to manage your code, collaborate with team members, and track changes. Implement automated testing and validation to catch potential issues early in the development cycle. Document your infrastructure configurations, dependencies, and deployment process to facilitate collaboration and troubleshooting.

Collaborate with team members

Collaborate with team members and stakeholders to ensure alignment with requirements, architecture, and best practices. Use shared repositories, code reviews, and CI/CD pipelines to facilitate collaboration and streamline the development process.

Monitor and maintain your infrastructure

Once your infrastructure is deployed, use monitoring and observability tools to monitor the health and performance of your infrastructure. Follow best practices for ongoing maintenance, including patching, updates, and security hardening.

Developer Collaboration with CDK

Developers rarely build something completely on their own. Building with others is more fun and leads to better, cleaner code. Developer collaboration is part of modern software development, and CDK can augment developers' collaborative efforts in the following areas:

Version control and code sharing

Use a version control system such as Git to manage your CDK application code. Git allows multiple developers to work on the same codebase concurrently, track changes, and merge code changes seamlessly. Create branches for different features or bug fixes, and use pull requests for code reviews before merging changes into the main branch. This enables collaborative development and ensures that changes are reviewed and approved by team members.

Continuous integration and continuous deployment

Implement a CI/CD pipeline using tools like AWS CodePipeline, Jenkins, or GitLab CI/CD to automate the build, test, and deployment processes of your CDK applications. This allows developers to continuously integrate and deploy their changes to a staging or production environment, enabling fast feedback loops and reducing the risk of conflicts or errors.

IaC best practices

Apply IaC best practices to your CDK codebase, such as using modular constructs, reusable patterns, and well-organized code structure. This makes it easier for multiple developers to collaborate on the same codebase without stepping on each other's toes. Define clear guidelines and conventions for CDK code development, documentation, and naming conventions to ensure consistency and readability.

Collaborative development using CDK libraries

CDK provides a wide range of built-in and community-contributed libraries, which can be used as shared resources across different CDK applications. Create reusable constructs or libraries that encapsulate common patterns or best practices for your organization, and share them among your development teams. This promotes consistency and accelerates development efforts by reusing well-tested and validated code across different CDK applications.

Collaboration using IaC tools

CDK allows you to define your IaC using programming languages, making it accessible to developers with different skill sets. Encourage collaboration among developers by leveraging CDK's language support (TypeScript, Python, Java, etc.) to enable developers to contribute to infrastructure code using their preferred programming language. This allows developers to collaborate more effectively, leveraging their existing skills and expertise.

Documentation and communication

Clearly document the design decisions, architecture, and implementation details of your CDK applications, including the purpose of different constructs, their usage, and any conventions or guidelines to follow. Use collaborative documentation tools like Confluence, GitHub Wiki, or Google Docs to capture and share important information among team members. Foster regular communication channels, such as team meetings, Slack channels, or email lists, to facilitate discussions, knowledge sharing, and issue resolution.

Training and onboarding

Provide training and onboarding sessions for new team members to familiarize them with CDK concepts, best practices, and development workflows. Encourage knowledge sharing and provide resources like tutorials, examples, and documentation to help developers get up to speed quickly. Foster a culture of continuous learning and improvement, where team members can learn from each other and share their expertise.

Be kind to new people joining your project. Give them the tools and documentation they need to be successful—this includes *future you*, who will have forgotten why you implemented this clever bit of code unless *current you* documents it.

Architecting for Multicloud Environments with CDK

Sometimes you have projects that work beyond a single cloud. Architecting for multicloud environments with CDK involves designing and developing applications and infrastructure that can be deployed across multiple cloud providers, enabling flexibility and portability. Here's an approach to architecting and developing multicloud applications and infrastructure using CDK and other tools:

Begin by abstracting cloud provider–specific logic

CDK allows you to define cloud resources using programming languages such as TypeScript, Python, or Java. One approach is to abstract the cloud provider-specific logic into separate constructs or classes, making it easier to swap out specific cloud providers as needed. For example, you can create separate constructs for AWS resources, Azure resources, and Google Cloud resources, and use conditional logic or configuration files to determine which set of constructs to use based on the target cloud environment.

To the extent that it makes sense, use cloud-agnostic services

AWS provides cloud-agnostic services such as AWS Lambda, Amazon S3, and Amazon RDS that can be used across multiple cloud environments. By leveraging these cloud-agnostic services, you can reduce the dependency on cloud-specific services and achieve portability across different cloud providers. CDK provides constructs for these cloud-agnostic services, allowing you to define them in your CDK applications and deploy them across different cloud environments.

Use cloud-agnostic deployment tools, like GitHub

CDK can generate cloud-agnostic CloudFormation templates, which can be used to deploy resources across different cloud providers. You can also use other cloud-agnostic deployment tools such as Terraform or Kubernetes to deploy your CDK applications to different cloud environments. These tools allow you to define your IaC in a cloud-agnostic way and deploy it to different cloud providers using their respective APIs or deployment mechanisms.

Manage cloud provider–specific configuration

While abstracting cloud provider–specific logic and leveraging cloud-agnostic services and deployment tools, you may still need to manage cloud provider–specific configuration, such as authentication, networking, and security settings. One approach is to use configuration files or environment variables to store and manage these cloud provider–specific settings, and use CDK's configuration management features to dynamically apply these settings during deployment based on the target cloud environment.

Test and validate everything works across different cloud environments to ensure compatibility, reliability, and performance

CDK provides testing frameworks and tools for validating your CDK applications during the development and deployment processes. You can also use cloud-specific testing tools and services, such as AWS CloudFormation StackSets or Azure Resource Manager templates, to test and validate your applications in different cloud environments.

Create a comprehensive monitoring and management strategy for your multicloud environments

CDK provides integration with cloud monitoring and management services such as AWS CloudWatch or Azure Monitor, allowing you to monitor and manage your CDK applications across different cloud providers from a centralized location. You can also use third-party monitoring and management tools that support multicloud environments to gain visibility and control over your applications and infrastructure.

Blue/Green and Canary Deployments

Handling blue/green and canary deployments is key to rolling out new versions of software or applications while minimizing downtime and risk. Both techniques effectively test changes in a controlled environment before fully committing to them. They are especially useful in cloud native environments, where continuous delivery and automated deployments are essential to the development cycle.

Blue/Green Deployment

Blue/green deployment is a technique designed to reduce downtime and the risks of releasing new applications. It works by creating twin identical environments. The program operates in two identical environments, but only one is active. The blue environment represents the production version, whereas the green environment holds the new version you intend to deploy. When you're ready to roll out a new version, you deploy the latest code (version) to the green environment while the blue environment remains live and keeps serving users. This allows you to completely test the new version in a green environment without harming current users.

Once testing is complete and the green environment is certified, traffic transitions from blue to green. This changeover can happen nearly instantaneously using DNS updates or load balancers, making the user transition painless. Essentially, the green environment becomes the new production, and the blue environment is kept inactive as a backup. If any complications develop with the green deployment, rolling back to the blue environment is as simple as diverting traffic. Since the blue environment hasn't been modified, it can swiftly serve users without downtime.

Blue/green deployment has both benefits and drawbacks:

Benefits of blue/green deployment
> The switch between blue/green environments is instant, meaning users don't experience noticeable downtime. This means that if something goes wrong, rolling back to the previous version is fast because the old environment is still fully functional. You can test the new version in a natural production-like environment (the green environment) before exposing it to all users. This ensures higher confidence in the release.

Drawbacks of blue/green deployment
> With blue/green deployment, you have to maintain two environments, which can be resource intensive. You must double your infrastructure, as both the blue and the green environments must be identical to ensure a smooth transition. For large-scale systems, this can get expensive. Blue/green deployment switches the traffic from one version to another all at once, which means that if something goes wrong, many users might be impacted before you roll back.

Blue/green deployments are a good choice when you have a mature, stable application with minimal modifications, and you're confident that the new version will not likely contain severe bugs. Blue/green deployment works effectively for critical applications where downtime must be avoided at all costs. With the capacity to roll back rapidly, the chance of introducing significant difficulties is lessened.

Canary Deployment

Unlike blue/green deployment, canary deployment is about gradually rolling out changes to a small subset of users first, allowing for more controlled and incremental testing in production before making the new version available to everyone. The term comes from using canaries in coal mines: just as miners used to release a canary to detect toxic gas, canary deployments release new features to a small group of users to detect problems early on.

Canary deployments are designed first to push out new modifications to a small percentage of customers. For example, only 5% of people may view the latest version, while the remaining 95% continue using the old version. Traffic is gradually switched to the new version in stages. You can start by routing a small amount of traffic to the latest version, monitoring the performance, and, if everything seems good, increasing the traffic share until the new version handles all user traffic. During a canary deployment, you actively monitor performance metrics, error rates, and logs to spot any concerns. If the new version behaves as expected, the distribution proceeds. If any abnormalities or significant difficulties are found, the rollout can be stopped, and traffic can be restored to the previous version. Similar to blue/green, canary deployments enable an easy rollback. Since most users are still on the old version, only a tiny fraction of users on the new version will be affected. You can immediately return traffic to the stable version, minimizing disturbance.

Like blue/green deployments, canary deployments also have benefits and drawbacks:

Benefits of canary deployment
> Since only a small group of users are initially exposed to the new version, any issues are contained. This allows for real-world testing with minimal impact if something goes wrong. The ability to gradually increase the user base on the new version means you can monitor for issues in real time and ensure that the latest version performs as expected before a full rollout. Since most users still use the old version, rolling back is relatively straightforward. Only a small portion of traffic must be redirected, reducing the blast radius of any failure.

Drawbacks of canary deployment
> Canary deployments are incremental, which means the entire deployment can take longer than a blue/green deployment. Each rollout stage involves testing and monitoring before proceeding, which might slow the release process. Canary implementations require careful monitoring, automation, and traffic control. You

need sophisticated load balancers or API gateways to route traffic in fine-grained percentages. Additionally, monitoring tools must be in place to detect performance declines or issues.

Canary deployments are a good choice for feature-heavy releases. Canary deployments are significant for apps that deliver new features or updates that may require progressive testing with real users to ensure reliability. For apps that update regularly, canary deployment decreases the chance of widespread failure with every new release. It's often used in agile development setups with CI/CD pipelines. Canary deployments are significant when you have a diverse user population, where different portions may respond differently to changes. By spreading out gradually, you can uncover concerns particular to specific groups and address them before a broader deployment.

Comparing Blue/Green and Canary Deployments

While both blue/green and canary deployments strive to reduce risk during deployment, they each offer various techniques to handle new versions in production. Blue/green is about switching over totally from one environment to another. It enables fast reversal and minimal downtime but can be resource heavy and doesn't allow for progressive deployment. Canary focuses on slow rollout and feedback, making it excellent for testing features and maintaining stability. However, it's more complex and requires regular monitoring and traffic management.

Why choose? In some circumstances, you can actually use both blue/green and canary deployments! For example, you could use blue/green deployment to maintain two environments, where one is the live production environment and the other is the testing environment. Once the new version is delivered to the green environment, do a canary release by directing only a tiny fraction of traffic. If the canary testing is successful, you may make a complete transition, routing all traffic to the green environment.

This hybrid strategy combines the benefits of both methods: minimizing downtime, assuring rollback options, and allowing incremental change rollout.

Several tools and services can help automate and manage blue/green and canary deployments. AWS CodeDeploy supports blue/green and canary deployment strategies and integrates with EC2, Lambda, and ECS services. Kubernetes' native support for rolling updates and service mesh tools like Istio makes canary deployments easier to manage in containerized environments. Reverse proxies can manage traffic distribution, helping to implement canary deployments with fine-grained traffic control. Tools like LaunchDarkly or Rollout let you manage feature releases through flags, allowing for canary-style testing of specific features before exposing them to the entire user base.

Managing Configuration Settings for Different Environments

Managing configuration settings for different environments is crucial to modern application development and deployment. Whether dealing with a local development environment, staging for quality assurance, or deploying for production, handling configurations properly helps ensure that your applications run smoothly across these environments. A poorly managed configuration can lead to deployment errors, data leaks, or performance issues, so it's essential to adopt practices and tools that help manage these settings effectively.

Getting Unstuck

I'm trying to contribute to CDK, but I'm not sure where to start. What's the best way to get involved?

Getting started with CDK contributions can be overwhelming. It is best to start by familiarizing yourself with the CDK codebase and documentation. You can find issues that need contributor help through the CDK GitHub repository—look for issues labeled "good first issue" or "help wanted." Join the CDK community on Slack or Discord to ask questions and get guidance. When you are getting started, try fixing a small bug or improving documentation as your first contribution. All well-structured repos will have guidance for contributing, so look for the *CONTRIBUTING.md* file in the CDK repository for specific guidelines. As you get started, we recommend working on constructs for AWS services that you've used.

I've made changes to a CDK construct, but my pull request was rejected. What should I do?

Don't be discouraged! There is usually a simple reason why a request is rejected. Start by carefully reading the feedback provided by the reviewers. If something isn't clear, ask for clarification. Address all the points raised in the review comments, and make sure your code adheres to the CDK coding standards and best practices. Run all tests locally to ensure that your changes don't break existing functionality, then update your pull request with the requested changes. If you disagree with any feedback, politely explain your reasoning. Be patient and responsive during the review process—the reviewers are human too.

I'm having trouble setting up the CDK development environment on my machine. How can I resolve this?

Setting up the development environment can be tricky at first, but it gets easier. Ensure that you have the correct versions of Node.js and npm installed. Follow the setup instructions in the CDK repository's README file closely. Run `npm run build` in the root of the CDK repository. If you encounter errors, check your Node.js version and try using `nvm` to switch versions. If you are still getting errors, clear your npm cache and *node_modules* directories. If all else fails, check for any OS-specific setup instructions that might apply to your system.

I've created a new construct, but I'm not sure how to properly document it. What's the best approach?

First of all, you are right to think about documentation because it is super important for CDK constructs. We recommend using JSDoc comments to document your construct's properties, methods, and parameters—include documentation for any default values or optional parameters. As you create your construct, write a clear and concise class description explaining the purpose of your construct. Please include code examples demonstrating how to use your construct and make these with the `@example` tags so that JSDoc knows these are examples. Run `npm run docgen` to generate API documentation, and review the generated doc to make sure it matches what you expect.

I'm trying to publish my custom construct as an npm package, but I'm encountering errors. What could be wrong?

Publishing npm packages can be tricky. If you are getting errors, then check that the *package.json* file is correctly configured with all required fields. The npm package has strict naming conventions, so verify that your package name is unique and follows npm naming rules. Sometimes these errors are caused by accidentally excluding required files in your package (use *.npmignore* or the files field in *package.json*). Run `npm pack` to create a tarball and inspect its contents before publishing. If you're using TypeScript, ensure that your *.d.ts* files are being generated and included. You can also check for any lint errors or failed tests that might be preventing publication. If you're getting a 403 error, make sure you have the necessary permissions to publish, and make sure that you're logged in to npm with the correct account (npm login).

How can I test my CDK construct across multiple AWS accounts or regions?

Testing across multiple accounts or regions requires some setup. We recommend that you use AWS profiles to manage credentials for different accounts. You can use environment variables to switch between accounts and regions. Create a test suite that uses different AWS profiles for different tests. We use AWS Organizations and AWS Config to manage multiaccount setups. It is helpful to implement integration tests that deploy to different accounts/regions:

- Consider using tools like AWS CloudFormation StackSets for multiregion deployments.
- Use mocking libraries to simulate different AWS environments in unit tests.
- Document the multiaccount/region testing process for other contributors.

Chapter Synth

In this chapter, you learned:

- How to package and publish your CDK constructs as npm libraries
- Best practices for writing, documenting, and testing reusable CDK components
- How to contribute to the AWS CDK open source project, including identifying areas for contribution, forking the repo, and submitting pull requests
- The differences between blue/green and canary deployments, and how each can help you roll out changes with reduced risk
- How to manage configuration settings across development, staging, and production environments
- Ways to collaborate with other developers using tools like version control, CI/CD, and shared CDK libraries
- Tips for working in multicloud environments and abstracting cloud-specific logic using CDK

Discussion

1. What are the key differences between blue/green and canary deployments, and when would you use each?
2. How can reusable CDK constructs improve developer collaboration in larger teams?
3. What are the challenges of contributing to open source projects like AWS CDK, and how can you overcome them?
4. What strategies have you used for managing infrastructure code across multiple environments (development, staging, and production)?

Extension Activities

1. Publish your first CDK construct as an npm package and share it with a friend.
2. Set up GitHub Pages for your construct repository and document your API using TypeDoc or JSDoc.
3. Create a reusable L3 construct that wraps multiple AWS resources for a common use case in your team or organization.
4. Try both a blue/green and a canary deployment in your own project. Compare the pros and cons of each.
5. Contribute a documentation improvement or bug fix to the AWS CDK GitHub repository.

## CHAPTER 14

Architecting, Building, and Publishing a Portfolio CDK Application

Whether you read the chapters sequentially and have successfully built your own CDK application, or you skipped ahead to this chapter, here you'll learn how to build something new and unique to you.

This chapter is a little different from the previous chapters because we don't have code examples or specific instructions for you. Instead, we will guide you through an abbreviated "working backward" process to help translate a business problem or opportunity for innovation into a cloud application that you will actually build.

Follow along to get started with defining and building your own application. We strongly encourage you to start your project by setting up a GitHub repository and your GitHub Actions workflows from the start so that you can test, publish, and share as you build.

Into the Working Backward Process

Working backward is a concept used frequently to develop new products at Amazon and AWS, but it is very similar to what is sometimes called "design thinking."

Solving problems that are worth solving takes time. We want to make sure we are solving the right problem, and to do that, we need to continuously get feedback from internal sources (like our systems) and external sources (like our customers). Figure 14-1 provides a structure we can use as we work backward from customer problems and convert business problems into technical solutions.

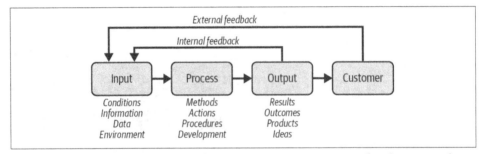

Figure 14-1. Approach to solving problems in an interactive way and seeking input from internal and external sources to improve the design

Step 1: Understanding the Core Problem

In the working backward approach, we start by identifying a customer-centric problem before considering solutions. This aligns with design thinking methodology, which emphasizes understanding the user and the challenges they face in their context. This phase is crucial as it sets the foundation for all subsequent innovation and solution development.

To deeply understand the problem, we engage in customer empathy, market research, and stakeholder analysis. This involves listening to customer stories, observing customers' interactions with current products or services, and identifying gaps in the market. The goal is not just to find a problem, but also to uncover the underlying needs that drive customer behavior.

> Activity: Conduct in-depth interviews with a diverse set of potential customers, including surveys and observation sessions. Analyze market trends and competitor offerings to identify gaps. Utilize tools like empathy maps and customer journey maps to visualize the customer's experience and pain points. By the end of this activity, you should have a comprehensive problem statement, empathy maps, customer journey maps, and a market gap analysis report.

Step 2: Defining the Customer and Their Needs

Building on the insights from step 1, we now focus on defining who our customers are and what they truly need. This step involves segmenting the market, creating detailed customer personas, and understanding the various customer archetypes that our solution might cater to. It's about going beyond demographic information to understand the motivations, frustrations, and aspirations of our customers.

In line with the design thinking approach, this step involves a lot of empathy and interaction with potential customers. The more we understand our customers, the better we can tailor our solutions to meet their needs and exceed their expectations.

Activity: Create detailed personas for each identified customer segment, including demographic information, behavioral patterns, goals, and pain points. Develop empathy maps for each persona to gain deeper insights into what they think, feel, see, and do. Conduct a day-in-the-life study for key personas to understand their daily interactions and pain points in context. By the end of this activity, you should have detailed customer personas, empathy maps, and a set of user stories that highlight the needs and challenges of your customers.

Step 3: Defining Ideas and Solutions

With a clear understanding of the problem and the customer, we now move into the ideation phase. This is where creativity and innovation come to the forefront. Using the working backward approach, we start by envisioning the ideal customer experience and work backward to identify the features and capabilities needed to realize this vision.

This phase involves brainstorming sessions, workshops, and prototyping, often utilizing design thinking principles such as divergence and convergence, where we generate a wide array of ideas and then narrow them down to the most viable solutions.

Activity: Organize ideation workshops with your team, stakeholders, and, if possible, customers. Use brainstorming techniques such as mind mapping, sketching, and SCAMPER. Develop low-fidelity prototypes to visualize the proposed solutions and test them with a small group of users. By the end of this activity, you should have a list of prioritized solutions, concept sketches, and low-fidelity prototypes that demonstrate potential ways to solve the customer's problem.

Step 4: Validate and Establish Success Metrics

Before moving forward with development, it's crucial to validate the proposed solutions with real users. This step involves creating high-fidelity prototypes or minimum viable products (MVPs) and conducting user testing sessions. The feedback collected during these sessions is invaluable for refining the solution.

In addition, defining clear success metrics aligned with customer needs and business objectives is essential. These metrics will guide the development process and help evaluate the solution's impact once it's launched.

Activity: Develop a high-fidelity prototype or MVP of your chosen solution. Conduct structured user testing sessions to gather qualitative and quantitative feedback. Refine your solution based on this feedback. Define clear, measurable success metrics that align with the customer's needs and your business objectives. By the end of this activity, you should have a validated solution prototype, a refined MVP ready for development, and a set of success metrics to evaluate the solution's impact.

Step 5: Go Build!

With a validated solution and clear success metrics, you're now ready to move into the development phase. This involves finalizing the technical architecture, setting up a DevSecOps foundation for efficient and secure development, and building the solution.

The development phase should be iterative, allowing for continuous integration of feedback and improvements. Regular testing and validation with users ensures that the solution remains aligned with customer needs and expectations.

> Activity: Finalize the architecture diagram for your solution, ensuring that it supports all identified features and is scalable. Establish your DevSecOps processes, including CI/CD, automated testing, and security practices. Develop the solution iteratively, integrating feedback from users and stakeholders. By the end of this activity, you should have a fully developed solution that is ready for launch and is available on GitHub with a live CI/CD pipeline.

Building Well-Architected Applications

The AWS Well-Architected Framework helps us design secure, highly available, cost-optimized, sustainable, operationally excellent, performant, and reliable applications.

The Well-Architected Framework is a set of best practices and guidelines developed by AWS to help architects build reliable, scalable, secure, and cost-effective cloud-based applications. The framework consists of five pillars, each representing a key area of focus when designing cloud architectures:

Operational Excellence
> This pillar focuses on optimizing the operation of your application, including monitoring, logging, and automation. It emphasizes the need for efficient management and operation of resources, identification and resolution of issues, and the use of automation to streamline operational processes.

Security
> This pillar emphasizes the importance of securing your application and data in the cloud. It covers best practices for protecting against unauthorized access, data breaches, and other security threats. It also includes guidance on encryption, IAM, network security, and compliance with industry regulations.

Reliability

This pillar focuses on ensuring that your application remains reliable and available, even in the face of failures or disruptions. It covers best practices for designing for fault tolerance, handling failures gracefully, and implementing backup and recovery strategies. It also includes guidance on testing, monitoring, and performance optimization.

Performance Efficiency

This pillar emphasizes the need for efficient resource utilization, cost optimization, and performance optimization. It covers best practices for optimizing compute, storage, and database resources, as well as techniques for monitoring and optimizing performance at different layers of your application stack.

Cost Optimization

This pillar focuses on optimizing costs associated with running your application in the cloud. It covers best practices for managing and optimizing costs across different AWS services, including pricing models, resource allocation, and cost monitoring. It also includes guidance on cost-effective architecture design, cost-aware development practices, and resource optimization techniques.

These pillars provide a framework to design applications that are well optimized in terms of operational excellence, security, reliability, performance efficiency, and cost optimization. By following the best practices outlined in the Well-Architected Framework, architects can ensure that their applications are designed in a scalable, reliable, secure, and cost-effective manner, ultimately leading to more robust and efficient cloud-based solutions.

Using the Well-Architected Framework with CDK

Building well-architected applications with AWS CDK involves following some key principles that align with the pillars of the Well-Architected Framework. You can use CDK to define your IaC, which allows you to version, test, and deploy your infrastructure just like you would with application code. This helps ensure consistency, repeatability, and traceability in your infrastructure deployments.

Well-architected applications are built of modular and reusable components. And lucky for us, CDK constructs are reusable building blocks for creating modular and reusable components for your infrastructure. This promotes consistency, reduces duplication, and makes it easier to manage and update your infrastructure over time.

The AWS Well-Architected Framework provides an opinioned structure for building reliable and maintainable infrastructure. These principles help guide decisions around automation, security, monitoring, cost management, and testing. Some of the ways we use these principles with CDK include:

Automation and orchestration
> Use CDK to automate the provisioning, configuration, and management of your infrastructure. This helps ensure that your infrastructure is deployed consistently, accurately, and efficiently. CDK also allows you to orchestrate complex deployments and manage dependencies between resources.

Security by design
> Follow AWS best practices for security when defining your CDK infrastructure. Use AWS IAM to control access to resources, encrypt sensitive data, and configure network security using Amazon VPC and other AWS services.

Monitoring and observability
> Use CDK to define and configure monitoring and observability capabilities for your infrastructure. This includes setting up logging, metrics, and alarms to detect and respond to issues proactively, as well as integrating with AWS monitoring and observability services like Amazon CloudWatch.

Cost optimization
> Consider cost optimization when designing your CDK infrastructure. Use CDK to define efficient resource utilization, implement cost-effective architecture patterns, and optimize costs by using AWS services like AWS Cost Explorer and AWS Budgets to monitor, analyze, and manage your costs.

Testing and validation
> Use CDK to define tests and validations for your infrastructure to ensure that it is built and configured correctly. This includes using CDK's built-in testing capabilities, as well as integrating with AWS testing and validation services like AWS CloudFormation StackSets and AWS CloudTrail.

Following these principles will help you build well-architected applications with AWS CDK that are scalable, reliable, secure, efficient, and cost-effective. This will help you achieve robust and optimized cloud-based solutions that align with the best practices of the Well-Architected Framework.

Operational Excellence for CDK

Operational Excellence is one of the pillars of the Well-Architected Framework, and it focuses on ensuring that applications are easy to operate and maintain. AWS CDK provides several tools and best practices that can help build operationally excellent applications:

Automation
> Use CDK to automate the provisioning, configuration, and management of your infrastructure. This helps reduce manual tasks and human error, making your applications more reliable and less prone to operational issues.

Infrastructure as Code

Use CDK to define your IaC, which allows you to version, test, and deploy your infrastructure in a consistent and repeatable manner. This enables you to manage your infrastructure as software, apply version control, and perform automated testing to ensure reliable deployments.

Monitoring and logging

Use CDK to configure monitoring and logging for your applications. This includes setting up logging, metrics, and alarms using Amazon CloudWatch, and integrating with other AWS monitoring and observability services to detect and respond to operational issues proactively.

Testing and validation

Use CDK to define tests and validations for your infrastructure to ensure that it is built and configured correctly. This includes using CDK's built-in testing capabilities, as well as integrating with AWS testing and validation services like AWS CloudFormation StackSets and AWS CloudTrail to validate your infrastructure's compliance with best practices.

Incident response

Define and implement incident response procedures using CDK. This includes setting up automated responses to detected issues, implementing self-healing mechanisms, and using AWS services like AWS Systems Manager Automation and AWS CloudFormation StackSets to quickly respond to incidents and minimize their impact.

Disaster recovery

Use CDK to implement disaster recovery strategies for your applications. This includes configuring backup and restore mechanisms, setting up cross-region replication, and using AWS services like AWS Backup and AWS CloudFormation StackSets to ensure data durability and application availability in case of disasters.

Cost optimization

Consider cost optimization when designing your CDK infrastructure. Use CDK to implement cost-effective architecture patterns, optimize resource utilization, and monitor costs using AWS services like AWS Cost Explorer and AWS Budgets to ensure efficient use of resources and cost-effective operations.

CDK gives you the tools and best practices needed to build operationally excellent applications that are easy to operate, maintain, and troubleshoot while ensuring high availability, reliability, and cost efficiency of your cloud-based solutions. Regular testing and validation of operational excellence using CDK's built-in capabilities, and integrating with AWS services can help you continuously improve the operational performance of your applications.

Security for CDK

Security is a critical aspect of building applications using AWS CDK, and it is essential to follow best practices to ensure the security of your infrastructure and applications. Here are some key considerations for building secure applications with CDK:

Identity and access management
Use CDK to define fine-grained IAM policies for your resources, ensuring that only authorized users and services have appropriate permissions to access and modify resources. Leverage AWS IAM to create and manage IAM roles, policies, and permissions, and follow the principle of least privilege to restrict access to only necessary actions and resources.

Encryption
Use CDK to configure encryption for data at rest and in transit. This includes enabling encryption at the storage layer using AWS KMS for services like S3, EBS, and RDS, as well as using encryption protocols like SSL/TLS for data in transit. Follow AWS best practices for key management, encryption algorithms, and data protection.

Security monitoring
Use CDK to configure security monitoring for your applications. This includes setting up logging, auditing, and monitoring using AWS CloudTrail, Amazon CloudWatch, and other AWS security services to detect and respond to security events in real time. Leverage CDK to define security-related alerts, alarms, and notifications to proactively respond to security incidents.

Compliance and auditing
Use CDK to implement compliance and auditing controls for your applications. This includes using AWS Config to continuously monitor and assess the compliance of your resources against predefined rules, leveraging AWS CloudFormation StackSets to enforce consistent security configurations across multiple accounts and regions, and using AWS Security Hub to aggregate and analyze security findings from various AWS security services.

Secure coding practices
Follow secure coding practices when using CDK to define your IaC. This includes avoiding hardcoded credentials, sensitive information, and other security vulnerabilities in your CDK code. Use CDK constructs that follow AWS best practices for security, and regularly review and update your CDK code to address security concerns.

Vulnerability scanning

Use CDK to configure vulnerability scanning for your applications. This includes leveraging AWS services like Amazon Inspector, AWS Security Hub, and other third-party security tools to scan your infrastructure and applications for vulnerabilities and security weaknesses. Address the identified vulnerabilities promptly to ensure the security of your applications.

Secure deployment

Follow secure deployment practices when using CDK to deploy your infrastructure and applications. This includes validating and testing your CDK templates before deployment, using AWS CloudFormation StackSets to deploy resources consistently across multiple accounts and regions, and implementing secure deployment pipelines using tools like AWS CodePipeline and AWS CodeBuild to automate the deployment process and ensure secure and controlled deployments.

Security starts with you. You can build secure applications that protect your data, resources, and applications from unauthorized access; comply with industry and regulatory standards; and proactively detect and respond to security threats with CDK. Remember to regularly test and validate the security of your applications using CDK's built-in capabilities and integrate with AWS security services to ensure the highest level of security for your cloud-based solutions.

Reliability for CDK

Reliability is a critical aspect of building applications using AWS CDK, ensuring that your applications are highly available, fault tolerant, and resilient to failures. Here are some key considerations for building reliable applications with CDK:

Fault tolerance

Use CDK to design and implement fault-tolerant architectures that can withstand failures of individual resources or components. This includes using features like Auto Scaling, Elastic Load Balancing, Amazon RDS Multi-AZ, and Amazon S3 cross-region replication to distribute workloads, replicate data, and automatically recover from failures.

Monitoring and alerting

Use CDK to configure monitoring and alerting for your applications. This includes setting up automated monitoring using Amazon CloudWatch, CloudTrail, and other AWS monitoring services to track the performance and health of your resources and services. Configure alarms and notifications using CDK constructs to alert on critical events and take automated actions to mitigate issues.

Backup and disaster recovery

Use CDK to define and implement backup and disaster recovery strategies for your applications. This includes using AWS services like Amazon S3 for data backups, Amazon RDS automated backups, and snapshots for database recovery, as well as leveraging AWS CloudFormation StackSets to create and manage backup resources consistently across multiple accounts and regions.

Testing for reliability

Use CDK to test the reliability of your applications by simulating failures and evaluating their impact. This includes using CDK constructs to simulate failures of resources or components, such as instance terminations, network failures, or service disruptions, and validating the behavior of your applications in such scenarios. Implement automated testing using tools like Chaos Monkey, Fault Injection Testing, and other techniques to assess the resilience and reliability of your applications.

Scalability and performance

Use CDK to design and implement scalable and high-performance architectures for your applications. This includes leveraging features like Auto Scaling, Amazon CloudFront, Amazon Route 53, and other CDK constructs to distribute traffic, cache content, and optimize performance. Follow AWS best practices for performance tuning, resource optimization, and capacity planning to ensure that your applications can handle varying workloads and traffic patterns.

Automated recovery

Use CDK to automate recovery from failures and errors. This includes using features like AWS CloudFormation auto-rollback, AWS CloudWatch Events, AWS Step Functions, and other CDK constructs to detect failures and automatically trigger recovery actions. Implement automated error handling, retries, and failover mechanisms in your CDK code to ensure that your applications can recover from failures and continue to operate reliably.

Load testing

Use CDK to perform load testing on your applications to evaluate their performance and reliability under heavy workloads. This includes using tools like AWS Load Testing, Apache JMeter, Gatling, or other load testing frameworks to simulate realistic workloads and validate the performance and reliability of your applications. Analyze the results and optimize your applications accordingly to ensure that they meet the desired reliability and performance requirements.

Regularly test and validate the reliability of your applications using CDK's built-in capabilities, implement automated recovery mechanisms, and optimize for scalability and performance to ensure that your applications are resilient and reliable in the face of failures and errors.

Performance Efficiency for CDK

Performance efficiency is a crucial aspect of building applications using AWS CDK, ensuring that your applications are optimized for performance, cost-effective, and efficient in their resource utilization. Here are some key considerations for building performance-efficient applications with CDK:

Resource optimization

Use CDK to optimize the allocation and utilization of resources in your applications. This includes right-sizing instances, storage, and other resources using CDK constructs, such as Amazon EC2 instance types, Amazon RDS instance classes, and Amazon S3 storage classes. Utilize features like Amazon EC2 Auto Scaling, Amazon S3 object lifecycle policies, and Amazon RDS automated backups to automatically manage the lifecycle of resources based on usage patterns and business needs.

Caching and content delivery

Use CDK to implement caching and content delivery mechanisms to improve the performance of your applications. This includes leveraging features like Amazon CloudFront, Amazon S3 static website hosting, Amazon ElastiCache, and other CDK constructs to distribute content, cache data, and reduce latency. Utilize CDK constructs to configure caching settings, content delivery network (CDN) behaviors, and cache expiration policies to optimize the performance of your applications.

Database optimization

Use CDK to optimize the performance of your databases for efficient data storage and retrieval. This includes using features like Amazon RDS read replicas, Amazon DynamoDB global secondary indexes, and Amazon Redshift sort keys and distribution styles to optimize query performance. Utilize CDK constructs to configure database settings, indexes, and caching options to improve database performance.

Performance monitoring

Use CDK to configure monitoring and logging for your applications to gain insights into performance and identify performance bottlenecks. This includes setting up automated monitoring using Amazon CloudWatch, AWS CloudTrail, and other AWS monitoring services to collect performance metrics and logs. Utilize CDK constructs to create custom metrics, dashboards, and alerts to monitor and optimize the performance of your applications.

Load testing

Use CDK to perform load testing on your applications to evaluate their performance and scalability. This includes using tools like AWS Load Testing, Apache JMeter, Gatling, or other load testing frameworks to simulate realistic workloads and measure the performance and scalability of your applications. Analyze the results and optimize your applications accordingly to ensure that they meet the desired performance and efficiency requirements.

Cost optimization
> Use CDK to optimize the cost of your applications while maintaining performance efficiency. This includes leveraging features like AWS Cost Explorer, AWS Budgets, and AWS Trusted Advisor to monitor and optimize costs. Utilize CDK constructs to configure cost optimization settings, such as instance sizes, storage types, and resource utilization, to ensure cost-effective operation of your applications.

Performance matters. Let CDK help you build applications that are optimized for cost, resource utilization, and performance. Regularly monitor and optimize the performance of your applications using CDK's monitoring and logging capabilities, perform load testing to evaluate performance and scalability, and implement resource optimization techniques to ensure that your applications are performing efficiently and cost-effectively.

Cost Optimization for CDK

Cost optimization is an important consideration when building applications using AWS CDK, as it helps ensure that your applications are cost-effective and efficient in their resource utilization. Here are some key strategies for building cost-optimized applications with CDK:

Resource utilization
> Use CDK to optimize the utilization of resources in your applications. This includes right-sizing instances, storage, and other resources using CDK constructs, such as Amazon EC2 instance types, Amazon RDS instance classes, and Amazon S3 storage classes. Monitor and adjust resource utilization based on usage patterns and business needs using CDK's monitoring and logging capabilities, and implement automated resource lifecycle policies, such as Amazon EC2 Auto Scaling and Amazon S3 object lifecycle policies, to optimize resource usage.

Cost monitoring
> Use CDK to configure cost monitoring and alerts for your applications. This includes setting up cost monitoring using AWS Cost Explorer, AWS Budgets, and AWS Trusted Advisor to track and analyze costs in real time. Utilize CDK constructs to create custom cost metrics, budgets, and alerts to proactively monitor and optimize costs for your applications.

Cost-effective services
> Use CDK to leverage cost-effective AWS services and features in your applications. This includes using features like Amazon S3 storage classes, Amazon RDS

reserved instances, Amazon EC2 spot instances, and other CDK constructs to choose the most cost-effective options for your workloads. Regularly review and update your CDK constructs to ensure that you are using the most cost-effective services and features that align with your application's requirements.

Serverless architectures
Use CDK to build serverless architectures that automatically scale based on demand, reducing costs during periods of low usage. This includes leveraging AWS Lambda, Amazon S3 events, Amazon SNS, and other serverless services to build cost-optimized, event-driven applications that scale automatically without the need for dedicated infrastructure.

Testing for cost optimization
Use CDK to implement automated testing for cost optimization in your applications. This includes using tools like AWS CloudFormation drift detection, AWS Config rules, and custom CDK constructs to test for cost optimization best practices, such as identifying unused resources, untagged resources, and overprovisioned resources. Implement automated tests using CDK constructs to ensure that your applications are cost-optimized throughout their lifecycle.

Cost attribution
Use CDK to implement cost attribution mechanisms for your applications. This includes using AWS Cost Allocation Tags, AWS Organizations, and other cost attribution features to track and allocate costs to specific applications, teams, or projects. Utilize CDK constructs to implement cost attribution settings and ensure that costs are accurately attributed to the relevant stakeholders.

No matter who is paying for your app, you want to make sure it is cost-optimized. CDK can help you meet the demands of any application.

Sustainability for CDK

Sustainability is an important consideration when building applications with AWS CDK, as it involves designing and building applications that are environmentally responsible, are energy efficient, and minimize their carbon footprint. Here are some key strategies for building sustainable applications with CDK:

Green computing
Use CDK to build applications that leverage green computing practices, such as using energy-efficient EC2 instance types, reducing unnecessary resource usage, and optimizing resource utilization. Utilize CDK constructs to automate power management settings, such as EC2 instance hibernation, to minimize energy consumption during periods of low usage.

Renewable energy

Use CDK to design and build applications that utilize renewable energy sources, such as AWS data centers powered by renewable energy. Leverage CDK constructs to deploy applications in regions or availability zones that are powered by renewable energy sources, and use AWS tools like AWS Compute Optimizer and AWS Cost Explorer to monitor and optimize the environmental impact of your applications.

Data center efficiency

Use CDK to design and build applications that use AWS data centers efficiently, reducing waste and minimizing environmental impact. Utilize CDK constructs to automate the provisioning and management of resources, such as Amazon EC2 instances, Amazon RDS databases, and Amazon S3 storage, to optimize data center usage, reduce waste, and minimize the environmental footprint of your applications.

Testing for sustainability

Use CDK to implement automated testing for sustainability in your applications. This includes using tools like AWS CloudFormation drift detection, AWS Config rules, and custom CDK constructs to test for sustainability best practices, such as resource efficiency, renewable energy usage, and data center efficiency. Implement automated tests using CDK constructs to ensure that your applications are sustainable throughout their lifecycle.

Sustainable architecture

Use CDK to design and build applications that follow sustainable architecture principles, such as designing for scalability, reliability, and performance efficiency. Utilize CDK constructs to implement cloud native architectural patterns, such as serverless computing, event-driven architectures, and microservices, that are inherently more sustainable in terms of resource utilization, energy consumption, and environmental impact.

Collaboration and education

Use CDK to foster collaboration and education among team members and stakeholders to promote sustainability practices in your application development process. Utilize CDK constructs to implement tools and processes for knowledge sharing, documentation, and communication, and educate team members and stakeholders about sustainability best practices, such as resource optimization, renewable energy usage, and data center efficiency.

Sustainability is a new trend in software development. In the past, we didn't think much about the environmental footprint of our applications. But now we have better tools to know what that footprint is, and we can design applications that get the job done while also keeping the carbon footprint low.

Thank You!

Thank you for reading this book! We hope you have learned a lot and are ready to build your own CDK applications. We would love to hear from you about your projects and any feedback you have about the book. You can reach us by email at *cdk@samwardbiddle.co.*

Index

About the Authors

Sam Ward Biddle is a principal product architect for Amazon Web Services (AWS). Sam works across industries to develop cloud native products that solve common industry challenges. Sam holds a Master of Science in Education from the University of Pennsylvania, and a Bachelor of Arts in Computational Sociology from Reed College.

Kyle T. Jones leads solutions architecture for power, utilities, and renewable energy in North America for Amazon Web Services (AWS). In his role, he works with leading new energy companies and investor-owned utilities to solve the most complex problems in the energy transition by using the cloud. He specializes in guiding companies through the cloud journey with solutions like the internet of things, high-performance computing, and artificial intelligence/machine learning. Outside of AWS, he is an adjunct professor of project management and analytics at American University. Kyle is a Project Management Professional (PMI-PMP) and Certified Analytics Professional (INFORMS CAP). He holds a Doctorate in Systems Engineering from George Washington University and a Masters in Applied Economics from Harvard University.

Colophon

The animal on the cover of *Hands-On AWS CDK* is an Arabian green bee-eater (*Merops cyanophrys*). Known for their dainty size and colorful feathers, these birds are found in the arid regions of the Arabian Peninsula, including Saudi Arabia, Oman, Yemen, and the United Arab Emirates.

Arabian green bee-eaters are small birds; they can weigh up to .88 ounces and grow to be around 9 inches in length, with a wingspan of up to 19.3 inches. They have bright green feathers, slender black bands that cover their eyes and throat, and a vibrant, electric-blue face and throat. Dust baths are essential for reducing the oil content in their feathers.

Arabian green bee-eaters are social birds and are often found in groups of up to 300 individuals; while foraging, they travel in groups of 20. These birds love to feast on bees and numerous bugs, including beetles, termites, flies, and crickets; they also eat butterflies, moths, caterpillars, and sometimes spiders. They are monogamous birds and build their nests on the ground; females can lay up to 8 eggs that hatch within 22 days. Both parents participate in feeding and raising their young.

Although many of the animals on O'Reilly covers are endangered, thankfully, Arabian green bee-eaters face no major threats and are currently listed as Least Concern by the IUCN. All animals featured on O'Reilly covers are important to the world.

The cover illustration is by Karen Montgomery, based on an antique line engraving from *Braukhaus Lexicon*. The series design is by Edie Freedman, Ellie Volckhausen, and Karen Montgomery. The cover fonts are Gilroy Semibold and Guardian Sans. The text font is Adobe Minion Pro; the heading font is Adobe Myriad Condensed; and the code font is Dalton Maag's Ubuntu Mono.

O'REILLY®

Learn from experts.
Become one yourself.

60,000+ titles | Live events with experts | Role-based courses
Interactive learning | Certification preparation

 **Try the O'Reilly learning platform
free for 10 days.**

www.ingramcontent.com/pod-product-compliance
Lightning Source LLC
Jackson TN
JSHW052333260425
83337JS00016B/187